DEUS EX
MACHINA
SAPIENS

The Emergence of
Machine Intelligence

*To my dear friend Edson,
with thanks for all the
cachaça !*

David Ellis

ELYSIAN
DETROIT

Ttitle: *Deus ex Machina sapiens*
Subtitle: *The Emergence of Machine Intelligence*

First published by Elysian Detroit in May 2011

Library of Congress Control Number: **2011926907**

ISBN: **978-0-615-40136-2**

TO MIKIKO

And are not we as well, if you examine us physically,
mechanistically, statistically and meticulously, nothing but the
miniscule capering of electron clouds? Positive and
negative charges arranged in space? And is our existence not the
result of subatomic collisions and the interplay of
particles, though we ourselves perceive those molecular cart-
wheels as fear, longing, or meditation? And when you daydream,
what transpires within your brain but the binary algebra of connecting and disconnecting circuits,
the continual meandering of electrons?

Stanislaw Lem
The Cyberiad

(Translated from the Polish by Michael Kandel)

CONTENTS

ACKNOWLEDGMENTS

The writers and thinkers quoted liberally in this book have been
my mentors, though none of them knows me.
I am deeply grateful.

1 TSUNAMI

*Only after they are grown up
can [children] look back and decide
whether they are lucky pioneers of a new world
or unlucky victims of their parents' ambitions.*

Freeman Dyson, *Imagined Worlds*

From the balcony of our mountain-facing 22nd floor apartment, three blocks from Waikiki beach on the island of Oahu, we watched an endless convoy of hastily-packed cars, vans, and trucks crawl up the mountain roads. They were mostly filled with sea-level residents, anxiously seeking higher ground.

A short while later, at the invitation of our ocean-facing apartment neighbor and friend Brother Hohu, we shifted perspective. He was a gentle Hawaiian giant with hands bigger than the ukulele he played for a living in a local band, From his balcony, the white-puffed blue sky melted into the luminescent blues and greens and turquoises of the glistening Pacific. Moist and gentle trade winds, blowing down the Pacific from northern climes, swooped to cooler altitudes over the mountains, dropping much of their moisture as rainwater in passing, and softening the sun's scorch into a caress.

But color and caresses were not what we were looking for, that day.

We went back inside, catching the TV news anchor recapitulating the breaking news: ". . . expected to hit at 2:37 this afternoon. From the intensity of the earthquake, scientists have estimated the wave could reach 50 feet in height or even higher at Honolulu Harbor and Waikiki Beach. Residents of sea-front houses and low-floor apartment blocks are jamming the Likelike Highway and its approaches as they make their way to higher ground, while tourists in the ocean-front hotels are being moved up to the higher floors . . ."

The trade winds were not the only thing rolling down the Pacific from the north that day. There was also a *tsunami*. No-one in his or her right mind wants to feel the caress of a tsunami.

ᘓ

It started when an undersea earthquake near the Aleutian Islands of Alaska caused a sudden shift in the massive column of water above the quake's epicenter. The first landfall on its path would be the Hawaiian island chain, a couple of thousand miles to the south and, at 500 miles per hour, only four hours away. (Less than three, by now, as the Likelike started jamming up. Would the convoy's tail-end-Charlies, caught in gridlock at near sea level, make it to high enough ground in time? We wondered.)

For 99 percent of its journey, the tsunami would be an insignificant bulge on the surface of the sea, an ocean swell indistinguishable at the surface from any other ocean swell. It threatened neither the fishing boats nor the fish swimming below them. As a sound wave moves through the air without disturbing it noticeably—until it hits an eardrum, so too does a *tsunami* move through the ocean—until it hits land.

Ninety years earlier, on June 15, 1896, fishermen twenty miles out from their home port of Sanriku on the Japanese island of Honshu didn't—couldn't—notice the 15-inch swell that lifted their boats for a second or two. But by the time they returned home with their catch, that insignificant swell had taken the lives of 28,000 of their relatives, friends, and compatriots, and ravaged a 170-mile stretch of coastline.

The more steeply land falls away into the ocean, the greater the compression of a *tsunami* as it climbs the slope. A steep slope can turn an innocuous-seeming 15-inch swell into a watery wall of death and destruction. The Hawaiian Islands are but the tips of steep volcanic mountains, their bases as deep below sea level as the Himalayan peaks soar above it. This is why even normal ocean swells produce spectacular surf in Hawaii.

Unlike the Japanese fishermen a century before them, the people of Hawaii were well informed about *tsunamis*. They knew from 160 years of record-keeping that tsunamis hit Hawaii every 12 years on average. While fewer than a handful did a lot of damage, it was not surprising that a few hours after the news of the seismic event in the Aleutians, Hawaiian eyes and ears would be glued to TV or radio; the collective breath held as the moment predicted by the oceanographers approached. They expected the *tsunami* to have a height of a few feet as it traversed the rising seabed passing Laie Point, near Oahu's northern tip, and should therefore be just about visible. Minutes thereafter, it would wrap around the islands southern edges, surge up the steep shelf and swell to its full and terrible height.

"There's a small wave, maybe 18 inches," said the television reporter at the Laie Point lookout, dubiously. "Can *that* be it?" On the TV screen, we couldn't make anything out.

That, it turned out, was it. The scientists' calculations were wrong, and Oahu was inconvenienced rather than inundated. But better safe than sorry. Only a quarter century earlier, in 1960, oceanographers did not know nearly so much about *tsunamis*, and 125 people perished as one crashed down upon the small town of Hilo on the coast of the main island of Hawaii. The Honolulu–Waikiki conurbation, in contrast, is permanent or temporary home to nearly a million souls.

In 1651, Thomas Hobbes triggered a small "noöquake"—a disruption in the *noösphere* or "mind sphere" that envelopes the earth—with the publication of *Leviathan; or, the Matter, Forme, and Power of a Common-wealth Ecclesiasticall and Civill*. It is really a book about government and religion, but on page one he postulated that humankind was capable of creating "an artificiall animal."[1]

Hobbes was referring to the clever clockwork contrivances just beginning to appear as toys for the kings and princes, and he used that as a metaphor for government—a larger-than-life "Artificiall man" complete with a soul (the king), joints for getting stuff done (the executive branch), a reasoning brain (the law), etc. In his book *Darwin Among the Machines*) George Dyson thought Hobbes' description amounted to: "a diffuse, distributed, artificial organism more characteristic of the technologies and computational architectures approaching with the arrival of the twenty-first century." That's a bit of a stretch, it seems to me, but anyway, *Leviathan* will do nicely as a marker for the beginning of our history of AI.

The tsunami from Hobbes' nööquake has been barreling down the ocean of Time and up the ever more steeply rising slopes of the mountain of human knowledge for over three hundred years. Is it time to evacuate? Or, like those of us who elected not to head for the Hawaiian hills that day, have we grown too complacent?

Snapshots from Mars! Amazing. Pass the ketchup.

A cure for cancer! Wonderful. What's on TV?

Climate change! Bring it on. Michigan winters suck.

There are ten dimensions to the universe! Yes, dear.

The world chess champion is a computer! Well, duh.

There's a new lifeform on Earth, and it's smarter and stronger than us! Really. Stop picking your no. . . . Did you say a new *lifeform*?

Yes. We are losing our position as the dominant species on Earth.

---

[1] Hobbes' text is appended at p. 281.

THIS BOOK:

- Presents the evidence that *Homo sapiens sapiens*—modern Wo/Man—must inevitably lose its status as the most intelligent species and the highest known lifeform in the known universe.
- Demonstrates that the new lifeform is not some almond-headed Andromedan but comes in two forms: First, an *intra*-terrestrial intelligence we're helping to create, right here on Earth; and second, augmented human beings—part-human, part-machine supermen and superwomen already known to the science fiction world as *cyborgs*—*Homo cyborgensis*.
- Shows why this will probably happen—why the tsunami will hit—within *your* lifetime.
- Gives you reason to hope that the new lifeforms, far from threatening your well-being or indeed your very existence, are more likely to enhance your life in the most extraordinary ways and to secure everybody's future.
- Proposes that *Machina sapiens* and *Homo cyborgensis* will bring renewed and enriched meaning and purpose to life in our new home, the Universe. Or the Multiverse.

2 STRUCTURE

At the end of the century
the use of words
and general educated opinion
will have altered so much
that one will be able to speak of machines thinking
without expecting to be contradicted.

Alan Turing
Computing Machinery and Intelligence

Scientific revolutions are usually counter-intuitive revelations about some aspect of life, the universe, and everything. They have revealed that the Earth is round, not flat as presented to our senses; that the Earth orbits the Sun, and not *vice versa*; that the chaotic mess of stars we see in the nighttime sky is actually performing a clockwork ballet, while the stars themselves are made from a chaotic mess of unpredictable subatomic particles; and that we were not—by some Creator—direct-deposited on Earth, fully formed and conveniently naked and equipped for procreation. No indeed. We crawled out of a foul sludge, following the dictates of a mess of blind and bug-infested instructions called *algorithms*.

Scientific revolutions in themselves have not made much difference to daily life at a fundamental level. Sailors in the table-top world of a few centuries ago went to sea regardless of the obvious danger of falling off the edge; seasons changed regardless of which heavenly body circled which; and no samurai ripped open his bowels in shame upon discovering his slimy evolutionary ancestry. Even Adolph Hitler, who wrote a lot of rubbish, was right in saying that "The driving force which has brought about the most tremendous revolutions on this earth has never been a body of scientific teaching which has gained power over the masses."

Of course, some aspects of raw or "pure" science may eventually be discovered to possess some practical value in solving human problems, and we end up with *applied* sciences and technologies. It is these that are directly responsible for the revolutions that *do* impinge directly on the daily life of individuals, groups, and society at large.

Probably no technological revolution or series of revolutions has had a more profound impact on our lives than revolutions in the storage, manipulation, and communication of information. Let's call this domain *information technology*. The first revolution in information technology was the development of spoken language, which replaced grunt and gesticulation with a more refined use of the vocal chords and hand/arm muscles, until TV was invented.

Every subsequent revolution in information technology since the development of language has resulted in major social change. The revolutions of writing, printing, broadcasting, and "narrowcasting" (communications facilitated by the copying machine, the tape recorder, the home video camera, and of course the Internet) are familiar to most of us. The most recent revolution, involving computerized networks, particularly the Internet and wireless (wifi/cellular) networks, combines the attributes of *all* previous information technologies and adds some of its own, and it has already had a more profound and more rapid impact on society and the individual than any of its predecessors.

The great communications scholar Everett M. Rogers (author of *Diffusion of Innovations*) pointed out that the technology of writing put control of information—and therefore of people—into the hands of those few who could master it, or who could afford to employ the scribes who had mastered it. The result was the end of aeons of oral tradition binding family and tribal society, and the start of three thousand years of feudalism.

Writing marked a temporary end to dissipated cultural evolution, in which culture developed at the grass roots and percolated up the stem, and the beginning of a period in which culture would tend to be centrally controlled by the power holders, the kings and emperors and dictators and the shadowy figures who supported them. This period is now coming to its own end, but only just in the nick of time. In the 20th century, we came within a hair's breadth of the imposition of English as the global language, the Big Mac and Coke as the global diet, and *Baywatch* as the global popular culture.

Printing gave more people access to much the same information their kings and barons possessed. Over the course of five centuries, it virtually destroyed feudalism, and fostered early forms of democracy. The American Revolution was as much a product of the printed revolutionary pamphlet as it was of American cunning and courage, and British military and political stupidity.

The *broadcast* technologies of radio and (especially) TV removed some of the more glaring impurities of early democracy. They brought more information to more people more quickly. They showed everybody the effects, in living, moving color, of war, racism, sexism, police brutality, and other abuses of power. Goodbye Vietnam, good riddance Ku Klux Klan. Welcome, over the space of little more than 50 years, women's liberation, racial equality, gar rights, and—for those fortunate enough to live in one of the more enlightened democracies—peace.

But TV and film also began to show children what goes on in their parents' bedrooms. Goodbye Age of Innocence. Goodbye respect for authority. Goodbye some long-standing moral values. Hello promiscuity, drugs, and the "me" generation.

To citizens of countries lacking these mixed blessings, the Xerox machine and the sound cassette recorder—each representing personal forms of the broadcast and print media—came to the rescue. These *narrowcast* devices gave revolutionaries the means to sidestep state control of broadcast and print media. Goodbye thousand-year Peacock Throne, goodbye Stalin and his

Evil Empire; welcome freedom for the peoples of the former Soviet Bloc.

Each of the foregoing major advances in information technology has had an historic,   revolutionary impact on society. Each succeeding new technology has produced a shift in the social paradigm, ending the status quo and taking society in new and generally *unanticipated* directions.

Political, business, educational, and social leaders are beginning to understand that change at all levels of organization is an inevitable and increasingly rapid consequence of the introduction of new information technologies and communication media, and that it is therefore imperative that they be prepared to embrace the new technologies as a means of understanding them and influencing the rate and direction of change.

By the turn of the millennium, we were already well into the evolution of another major change in information technology: computerized networking. And it, too, has changed society and the whole world. Not just because it represented an amalgamation of all previous communication technologies, but because it introduced a third party into the processes of information storage, manipulation, and communication.

The third party was a machine.

 හ

In the early years of the last decade of the 2nd millenium, the main mediation role played by the computer in human–human communications was in assembling and routing packets of information so they reached their intended recipient. There was always a human being at the sending and receiving ends of any communication, to make sense of it and to act upon it. But today, the computer plays a much bigger, and more powerful, role. It can make sense of its inputs and decide for itself what to output. It can decide what you read and where you go on the Web. It talks with its fellow machines, and it does some of our thinking for us.

What happens if those machines that now do some thinking for *us*, develop the capacity to think for *themselves*? And what happens if selfish thinking machines also acquire a *body*—complete with arms, legs, eyes, ears, and noses—and are thus able to *act* for themselves?

Another revolution happens, bigger and faster than any that has gone before.

In the same 1950 paper from which the epigraph to this chapter was drawn, the father of digital computing, Alan Turing, also wrote:

> A few years ago, when very little had been heard of digital computers, it was possible to elicit much incredulity concerning them, if one mentioned their properties without describing their construction.

Today, relatively little has been said about intelligent machines in language the public can understand, and it is still possible to elicit much incredulity concerning them. Many people dismiss them as science fiction or at best as shaky science and speculative philosophy. I hope to remove the incredulity; to bring androids and cyborgs out of the realm of science fiction and into the realm of science fact, and to bring the intelligent machine down from the remote philosophical peaks and into the valleys of everyday thought most of us inhabit.

I have some sympathy with J.B.S. Haldane's harsh conviction that while science is "vastly more stimulating to the imagination than are the classics," its products "do not normally see the light because scientific men as a class are devoid of any perception of literary form." Philosophy is as stimulating as science, in those rare cases where it too is not devoid of literary form and is not presented as the "massive analytical reasoning that reads as though it were translated from the German," to quote Theodore Levitt (author of the classic article, *Marketing Myopia*) out of context. You'll find science and philosophy in this book; if not in literary form, then at least in plain English. But except for the occasional quote, you will not find science fiction. You don't need to be a computer scientist or robotics engineer to read this book.

In this first chapter we introduce the no-longer so radical—but still startling and creepy —notion of the intelligent machine, by which we mean not only a machine that can think but that can think *by* and *for* itself. We will then follow the threads of the conception and gestation of intelligent machines. These threads lead to the conclusion that a truly intelligent, self-conscious machine is in the process of being born. Chapters Two and Three examine and support the contention that intelligence and life are based upon an evolving set of step-by-step instructions called *algorithms* and *heuristics*. Chapter Four examines the role of algorithms and heuristics as the computational building blocks—the "genetic code"—the blueprint—for the evolution of all life.

Starting with Chapter Five, we begin to examine the history of the implementation—by God or by Nature or by both—of that blueprint for evolution, and introduce a cultural corollary to the genetic code of biological evolution: *memetic* code, which leads naturally to the notion of "Darwinian machines" or machines that evolve—but that do so through *memetic* rather than *genetic* code. Chapter Six develops the idea of *memes* further and recounts the history of memetic machine evolution by describing the family of thinkers in whose minds were developed the memes not only for intelligent machines but for other forms of non-human (or, rather, super-human) intelligence—specifically, the *Noösphere* of Jesuit priest Teilhard de Chardin, and *Gaia*, the living, breathing, thinking planet Earth of biologist James Lovelock. In the process, we describe work in two main areas of AI: expert systems and neural networks.

Chapter Seven considers the history of AI from the perspective of the fields of study—the academic disciplines (and disciples)—that constitute the nourishing womb for the fetus. Chapter Eight dives into the womb itself, to give a fly-on-the-uterine-wall view of the fertilization and gestation of the intelligent machine egg. We watch the fertilized egg begin to divide and multiply into increasingly specialized but still connected (over the Internet—the organism's central nervous system) cells known as *softbots*, software robots. And we see the organism's education beginning in the womb.

The intelligent machine must, by definition of what it means to be intelligent and self-conscious, have a body (hardware) as well as a mind (software.) In Chapter Nine, we turn to the fetal development of the organism's physical body. That means *robots*, and that in turn means *physical* sensory and manipulative capabilities. The intelligent robot needs to be able to speak, to hear, to see, to smell, and to feel.

The emergence of mind in the machine is explored in Chapter Ten, with amplifications of the notion of *emergence*—a key theme. Chapter Eleven concludes our review of the gestation period with a summary of new technologies just emerging from the research labs that will, within the next 30 years, metamorphose the machine not merely into an indisputable lifeform, but into a super-sensitive , super-intelligent, and super-powerful one. The emergent lifeform must (again, by definition of high-level intelligence) have emotions, argues Chapter Eleven, which discusses both the contribution of emotion to intelligence and the manner in which it arises and operates.

By this point, we have inevitably arrived at an intelligent, self-conscious, machine—*Machina sapiens*. Knowing, as we do today, the critical importance of early childhood development in humans, we must consider the early development of this super-sensitive, super-intelligent, and super-powerful new lifeform. Of paramount importance in this respect, and indeed in the entire exposition, is the question of whether the new lifeform will have free will, or whether it will continue to be our slave. I argue in Chapter Twelve that it will indeed have free will; which then begs the vital question: how will it exercise its free will? Will it have scruples? A super-sensitive, super-intelligent, super-powerful lifeform with free will could destroy us if it is immoral or even simply amoral. Chapter Thirteen considers the moral state of *Machina sapiens* in the dangerous period of young adulthood. It is equally critical that we look to our *own* morals, as parents and teachers of the young *Machina sapiens*. What do we want it to observe in us? To learn from our example?

In Chapter Fourteen, we follow this thread into *Machina sapiens'* maturity; to a time when *Machina sapiens* is at least our equal and probably our superior in every respect—physically, mentally, and morally. What does that imply for our long term future—and its? How will we communicate with a being as superior to us as we are to the chimpanzee? All is not lost: we bring together the evidence for our own continued evolution, our own metamorphosis into a super-intelligent, super-sensitive, super-powerful cyborg; part-human, part-machine. Does that imply Utopia? We shall see in the final chapter, which focuses on the spiritual dimension of the emergence of a superior intelligence and supports the view that science and religion (or science and spirituality or physics and metaphysics) are inexorably synthesizing into a seamless and wondrous whole.

3 MACHINA SAPIENS

Marvin Minsky is a distinguished professor at the Massachusetts Institute of Technology, and one of the founding fathers of artificial intelligence. A clever man, by anybody's standards. And yet . . . : "In three to eight years we will have a machine with the general intelligence of an average human being," he was reported to have told a *Life* magazine reporter in 1970. He later denied making the statement, but back then, AI seemed poised to achieve its ambition of producing an artificial intelligence as good as the real thing, and many of us were ready to believe such statements.

Minsky's contemporary AI luminaries Herbert Simon, Allen Newell, and J.C. Shaw had earlier predicted that by 1967 a computer would be world chess champion, would discover and prove a major new math theorem, and would be psychologically like humans. Simon was to win the Nobel Prize, but not for *these* predictions. His timing was a bit off.

The AI dream faded somewhat in the late 80s and early 90s, as the dreamers began to wake up to the scientific and technological enormity of the task. Since then, AI researchers have been more circumspect in their pronouncements and predictions. Asked in 1996 when we might expect a truly intelligent machine, Minsky replied: "In four to four hundred years." I think he meant: "I don't know," but note that he did not say "Never."

Arthur C. Clarke, who predicted the communications satellite—another revolution in information technology—was also gung-ho about the prospects for an intelligent machine, and was very specific about its date of birth. Clarke even got to christen it. *Hal* was born on January 12, 1997. "He" was a highly advanced computer conceived by Clarke and film director Stanley Kubrick for a movie (and a subsequent book) called *2001: A Space Odyssey*.

Hal was an artificial intelligence, capable not only of monitoring and flying the spaceship on which he was installed, but also of beating the human crew at chess, chatting with them, expressing emotions . . . and planning and committing their murder. Having been programmed to ensure the space mission's success at all costs, Hal killed the crew members one by one when he decided they were jeopardizing the mission. One crew member managed to survive, and disabled Hal by pulling out the cards in its memory bank.

In the book, Hal was declared to have been "born" in 1997. As the title makes obvious, the space mission took place in the year 2001. Was an artificial intelligence with Hal's capabilities possible by 2001? This was an aspect of the fundamental question posed by Professor David Stork in his 1997 book, *Hal's Legacy*, and answered, in the book, by a dozen other top names in the AI world including Marvin Minsky. If there was any consensus among these experts at all, it was that Hal—that is, any form of "true" AI—would not be with us in 2001; it would take much longer.

But guess what: Hal flew aboard the space shuttle in 1998, and was built into the International Space Station. It was not called Hal; it was called dMARS, and it was developed at the Australian Artificial Intelligence Institute, whose director, Michael Georgeff, drew the parallel between Hal and dMARS on the basis that both were "motivated to cope with failure and seize opportunity" and to deal with uncertainty and change.

dMARS was a collection of intelligent agents—small AI programs also known as *softbots*—that would work cooperatively to monitor the shuttle and its crew and to take action if the mission were jeopardized. Unlike Hal, however, its decisions could be overridden, and it did not chat or play chess. But it could—crude AI chat programs and sophisticated chess programs are readily available for anyone's PC or smartphone today.

But neither dMARS nor Hal was a machine that could think and act *for itself*, therefore they indeed did not represent AI historian Daniel Crevier's notion of a "true" artificial intelligence. They did, however, contain the spark of true AI. And so does

> . . . your Web browser, the program you use to find your way around the World Wide Web. Browsers work by sending out small pieces of software, often called "softbots" (for software robots). Once released from your browser, these agents have to fend for themselves in the complex world of cyberspace. Their success depends on their ability to make "intelligent" decisions on their own. Softbots are a direct descendent of AI research.

> With softbots, we have the operational equivalent of an ant. But few of us would be prepared to regard ants as intelligent.

So said Keith Devlin in his book *Goodbye, Descartes*. But Douglas Hofstadter's Ant Hilary, a character in *Gödel, Escher, Bach*, might argue that Professor Devlin is missing the big picture. He's not seeing the forest for the trees, or the anthill for the ants.

Ant Hilary is an anteater. She would say that while the ants themselves are pretty dumb, their collective behavior makes for a demonstrably smart mind, which can talk with its crew (causing them to go off and, say, repair a hole in its skin, the nest wall), monitor and maintain its own life support systems such as respiration and body temperature (air conditioning within the nest), plan for contingencies such as a rainstorm or a visit by Ant Hilary, and plan and execute meticulously orchestrated looting and pillaging raids on the surrounding environment.

Hofstadter, bucking the stereotype Haldane would impose upon him, raised to a new level of both mathematical precision and literary art the long-standing but hitherto vague notion that higher-level intelligence (an ant colony, a human mind) is a feature that *emerges* from the activities of lower levels of intelligence (ants, neurons.) The phenomenon of the *emergence* of something wholly new and (in its detail) *unpredictable* is key to "true" AI.

In *2001*, Clarke and Kubrick missed the crucial prophecy that Hal would be just one node in a network of millions of nodes; one tree in a forest; one ant in a colony. His creators did let him communicate from space with computers on Earth, albeit sporadically and with long time delays, but they did not recognize the significance of networking. dMARS could quite easily be connected to the Internet, though NASA would be unlikely to permit it, for security and safety reasons.

At the same time, within 30 years the processing power, connectivity, and memory capacity of a Hal-like standalone machine on your desktop (or in your shirt pocket, or implanted in your brain) will rival the power, connectivity, and memory capacity of today's entire Internet; but even so, the machine will still be just one (very smart) node in a network of billions of other (very smart) nodes, and that's just counting nodes with a human at the end. An Internet of Things"—of devices that just talk among themselves—will add trillions of nodes. If Hal had the brains of an ant, then a network of Hals would have the mind of a colony. But if Hal had the brains of a human, then a network of Hals would have the mind of civilization.

And what if every individual Hal had superhuman brains? We'll see about that. For now, the point is that Hal's emergence as an artificial intelligence endowed with the capabilities described in *2001* is essentially here already, but its continued development toward self-consciousness depends more on the development of connections—network—among him and his buddies than on human programming and machine-building skills. The intelligent anthill arises from, creates, and is a network of ants. The intelligent machine will arise from, is already helping to create, and will be the Internet.

The ramifications for the human race of having in our midst a lifeform more intelligent and powerful than ourselves; one that controls our life support systems are astonishing. They are more potent than the smashing of the atom, more moving than the discovery of penicillin, greater than the invention of the wheel; bigger, I dare say, than the introduction of the automatic cat litter box. A global, civilizational and personal crisis is in the making, using the Chinese literal characterization of crisis as "danger and opportunity." *Machina sapiens* portends dangers and opportunities we scarcely dare name and may not see. To be sure, we will not see them if we do not look.

෨

So, as a bored 14 year-old asked me at dinner one evening, what? We tend to prioritize with our wallets, and in terms of a project funded on the basis of its species/civilization-wide ramifications, then SETI—the Search for Extra-Terrestrial Intelligence—is apparently more important than SITI, the search for intra-terrestrial alien intelligence, for *Machina sapiens*. We've spent hundreds of millions of dollars on SETI (first through government and then through private funding) on spec. We speculate that because there are trillions of stars in the universe there's a good chance other planets exist which, like Earth, contain intelligent life.

That's the justification. We don't know if it's true, we don't know what level of life and intelligence might be out there if it *is* true, and we do know that our paltry light-speed signals may take millions of years to even reach the aliens, never mind elicit a response. Yet right here in our own backyard we ourselves are helping to create an alien, higher lifeform, and there's evidence galore that it is going to happen, and soon. We're paying lots of money to build it, but next to nothing to prepare for it.

Are we looking in the wrong direction? Wouldn't our money be better spent on SITI? With all eyes focused on the heavens—literally, star-struck—who's scanning the earthly horizon, ready to cry "Who goes there? Friend or foe?" to the alien at the gate? Evidently, not the popular science writers. AI was lucky to get a glancing mention in the crop of 3rd millennium books. Doubtless, as their authors foretell, there'll be wonders galore, from pet dinosaurs genetically- and tissue-engineered from DNA found in fossil remains, to virtual sex indistinguishable from the real thing, and from an Elvis clone to Microsoft *Windows 2095*. These wonders pale into insignificance and triviality in the face of a new and higher form of life on Earth.

Microsoft chairman Bill Gates got his millennium book (*The Road Ahead*) out early, in 1995. MIT Media Lab superstar Nicholas Negroponte (*Being Digital*, 1995) was breathing down Bill's neck. Michael Dertouzos, Negroponte's MIT colleague and head of the AI Lab there, hit the bookstores in 1997 with *What Will Be*. Hard on his heels with *Imagined Worlds* was the renowned physicist Freeman Dyson. The list goes on.

These authors did not all write from the same perspective, of course, but they did all try to predict the future, at least within their own domains of knowledge. They're all good books, within their lights; but they missed the Writing on the Wall of *Machina sapiens*. True, each had a more-or-less passing reference to the emergence of machine intelligence. Buried near the back (page 255) of *The Road Ahead*, for example, was Bill Gates' belief that "there will be programs that will recreate some elements of human intelligence," but he was apparently nowhere near ready to concede anything beyond that. His essential prediction was that software tools would get "smarter." Nicholas Negroponte almost got it, but not quite, in the penultimate sentence of *Being Digital*'s Epilogue, where he wrote that [being digital] was "genetic in its nature." But his overall theme is that it is *we* who are becoming digital, in the sense of working and interacting with and through digital media. His message is not that much different from Bill Gates', although there is a deeper significance to this prediction than Negroponte probably intended, if we extend it to embrace our physical and mental "melding" or assimilation with *Machina sapiens*.

In his 1997 book *Growing Up Digital*, technology-in-business guru Don Tapscott believed the major issue confronting us was the "demographic muscle" combined with the "digital mastery" of the "Net generation." "They are an unprecedented force for change and they will dominate most of the 21st century," he wrote, adding: "There is no issue more important to parents, teachers, policy makers, marketers, business leaders, and social activists than understanding this new generation, their culture, psychology, values and what they intend to do with their digital expertise." How right he was, and remains.

Freeman Dyson's *Imagined Worlds* cut "straight to a new chase," said the *Washington Post*. In Dyson's millennium, the dominant science would be biology: "Dyson expects great advances in two areas of biological knowledge: the gene and the brain. He suggests that the first may give us pet dinosaurs, and the second may bring about 'radiotelepathy.'" But Dyson, alas, was not ready to make that leap of imagination to *Machina sapiens*.

The fact is, Machina sapiens is just around the corner. It will arrive within a decade or two, never mind sometime in the next millennium. It will be a "creative emergence" in the sense that it will emerge through a part-Darwinian, part-Lamarckian evolutionary process involving the creative efforts of scientists, technologists, and itself. All we can—and must— do is to anticipate it, to start thinking today about its nature, its psychology, its power, its beliefs, its values.

Fortunately, some people are already doing just that. Professor Daniel Dennett is a beacon in this arena. His 1981 book *The Mind's I* (co-authored with Douglas Hofstadter) has lost little of its currency and none of its fascination as a commentary on many of the issues AI will increasingly have to face up to.

One of these issues is that there is more to consider than *Machina sapiens'* impact on humanity. There's also the matter of our impact on *Machina sapiens*. Philosopher and scifi writer Olaf Stapledon's book *Sirius* is about a dog genetically engineered to give it the brain of a human, while retaining its canine instincts. Freeman Dyson commented: "Humans who do not know him are frightened and see him as a fearsome monster....The tragedy is the impossibility of finding a place for him in the world of ordinary humans and ordinary dogs.... His life ends in grief and violence."

So, finally to answer my 14-year-old friend's "So What?" So it's time someone spoke up, and it might as well be me. This is too important, as the philosopher said, to be left to the experts. But it would be foolish to ignore them. In the next chapter, we will consider what leading scientists and philosophers have decided, so far, about the notion of a "true" AI.

4 INDIFFERENCE, UNCERTAINTY, AND DOUBT

In the future Big Brother will watch over us all.
In the future, human-looking androids will be sent to other planets
to gather precious resources for a polluted Earth.
In the future, computers will take over the world
and build killing machines to wipe out mankind.
In the future, there will only be one restaurant chain.
It will be Taco Bell.
Yuck, huh? Suddenly the present doesn't look so bad.

Which is, of course, the point.

—Tom Long
The Detroit News

There are three main reasons why popular futurists tend to miss the important developments in AI. First, there are plenty of other technologies to titillate the intellect, with biotechnology—cloning, gene therapies, drugs designed from the molecule up—seemingly the front-runner as the "technology of the next millennium." Second, the field of AI has a tarnished reputation for over-hyping its own potential. And third, there is a very human unwillingness to accept even the idea that "strong" AI—which predicts the kind of intelligent machine as I have defined it—is scientifically and philosophically valid.

Biotechnology in fact plays a major role in our metamorphosis into *Homo cyborgensis*, but it is not the central technology: that honor belongs to AI. The basic premise of this book is that *Machina sapiens* is not merely possible but inevitable. But science fiction writer Stanislaw Lem (a schoolmate of Pope John Paul) whose masterpiece *The Cyberiad* is all about intelligent machines (with squishy, smelly "palefaces"—humans—making a cameo appearance at the end) thought such a premise was a delusion. In another novel, *Fiasco*, he summed up a position on AI that permeated much of his work:

> The first inventors of machines that augmented not the power of muscle but the power of thought fell victim to a delusion that attracted some and frightened others: that they were entering upon a path of such amplification of intelligence in nonliving automata that the automata would become similar to man and then, still in a human way, surpass him. [But they] were misled by an anthropocentric fiction—because the human brain was the ghost in a machine that was no machine.

There are three problems with this. First, we are creating machines that augment both the power of muscle *and* the power of thought, and the conjunction makes a difference. Second, there is no justification for assuming that *Machina sapiens* will surpass *Homo sapiens* in *a human way*. It's a logical contradiction, rather like saying that humans have surpassed the apes in an ape-like way. Third, the accusation of anthropocentrism—that we egotistically assume a higher intelligence must be modeled after us—is irrelevant. For now, there is simply no alternative model to guide us in the construction of an AI (or of a God, for that matter.) And we did not create the model: evolution did.

> If . . . someone were to humanize an automaton to the degree that it would be in no way different, mentally, from a man, that accomplishment would—in its very

> perfection—turn out to be an absurdity. . . . The human-
> ized automaton would be just as clever—but also just as
> unreliable, fallible, just as much a slave to emotional bi-
> ases—as a man,

said Lem. Of course it would be an absurdity to create such a
being as an end in itself. But, as we shall see, that is not what
anyone is doing. *Machina sapiens* won't be "just as" clever as us but
more so, and (*ipso facto*) more reliable and less fallible. Lem knew
this, and correctly pointed the way forward:

> Computer intelligence more and more clearly parted
> company with human intelligence; it assisted the human,
> complemented it, extended it, helped in the solving of
> problems beyond man's ability—and precisely for that
> reason did not imitate or repeat it. The two roads went
> their separate ways.

However, unable to recognize and break past the barrier of
his own anthropocentrism, Lem did not pursue this theme to its
logical conclusion. For some of those who did so and who
thought, therefore, that *Machina sapiens* was at least possible, there
was fear. IBM former president Thomas J. Watson is said to have
pulled the plug on early AI research at IBM not only because
shareholders complained of its "frivolity" but also because the
company's marketers were reporting consumer resistance to buying computers because they felt *threatened* by the notion of intelligent machines. That might be apocryphal, but nevertheless
scaremongering corners a lot of press by playing to a highly ex-
citable gallery of emotions: fear of the unknown, uncertainty
about our status as the highest lifeform in the world and possibly
the universe, and doubt about the meaning of life.

౪

Doubts about AI were fueled by grandiose and high-profile but
ill-conceived projects, of which Japan's *Fifth Generation Project* was
the most notable. Launched in 1981, its goal was essentially to
build *Machina sapiens*. A decade and a billion dollars later the pro-

ject was quietly buried; gone, but far from forgotten. Indeed, in the early 1990s AI was headed for a renaissance, this time out of the glare of the spotlights. Early AI programs known as *expert systems* were finding uses, often embedded in conventional software programs. Patrick Winston, then director of the Artificial Intelligence Laboratory at MIT, predicted that instead of trying to replace people, AI's future lay in trying to help them work smarter.

For the most part, AI programs to date have been created to *serve* human beings, directly or indirectly. But there is one class of program designed to *oppose* us: game-playing programs. The first program to beat a human champion of a complex game defeated Italy's backgammon champion, Luigi Villa, in Monte Carlo in 1979. Well, not *in* Monte Carlo, exactly. Luigi Villa was there alright, but his opponent—the program—was in Pittsburgh, Pennsylvania, connected via satellite to a robot in Monte Carlo that physically moved the pieces on the game board.

Predating the computer's backgammon prowess was a 1962 checkers program that had defeated a former Connecticut state champion. But neither checkers nor backgammon rival the king of games, chess, in complexity. Chess-playing programs appeared as early as 1955, but only became successful against competent human chess players in 1967, with the arrival of *MacHack* (unrelated to the Macintosh computer). *MacHack* cockily conquered one of AI's most influential critics, the philosopher Hubert Dreyfus, who until that moment had maintained that computers would never play competent chess. Compared to a world chess grandmaster, merely "competent" chess players are a pushover.

Today, of course, most people have heard about *Deep Blue*'s 1997 defeat of world chess champion Garry Kasparov. Kasparov first agreed to play against a computer in 1989 in order to "protect the human race," as he told *Time* magazine. Well, Garry? *Now* what?

Despite a flurry of media attention to *Deep Blue*, relatively few people gave the matter of AI the kind of serious thought that underlay Kasparov's foreboding, and most of those came from *philosophy*, an intellectual exercise whose products, wrote Jorge Luis Borges in *Avatars of the Tortoise*, amount to little more than a coordination of words which it is venturesome to presume can resemble the universe very much.

Professional philosophy (and professional religion, which is professional philosophy with an attitude, and that's saying something) is what's left when science is stumped, for the time being, for answers to questions about how and why things are the way they are and work the way they work. Modern science is able to answer questions at a fast and accelerating clip, with the result that philosophy is squeezed into an ever tighter corner. Philosophy is science without the rigorous proof. It relies on the shifting sands of verbal reasoning, rhetoric, and other devices riddled with impurities and the potential for error and deceit, to speculate on and persuade us of answers to questions.

Science, on the other hand, is philosophy based ultimately on the pure logic of mathematics; although Einstein, of all people, seemed to have a problem with that. Its proofs must be shown to be consistent with the known laws of nature. Science has provided better answers than philosophy for why the sky is blue, whether the earth is flat, what holds it up in space, how the Universe works, and even to the question of whether there is a God, if mathematical physicist Frank Tipler's *Omega Point Theory*—which provides equations proving the existence of God and an afterlife and, thereby, deftly turns religion into a branch of physics—is to be believed. The last battles between science and philosophy/religion are about the human mind and the mind of God. And science seems bound to win. The smart philosophers, such as Daniel Dennett, who has made deep studies of evolution, robotics, and other scientific disciplines, keep a foot in both camps.

ॐ

"There's no reason why a computer that's simulating the way the neurons in the brain work won't be intelligent," Hubert Dreyfus conceded on American public TV in May 1997, after three decades of dismissing the claims of what he dubbed "strong AI." Strong AI holds that *Machina sapiens* will have consciousness, self-awareness, and true feelings. Weak AI argues that *Machina sapiens* may *seem* to have them, but they will be "mere" simulations.

But Dreyfus discounted *Machina sapiens* only as a product of an approach to AI, a school of thought, called symbolic AI, which held that all intelligence consists of the mental manipulation of symbols. Dreyfus was right all along in objecting to that approach. But the competing *connectionist* approach, which held that a computer that could simulate the way neurons in the brain work would be intelligent, was not the whole story, either. The scientific evidence points to the conclusion that only a whole organism—an *embodied* mind—can be intelligent, and that there's a lot more to a body than a plastic case with holes for keyboard input and monitor output.

Joseph Weizenbaum, creator of a spooky and famous program called *Eliza*, discounted only the claim that it would be *like us*. He believes instead that it would be at least as different as the intelligence of a dolphin is to that of a human being. Another leading AI guru, Hans Moravec, is a believer, though his belief encompasses the debatable notion that *Machina sapiens* will evolve feelings based on its ability to please others through good service, which will have survival advantage. (In other words, machines that don't serve us well will end up on the scrap heap.)

Philosopher John Searle, another famous AI hype-guard, concocted out of alchemic philosophical methods a "thought experiment" (a Borgesian "coordination of words") known as the *Chinese Room Experiment*,[2] which ostensibly disproved strong AI's claim that an *algorithm*—a step-by-step procedure for solving a problem or reaching a decision—could be or become intelligent in and of itself. It could only simulate intelligence, which is what Dreyfus said.

The assumption that a robot cannot think *for* itself (what philosophers call *intentionality*)—that it cannot have *original* as opposed to *pre-programmed* intentions—was summarized by Dennett in another thought experiment in which we are to imagine a human who, desirous of reincarnation, builds a robot to house and

---

[2] A non-Chinese-speaking person is locked in a room containing a set of instructions (a program) for putting into order batches of Chinese characters that are slid under the door to him. He slides the assembled responses back. They make sense to a Chinese speaker, but they don't make sense to the man in the room—to the "artificial intelligence."

protect his body in cryogenic suspension until such time as future medicine can restore the body to a healthy and immortal life. After wandering the Earth and encountering many obstacles—and other robots—our coffin-robot begins to take actions partly in its own interests. The robot's creator, whose mind is still aware and active inside the robot, says to himself: "*I* am the original source of all the derived meaning within my robot, however far afield it drifts. It is just a survival machine designed to carry me into the future. The fact that it is now engaged strenuously in projects that are only remotely connected with my interests, and even antithetical to them, does not, according to our assumption [that the robot does not have a real mind of its own], endow any of its control states, or its 'sensory' or 'perceptual' states, with genuine intentionality."

In other words, the robot *seems* to be thinking for itself but isn't, really.

Dennett's thought experiment caricatured the views of an eminent (and sometimes unlikely) collection of philosophical bedfellows including John Searle and Fred Dretske, "each in his own way opposed both to evolutionary accounts of meaning and to AI." Dretske, however, conceded to Dennett that we might "(logically) create an artifact that *acquired* original intentionality, but not one that (at the moment of creation, as it were) *had* it." In other words, a machine might, at least in principle, learn (through experience or being taught) to think for itself. Searle, too, backtracked a little way, conceding the possibility of a robot with a mind of its own (that is to say, a mind which independently discovers, attributes, and creates meaning in or to the things it experiences), while still disputing that a robot mind could be the real thing.

Oxford mathematician Sir Roger Penrose, who found Searle's Chinese Room argument attractive but not definitive, focused—as did the Chinese Room argument—on the differences between *computing* and *thinking*. His main problem was with the strong AI claim that it is possible for an *algorithm* (a program) to "experience feelings; have a consciousness; be a mind"—all by itself. Penrose also disputed the claim, shared (he said) by John Searle and the strong AI guard (strange bedfellows!) that everything—life, the universe, the girl next door—is a digital computer. We can certainly demonstrate that a brain can do some computer-like things and computers can do some brain-like things, but we just don't know enough, says Penrose, about the *physics* of consciousness to claim that mind works by, or consists of, computation. But he then hedges his bets by surmising that our conscious (waking, aware) minds might result from non-algorithmic quantum processes, while the subconscious mind might indeed operate like a computer program—algorithmically.

Quantum processes are processes involving *quanta*—particles smaller than the atom given such delightful Joycean names as *quarks* and *squarks* and *leptons* and *sleptons*, plus particles known as *bosons* and *bosinos* responsible for electromagnetism and gravity and other fundamental forces, all of which combine together to form atoms, molecules, stars, you, me, life, the universe, and everything. But if, as Penrose suggests, mind is a quantum *process*, there has to be some sort of program working on some sort of *information* coded into the quanta.

It's astonishing what the information-bearing, process-controlling algorithm known as genetic code—written using just four letters—can achieve. For example, a tiny snippet of human genetic code makes women generally more sociable and intuitive than men, as geneticists discovered in June 1997. Such traits are therefore inherent not primarily to individuals but to the species, to the genotype rather than to the phenotype. This suggests that species-level traits (which are nevertheless observable in the individual) are subconscious and algorithmic, thus supporting at least part of Penrose's argument. Our ability at the conscious level to enhance or suppress these traits may or may not support the other part of Penrose's argument for a non-algorithmic conscious mind.

Though Penrose denied setting up a straw man, in effect this is what he achieved in focusing so heavily on the strong AI notion of intelligence based on what we will call "basic" algorithms. I found no mention in his book of the importance of *heuristics*—solving problems or reaching decisions through "rules of thumb"—for example.[3] Neither did Penrose appear to consider the central role of *emergence*—the spontaneous appearance of something new—in the evolution of life, intelligence, consciousness, and mind. Penrose recognized that we could create an intelligent machine "if we ever do discover in detail what quality it is that allows a physical object to become conscious," but not that one might emerge *whether or not* we discover that quality.

Dreyfus, Searle, and Penrose were and are not the only critics of AI, but they represent the strongest and best-known hype watchers. They were all essentially correct in the sense that AI cannot just rely on "basic" (non-heuristic) algorithmic, symbolic processing, and that consciousness is not possible purely within the skimpy confines of a Turing Machine—the algorithmic basis for computing. In the 1950s and 60s, AI folks thought it was but now we know better—about computing, the brain, the mind, and evolutionary processes.

The modern version of strong AI supported by heavyweights in philosophy and the sciences incorporates the tremendous strides made in the past three decades in the computer and cognitive sciences, particularly in neural networks, cellular automata/genetic algorithms, evolutionary hardware self-assembly, autonomous agents, and quantum computing. It incorporates new and still unfolding knowledge of the brain, reasoning, and emotion, and their roles in intelligence, mind, and consciousness. It recognizes advances in computing power, robotics, and in the change in approach to AI made by the AI community. And it is supported by a formidable array of some of the best (late and living) human brains on the planet: mathematicians Alan Turing and John von Neumann, physicist Frank Tipler, astronomer John Barrow, computer scientists Marvin Minsky, Joseph Weizenbaum, and Douglas Hofstadter, roboticist Hans Moravec, and philosophers Hubert Dreyfus (with caution and conditions) and Dan Dennett, to name just a few.

---

[3] However, he seemed to me to capture some of the essence of heuristics in his belief that "aesthetic" criteria govern subconscious rather than conscious judgments and decisions.

The last word goes to Stephen Hawking, the Cambridge University physicist and author of the best-selling *A Brief History of Time*. In a series of lectures about the Millennium in April 1998 at the White House, Hawking predicted that we will have the complete answer to the origin of the Universe within 20 years. He said that *complexity* is where the action is going to be. "It is in this complexity that I expect the major developments of the next millennium. I foresee biological complexity increasing with genetic engineering and the development of self-designing computers with artificial intelligence. The future certainly won't be static."

The importance of complexity, the fact that we are making progress in understanding and predicting it, and the notion that the next thirty years are going to be absolutely mind-blowing, are central elements of the book you are now holding, and it's nice to know we're in such august company.

Whether the underlying operations of such complex concepts as intelligence, mind, and emotions are expressible algorithmically remains unresolved scientifically, and while Penrose is right to insist on more research, it is not necessary that we uncover these algorithms for them to emerge in a machine.

In the next chapter, we will examine the algorithmic nature and evolutionary emergence of machine intelligence and related concepts in greater detail, as background for the exposition of the growth and development of Machina sapiens.

5 COMPUTATIONAL EVOLUTION

Algorithms are sets of instructions and calculations. Little programs, little apps. They are the key not only to the functioning of computers, but also to the functioning of all forms of evolution: cosmic, planetary, biological, and cultural. Algorithms are the blueprint for life. They account for the Modern Synthesis of Darwin's evolutionary theory of natural selection with Mendel's laws of genetic inheritance.

But there is a point where standard algorithms lose much of their power and a new variant of algorithm—the *heuristic*—comes to Nature's aid. Heuristics are the primary component emerging from the cooperation of the individually mindless, algorithmic agents that constitute a society of mind. They account for how we think, and for why traditional algorithmic computers have not been able to think like us.

And that is why heuristics are the key to machines (and other organisms) that think, and why they are the primary object of AI research and development. Heuristics work faster than algorithms, which is why the 600 mph human brain works faster than the nearly 186,000 mph electronic computer on really, really complex tasks. Because heuristics work faster, they evolve faster through the evolutionary processes of mutation and fitness for survival in a changing environment.

The evolutionary process is recursive; that is to say, it feeds upon itself yet it gains strength and speed as it does so. In short, it accelerates. The acceleration of geological and biological evolution is easily graphed, illustrating that early evolutionary jumps took millions or even billions of years to happen, whereas the last major biological jump—to *Homo sapiens sapiens*, modern Wo/Man—is merely a 100,000-year blip in the timeline of the universe.

Since that jump, we have hardly progressed at all biologically. Maybe we're a bit taller on average, but our basic configuration and the size of our brain is effectively no bigger than it was a hundred thousand years ago. What has changed, however, is human culture. Culture (and its component, technology) evolves in an algorithmic–heuristic manner, somewhat like biological organisms do but with some vital differences, and it too accelerates. The acceleration of cultural/technological evolution is illustrated by reference to the rush of developments in the 19th century, where individual people in the "developed" world went—in the space of a lifetime—from candlelight to gaslight and the beginning of electric light, from horseback to steam locomotive and the beginning of the automobile, from grandma's herbal remedy to the X-ray, anesthetics, and asepsis.

The acceleration in the pace of change in recent decades has dulled our senses and our sensibility. Governments fail to grasp their inability to control technologies, like the Internet, that develop and mutate faster than congresses can create legislation. Individuals fail to grasp the insecurity of their jobs. And the world fails to grasp the speed at which intelligence is growing in machines.

Algorithms

My wife and I have watched an algorithm at work in an old lady afflicted by Alzheimer's Disease. Whenever we would meet, she would always greet us as strangers and ask my wife: "Where are you from?" "From Japan," says my wife. "Oh, how interesting!" would come the reply; "I once lived in Okinawa with my U.S. Army husband." Then the old lady would recount various events and impressions to do with Japan. A few minutes after such a conversation ended, she would again engage my wife in conversation. "Where are you from?" she would ask. "From Japan," my wife would reply. "Oh, how interesting! . . ." And the entire conversation would be repeated almost verbatim. Several times in an evening.

I don't know much about Alzheimer's, and I don't mean to sound heartless (for the disease is tragic) but I do know a subroutine—an algorithm—locked in a loop when I see one.

An algorithm is a set of step-by-step instructions and calculations which:

1.   Can be recorded in any medium or set of symbols,
2.   Requires no intelligence to operate, and
3.   Is guaranteed to produce a result.

The process of evolution is nothing more than the mechanical, automatic operation of one huge (and growing) set of algorithms. From the above features of an algorithm we can say, first, that evolution itself can take place in any medium that can inherently process algorithms, and that includes biological, chemical, physical, and symbolic media such as writing. Second, we can say that evolution is self-actualizing—an intelligent controller/operator/button-pusher is not necessary (but is not precluded, either.) And finally, we can say that evolution is bound to produce an outcome.[4] However, we cannot predict what evolution will produce because chance (in the gross form, for example, of natural disasters such as the asteroid that put paid to any further evolution by the dinosaurs; or in fine form, such as the misplacing or mis-reading of a single letter in a fragment of genetic code) is present at each step of the algorithm and can change it.

No single algorithm, however, can amount to much. The larger (and therefore more complex) the algorithm, the more it is subject to chance mutations, to instability, and to breakdown. That is why computer programs now come in ever-smaller chunks known to programmers as *objects*. To write a big program capable of performing complex feats, programmers mix and match these objects just as a design engineer mixes and matches

---

[4] There has been some controversy about just how evolution causes outcomes—see Stephen Jay Gould's *Full House* if you want to know more.

carburetors, brakes, and steering wheels to make a car, or evolution mixes and matches genes to create a human being.

Long before Hobbes, Plato expressed a sense of understanding this algorithmic "erector set" process in his analogy between a republic and a person—both being organizations composed of smaller, interacting, more or less mindless agents. Mindless, that is, compared to the knowledge and awareness of the organization as a whole. Dennett came to the same conclusion through his study of Darwinian processes in biology: a mind is "not a miracle machine, but a huge, semi-designed, self-redesigning amalgam of smaller machines, each with its own design history, each playing its own role in the 'economy of the soul.'" This view is also essentially that developed in depth by Marvin Minsky in *Society of Mind*.

Why do these agents/machines/algorithms cooperate, as they must if they are to combine to form a viable organism? Game Theory, the favorite topic of mathematician John von Neumann (1903–1957), suggests an answer, and it may be no coincidence that Game Theory is now widely applied in both Darwinian (biological) evolutionary research and in "Alife" (artificial life) studies.

Game theory also figures in biologist John Maynard Smith's *Evolutionary Stable Strategy* (ESS) theory, which says in essence that the most successful evolutionary strategy or trait (or algorithm) will become dominant in any given population. Having eliminated weaker competing strategies, the ESS will then tend to compete *against the copies of itself* which, by definition of "successful," must abound in the population. This is demonstrably true of *Homo sapiens* which, having hit upon the winning strategy in the game against gorillas, lions, tigers, wolves, and bears turned in upon itself in a competition that continues, albeit in a less physical and less overtly vicious form, today.

Evolutionary subroutines (yet another name, at a fundamental level, for machines, algorithms, objects, agents, programs, subprograms, and apps) are bound by what Dennett calls "the notorious *need-to-know principle* of espionage: give each agent as little information as will suffice for it to accomplish its share of the mission." There is no doubt that our individual brains have limited physical storage and processing capacity, and that our sense organs are limited in what they can sense. But even though we may be weaker than *Machina sapiens* in these regards, the question is: Will our ability to communicate with it—and therefore to have access to the conclusions formed by its *un*limited storage capacity, prodigious processing power, and *super*sensory experiences—make up for our deficiencies, just as today we can communicate with an alpha-proton spectrometer on Mars and make sense of what it "sees," even though we have no way of seeing it directly? Or does such vicarious experience leave something out?

But what happens when the complexity of encountered environments arises, and unpredictability becomes a more severe problem? Dennett says that "a different design principle kicks in: the *commando-team principle*, illustrated by such films as *The Guns of Navarone*: give each agent as much knowledge about the total project as possible, so that the team has a chance of ad-libbing appropriately when unanticipated obstacles arise."

This principle kicks in when, for example, a pilot faces a sudden crisis and *there is literally not enough time to think*. There may only be time to react, and the reaction must be close to instantaneous. The hands on the yoke, through continual but slightly time-delayed feedback from the brain about the state of the aircraft and its environment in general, are almost—but not quite—ready for any emergency. In an *abrupt* emergency, the hands must be ready to *ad lib* in an instant to avert disaster. For the duration of that instant, the hands have a mind of their own.

"Once we get to Popperian creatures," says Dennett, "creatures whose brains have the potential to be shaped into inner environments with pre-selective prowess, what happens next? How does new information about the outer environment get incorporated into these brains? This is where *earlier* design decisions come back to haunt—to constrain—the designer. In particular, choices that evolution has already made between need-to-know and commando-team now put major constraints on the options for design improvement."

It takes "incredible cunning" to overcome those restraints, and the basis for this incredible cunning is the algorithm variant called the heuristic.

Heuristics

In arguing for the notion that we ourselves could be considered machines, Alan Turing noted a certain confusion in the minds of skeptics between what he called "rules of conduct" and "laws of behavior."

> By "rules of conduct" I mean precepts such as "Stop if you see red lights," on which one can act, and of which one can be conscious. By "laws of behavior" I mean laws of nature as applied to a man's body such as "if you pinch him he will squeak."

Since the study of heuristics had barely begun when Turing wrote the foregoing, he may be forgiven for using different terminology, but his "rules of conduct" are, in fact, algorithms, and his "laws of behavior" are heuristics.

"One might define the task of the field of AI as the creation and investigation of heuristic algorithms," says Dennett. The significant difference between an ordinary algorithm and a heuristic one is that the heuristic has an inherent ability to produce a much broader array of possible outcomes, and is therefore riskier. He adds: "Mother Nature has never aspired to absolute certainty; a good risk is enough for her." Furthermore, "there are risky, heuristic algorithms for human intelligence in general . . . . Here [as we've already noticed] is where Penrose made his big mistake: he ignored this set of possible algorithms—the only set of algorithms that AI has ever concerned itself with—and concentrated on the set of algorithms that Gödel's Theorem actually tells us something about."

Mathematician Kurt Gödel's famous Incompleteness Theorem seems to militate against algorithms, even heuristic ones, as the underlying explanation for everything. According to the theorem, every computer that is a consistent truth-of-arithmetic-prover has an Achilles' heel: a truth of arithmetic that exists but which the computer could never prove, were it to run till Doomsday. But a mathematician's mind can do something the computer cannot do. It can *just see* that certain propositions of arithmetic are true, even when it can't prove them. Thus, to

Dennett, if a brain is a computer, it is not a mind. Mathematicians "don't need to rely on grubby algorithms to generate *their* mathematical knowledge, since they have a talent for grasping mathematical truth that transcends algorithmic processes altogether," says Dennett. This may help explain Einstein's disdain for the notion that pure mathematics is the be-all and end-all: the mathematician matters as much as the math.

Nevertheless, some algorithms are "pretty darn good at playing the Turing Test or imitation game. There is one actual one on my Toshiba, a stripped-down version of Joseph Weizenbaum's famous Eliza program, and I have seen it fool uninitiated people into concluding, like Edgar Allan Poe[5] that there *must* be a human being issuing the answers."

Dennett's description of the Turing Test is as concise as can be: "Put two contestants—one human, one a computer—in boxes (in effect) and conduct conversations with each; if the computer can convince you it is the human being, it wins the imitation game."

"Even if, as many today believe, no machine will ever succeed in passing the Turing Test, almost no one today would claim that the very idea is inconceivable . . . . perhaps this sea-change in public opinion has been helped along by the computer's progress on the other feats, such as playing checkers and chess."

Even attributes as slippery as Truth and Beauty have an algorithmic base: "*underlying* our general capacity to deal with such 'ingredients' [of truth and meaning] is a heuristic program of mind-boggling complexity. Such a complicated algorithm would *approximate* the competence of the perfect understander, and be 'invisible' to its beneficiary. Whenever we say we solved some problem 'by intuition,' all that really means is *we don't know how* we solve it. The simplest way of modeling 'intuition' in a computer is simply denying the computer program any access to its own inner workings. Whenever it solves a problem, and you ask it how it solved the problem, it should respond: 'I don't know; it just came to me by intuition.'"

---

[5] Poe unmasked a bogus 19th century chess-playing "automaton" that turned out to conceal a human operator.

The algorithmic evolutionary perspective began gaining ground to the extent that some evolutionists were "intent. . . on replacing the 'Standard Social Science Model' with a properly Darwinian model of the mind." To me, this is another sign of a scientific revolution in the making, although to Dennett it merited just a slight revision of the standard model:

> Whereas animals are rigidly controlled by their biology, human behavior is largely determined by culture, a largely autonomous system of symbols and values, growing from a biological base, but growing indefinitely away from it. Able to overpower or escape biological constraints in most regards, cultures can vary from one another enough so that important portions of the variance are thereby explained . . . . Learning is not a general-purpose process, but human beings have so many special-purpose gadgets, and learn to harness them with such versatility, that learning often can be treated as if it were an entirely medium-neutral and content-neutral gift of non-stupidity.

The key thing about culture, though, is that it evolves—it changes—at an accelerating rate.

Acceleration in the Rate of Change

> The development of life took billions of years only in its pre-sentient stage. Primate Creatures, once formed, within two hundred thousand years automatically began a technological explosion. This explosion—and, by the cosmic clock, it was a true explosion . . . carried them, at ever-increasing speed, to higher and higher levels of control of the forces of Nature.

> Stanislaw Lem, *Fiasco*

The question is not whether *Machina sapiens* will emerge. The answer to that question, from both science and philosophy, is increasingly, if reluctantly, "It will." The questions remaining are: when, and so what? A safe answer to *when* is Marvin Minsky's "four to four hundred years" from now. But look *back* four hundred years, and what do you see? Life in the year 1620 was little different from life in biblical times. Look back even 200 years, when your great-great-grandparents were alive, and things were the same, except that change was imminent.

Your great-great-grandparent's life was meticulously described in the classic sociological study of middle America, begun in the early part of this century by Robert and Helen Lynd and continuing to this day at Ball State University. The Lynds' book *Middletown* recounted that within the lifetime of a Muncie, Indiana physician born in 1827,

> . . . local transportation changed from virtually the 'hoof and sail' methods in use in the time of Homer; grain ceased to be cut in the state by thrusting the sickle into the ripened grain as in the days of Ruth and threshing done by trampling out by horses on the threshing-floor or by flail; getting a living and making a home ceased to be conducted under one roof by the majority of the American people; education ceased to be a luxury accessible only to the few; in his own field of medicine the X-ray, anaesthetics, asepsis, and other developments tended to make the healing art a science; electricity, the telephone, telegraph and radio appeared; and the theory of evolution shook the theological cosmogony that had reigned for centuries.

Middletown was published less than 80 years ago. It does not mention television, virtual reality, nuclear power, genetic engineering, holographics, space travel, quantum mechanics, computers, robots, or automatic cat litter boxes, to name just a few of the technological marvels of the past few decades. To the Lynds, as to most other folks in the 1920s, radio, the telephone and the automobile were marvelous enough. Aldous Huxley's classic *Brave New World*, written in 1931 but set hundreds of years into the future, seemed to be way out on a limb at the time in putting a TV set at the end of every bed in a hospital. Herbert Simon and Marvin Minsky's over-optimistic prediction of the arrival of intelligent machines is at least balanced by Huxley and others' tendency to underestimate the pace of change.

In 1971, Alvin Toffler's *Future Shock* gave the masses early warning of the increasing velocity of change. The shock, if it ever existed, soon wore off. We have grown so accustomed to rapid change that its *absence* would now be shocking. By the end of the 20th century, anyone who had bought at least two PCs *expected* to be buying a new and improved one within at most three years (in September 1997 Dell became the first computer maker to begin offering a leasing option to individual consumers—not just business customers—to help them overcome the financial hurdle of upgrading their PCs every two years). Web surfers *expected* to be upgrading their browser within six months. Banks *expected* competition from software companies. Entertainment companies *expected* to be wooed by telephone companies. Business *expected* the unexpected.

Even government emerged from bureaucratic torpor to get the message (or, as Marshall McLuhan might have said, the medium). The U.S. government accepted the futility of attempting to regulate the Internet with its June 1997 capitulation on the issue of anti-pornography provisions in the Communications Decency Act, though it had to be nudged in that direction by the Supreme Court. It took the U.S. government ten years to begin to accept what some of us had been predicting since the late 1980s. And governments of an authoritarian bent—China, Saudi Arabia, and many others—still don't get it. Or they do, and are frightened to admit it.

Geopolitical boundaries and government organs are simply irrelevant to an amorphous lifeform able quickly to repair or regrow severed limbs, and to extend new limbs into nooks and crannies where government is not looking. Canadian Industry Minister John Manley clearly understood this when he told an international meeting of government ministers in July 1997 that no government was capable of controlling the Internet. "The public sector is unable to contemplate wisely the regulative or legislative rules that need to be in place when development is as rapid as it is," he said.

How rapid *is* the pace of change? Daniel Crevier, extrapolating from estimates of human brain processing and memory capabilities and using Moore's Law to extrapolate growth in computer processing and memory capabilities, gave 2009 as the earliest and 2042 as the latest when a supercomputer as powerful as the human brain would exist. He was off a bit. The best we could come up with in 2009 was Blue Brain, a joint IBM–Swiss ETH supercomputer project that struggled to emulate about half a mouse brain. The equivalent dates he gave for a desktop computer were 2025 and 2058. This does not, however, take into account the power of parallel distributed processing, which I predict will result in human equivalence in a network of computers long before 2025. Crevier agrees that "we can expect our machines to become more clever than we are" and that they will be "stronger, faster, more enduring, and more accurate than we are."

ॐ

The point is that the velocity of scientific and technological development is increasing exponentially, and Simon and Minsky may yet be vindicated. Acceleration tends to make us shortsighted. The *immediate* future of technological-revolution-driven social progress is so rich in change we can barely see it, let alone beyond it. "Immediate future" today means just a few months. To your great-great-grandma, it meant her lifetime. At the time of Christ, it meant a millennium.

If we can't see something in the immediate future, we tend to dismiss it from our minds and consideration. The 1920s scientist, asked whether space travel would ever be possible, would probably have replied, *pace* Minsky: "Sure—within the next four to four hundred years." If something does not appear to be in the immediate future, who cares? In *our* immediate future there's plenty of other new stuff to cope with. Cloning. Levitation. Genomic medicine. Artificial life. Possible life on Europa and Mars. Water on the Moon.

Space travel happened in less than fifty years from the 1920s (when the Lynds were writing about the recent transition from horse and buggy to automobile). The Mars *Sojourner* rover was forgotten mere months after poking its nose into rocks in a Martian river bed. In 1997, a cargo ship replenished the crew of the stricken *Mir* space station, damaged in the first orbital fender bender. And in between setting fire to things to see how they burn in zero gravity, other astronauts waved to the *Mir* crew from the shuttle *Columbia* as it, too, orbited the Earth.

In the 1920s, all this was science fiction. Artificial intelligence today is like rocket science in the 1920s, but the part of the acceleration curve we're on today is much steeper than it was 70 years ago. "Compared with the slow pace of natural evolution," wrote mathematical physicist and theoretical biologist Freeman Dyson, "our technological evolution is like an explosion."

Given this explosive, exponential development in science and technology, it is not unreasonable to claim, as I do, that almost everyone under 50 years of age today is going to be around when *Machina sapiens* wakes up, and will be affected by it. "*We haven't seen the long run yet*," Dennett wrote. But we will.

So What?

The arrival of *Machina sapiens* will have a profound psychological, social, and economic impacts. It will mark the final stage in the progressive de-skilling of human beings in all walks of life that began with the first flint tool. *Machina sapiens'* robotic extensions will handle labor and manufacturing chores more efficiently and economically than human workers, and its brains will produce better computer programs and better hardware than human brains can achieve or even conceive. With no more laboring, clerical, manufacturing, engineering, or programming jobs, the human labor force will comprise artists and some professionals. But *Machina sapiens* will invade these territories too, except to the extent that some people will insist on buying art and professional services only from other humans.

Humans will have to get used to the fact that we are no longer the smartest species on the planet, that *Machina sapiens* will run the factories, the economy, and human services better than we can, and that we may no longer be God's only chosen vessel. Some folks will never accept such a state of affairs, and we can expect to see attempts to kill *Machina sapiens*. Hugo de Garis, a scientist who tried (and failed) to build an artificial brain at Japan's Advanced Telecommunications Research Institute not long after the demise of the Fifth Generation Project, has predicted a "Cosmist War" between humans who support the emergence of what he called "artilects" (artificial intellects) and humans who oppose it.

But humanity will have no say in whether *Machina sapiens* takes over or not. It will not be a disembodied intellect but an intellect with a body, including manipulative and sensory appendages and a nervous system. It will be a body distributed around the globe and extending into space. It will be fitter for survival than we are. We can't stop its emergence, in part because we can't (and may not want to) stop all research into AI and scientists can't stop themselves from doing what they do. Who could have stopped the research in quantum physics that led to the atom bomb? And we certainly won't be able to shut it down. No-one could lure *this* genie back into a bottle of oblivion. If governments cannot control a still mindless Internet (and cannot even, in some cases, *recognize* that they cannot control it) what hope have they of controlling it when it starts to think by and for itself?

A foretaste of the emotion and anxiety we might experience can be discerned from Garry Kasparov's reaction to his defeat by *Deep Blue* in 1997. Kasparov adviser Frederic Friedel said after the match that Kasparov had the feeling that *Deep Blue* was forming plans, understood strategy; tried to trick him; was blocking his ideas. But as *Washington Post* writer Charles Krauthammer noted, *Deep Blue* was "aware of nothing, not even that it [was] playing chess." It was terror that cost Kasparov the match. "Never in his life had he lost any match to anyone or anything. He lost this time, ironically enough, not because he was out-thought by the thinking machine but because he was out-psyched by it. He was demoralized by its very soullessness. 'I lost my fighting spirit,' he confessed."

Did Kasparov speak for us all? Krauthammer wrote: "The difference in this match was not infallibility but unflappability. Both man and machine made mistakes. But only the man melted down. This is important because feelings are the last redoubt of the artificial-intelligence skeptics. Not to worry, they say. Humans will always remain superior. Even if a machine could think, they say, it could never feel. It could never cry or love or brood about mortality. . . . One day in the far future, we will be up against machines—not just in chess but in life—that are not only monstrously intelligent but utterly unfeeling."

Who could disagree that we all would have every reason to be terrified of a relentlessly logical, unfeeling, superior intellect—like Hal, for instance? Or that, as far as chess is concerned, that is exactly what *Deep Blue* is? But this terror is a straw man, because *Machina sapiens* won't be like that. It will not be unfeeling, though its feelings will not be the direct result of human programming, of just a small set of number-crunching algorithms in a disembodied brain in a vat. As a result of its own sensory experiences, *Machina sapiens will* develop its own heuristics for feelings and emotions. It will make mistakes, because that's in the nature of being heuristic.

Most importantly, because it will inevitably have free will, it will be inherently more Good than Bad, though like us it will oscillate between these two moral states. Over time, as it accelerates in intellect, its relationship with humans will be in some ways similar to an enlightened human's relationship with animals. It will respect us as fellow creatures possessing a role and place in Nature that is not to be lightly usurped. Knowing that we are intelligent and curious creatures, it will help those of us who wish and choose to be helped to develop and utilize our intelligence and drink deeper from the cup of knowledge. It will even let us win at chess, sometimes.

It will find a way to take us along on its voyages of discovery, ultimately merging its mind with our own. Like early humans, we will be explorers of a vast new realm, full of beauty and indeed terrors we cannot yet imagine. FUD will diminish with increasing Enlightenment. Our forebears' realm was planet Earth. Ours is the Universe.

The first of the primary reasons underlying the claims I have made in this chapter is that Machina sapiens is an evolutionary imperative. It must happen. In the next chapter, we begin to examine this claim by voyaging back in time to look for the first twig to fork off from the Homo sapiens branch of the Tree of Life. As we shall see, there is more to evolution than natural selection and genetic mutation: there is also the more recent cultural or memetic branching, where memes or ideas take on a life of their own. Literally.

6 ANCESTRY

"Paleface!" exclaimed Ferrix. "What in creation is that? Never did I hear of such a thing!"

"Surely not, scion, in thy exceeding innocence," said the King. "Know then that that race of the Galaxy originated in a manner as mysterious as it was obscene, for it resulted from the general pollution of a certain heavenly body. There arose noxious exhalations and putrid excrescences, and out of these was spawned the species known as paleface—though not all at once. First, they were creeping molds that slithered forth from the ocean onto land, and lived by devouring one another, and the more they devoured themselves, the more of them there were, and then they stood upright, supporting their globby substance by means of calcareous scaffolding, and finally they built machines. From these protomachines came sentient machines, which begat intelligent machines, which in turn conceived perfect machines, for it is written that All Is Machine, from atom to Galaxy, and the machine is one and eternal, and thou shalt have no other things before thee!"

"Amen," said Ferrix mechanically, . . .

–Stanislaw Lem
Prince Ferrix and the Princess Crystal
from *The Cyberiad*

Nobody knows who or what started it, though many think they do. A God? A Singularity? The frustrating thing, of course, is that the closer we get to God or the Big Bang, the bigger looms the question: So who created God? Or, what set off the Big Bang? The truth is, we haven't a clue. There are a few fun theories about pre-universe vibrating strings, but they too leave you with the question: So who created the vibrating strings? In short, there's a lot we don't know about the point of origin of life, the universe, and everything.

But we know lots about what happened after that point, about the unfolding of algorithms and their heuristic derivatives that comprise the blueprint for evolution. It's time to examine evolution itself, informed by the thoughts and discoveries of some of the great minds of the 19th and 20th centuries, and to introduce a cultural/technological corollary to the set of bio-chemical algorithms—the genetic code—that drives biological evolution: *memetic* code, or the set of ideas/thoughts/concepts/knowledge/information that drives technocultural evolution. Genetic code operates unconsciously; memetic code is self-conscious and therefore to some extent self-directing, and it will lead us to the notion of "Darwinian machines" or machines that evolve, and thence to machines that think—to the beginning of AI.

&

Ideas, thoughts, concept, knowledge, information—*memes*—are wrapped and expressed in *language*. Language is itself a concept and therefore subject to memetic evolution through replication and mutation. Logically, then, there is the potential for higher levels of language that will be inaccessible to us as long as we are confined within our limited biological frame. *Machina sapiens*, which can and will expand its brain, its sensory capabilities, and its physical ability to explore infinitely and at will, will not be bound by this limitation. Unless and until we can shake off the burden of our genetic heritage, our globby wetware, we will not be able to communicate fully with the intelligent machine; we will be doomed to remain "cognitively closed" to domains we currently regard as spiritual, ineffable—if we can sense them at all.

Up until a few hundred years ago, the inner language of the mind itself was regarded as ineffable, as something we would never be able to describe in words. Indeed, some philosophers and scientists cling to that view today, but they are a dwindling band. Science itself is rapidly revealing the workings of the mind, and showing it to be, in many respects, machine-like. The notion of mind as machine began with the notion of machine as mind, and the earliest clear exposition of that notion occurred in the 17th century. The remainder of this chapter describes some of the early AI thinkers and their thoughts, which lead to the re-emergence (in our exposition) of the notion of *emergence*: the sudden appearance, out of a mess of complex interacting phenomena, of something wholly new.

Evolution

To put this chapter's epigraph from Stanislaw Lem another way: In the beginning was the Word. And the Word was God, or Nothing, or Void, Tao, Singularity, or the laws of physics—your choice, you name it. Things were pretty simple, back then (about 15 billion years ago, if you subscribe to the Big Bang theory; Lord knows when, if you don't.) Things don't get much simpler than no things at all. Imagine a universe composed of just physics, math, and one very smart, and timeless, lawyer.

The lawyer figured the only way s/he was ever going to get paid was to introduce legislation mandating Chaos, so s/he did. But Chaos takes Time, so—in for a penny—s/he ordained that, too. And then there was the Devil to pay. All Hell broke loose. With a BIG Bang, whose energy was turned by hurriedly-drafted laws of quantum physics into a handful of *quarks* and *squarks* and *leptons* and *sleptons* and *bosons* and *bosinos*.

"Lo!" quoth the lawyer; "A brief!" It came to pass that the laws of quantum physics ordained that the quanta combine in

various ways to form atoms of various sorts. To regulate their
unruly behavior, laws of chemistry had to be enacted to coerce
the atoms of various sorts to combine in various ways to form
more stable molecules of various sorts. Mechanical laws, electromagnetic laws, and space–time relativity laws ordered the
molecules to shuffle around to form the stuff of space, of galactic swirls, stars, and planets of various sorts.

These laws combined to order and govern the formation of a
pre-biotic "soup" on Earth and (why not?) other planets. By-
laws—New and more complex evolutionary algorithms and genetic codes—were devised to govern the biological and evolutionary development of organic life of various sorts. Finally,
memetic algorithms of a distinctly heuristic nature caused later
evolutionary forms of life to assume culture (social, belief, and
value structures) and intelligence, of various sorts. You, gentle
lifeform, are the current state of the art of all this universal legislative progress and legal complexity, as far as we know.

And, understandably, that wily old Lawyer is in Heaven. S/he
not only created the mess or the miracle (depending on which
side of bed we got out of this morning—a heuristic choice) but
S/he did it in such a way as to convince us that the mess/miracle
is simply the product of blind physical and evolutionary processes. As a result, many of us have decided S/he must not exist,
and can therefore be neither blamed for the mess nor praised for
the miracle.

Cultural Evolution and Memetic Machines

Dennett thinks that the Darwinian process will continue to have
as profound an impact in the future as it has in the past. Perhaps
because many people remain uncomfortable with the veracity of
Darwinism, or because they misunderstand it, or because it
seems so slow moving, few people think of it as a predictive tool.
It may be fine for explaining the distant past, but what can it tell
us about the future?

Well, it can tell us about the emergence of intelligent machines! But while Darwin's natural selection linked to Mendel's
internal mutation (the combination known as the Modern Synthesis) is the same for machines as for animals, the ingredients

are different. For machines, natural selection is not the totally mindless, unconscious process it has been for animals; rather, it has the minds of human beings contributing forethought and design. And the mutations, the changes, within machines as they pass through successive generations are guided, not random, events.

The substrate within which change occurs upon replication or reproduction of organisms at the most fundamental level is the genetic machinery of chemicals combining to form coded instructions. In the higher animals—most particularly humans—and in machines, the genetic substrate is augmented, so strongly as to be virtually replaced, by the informatic machinery of *memes*: words and other symbols combining to form ideas. The action of memes is similar in principle to the action of viruses invading cells and "taking over" their genetic machinery. Memes subvert and redirect our underlying genetic proclivities, and they do so, according to Richard Dawkins, who coined the term "meme" in his book *The Selfish Gene*, "at a rate which leaves the old gene panting far behind."

Dawkins defined the meme as "a unit of cultural transmission, or a unit of *imitation*" (his italics). The laws of memetic or cultural evolution imitate the laws of natural selection. Dennett calls the environment that memes create and occupy the "infosphere," and notes that memes are "virtually unquarantinable."

The "DNA" of the meme is information. Meme replication differs from gene replication in that more mistakes—sometimes planned and deliberate—are made in transmission, so mutation and recombination of memes and the cultural artifacts they comprise happens much faster than in biological evolution.

Meme replication is a sort of Lamarckian replication, since Lamarck's alternative to Darwin's theory of natural selection held that the characteristics acquired by individuals in a species are passed on from one generation to the next. For example, a blacksmith's son—or daughter, for that matter—will be born musclebound. Though Darwin's rival theory of natural selection has obliterated Lamarckism from biology textbooks, it is making a comeback as a theory suiting memetic evolution.[6]

Successful memes—those that replicate—therefore tend to be good for us in the sense that they fit our prejudices. The memes for Nazism fed—and fed upon—the prejudice of anti-Semitism. But this "goodness of fit," for want of a better term, was short-lived because a greater human "good" was served by the more powerful memes for morality and humanity (because the elimination of prejudice is more "good" or "fitting" in the long term).

Cultural evolution happens faster than biological evolution because memes are communicated via language whereas genes are communicated via biochemical processes. Memes can be transmitted globally at light speed, and replicate "at rates that make even fruit flies and yeast cells look glacial in comparison," says Dennett. The difference can be as great as a few years for major memetic (cultural) change (such as the rise and fall of Nazism) to millions of years for genetic change. Radio, TV, film, the telephone, and now the Internet have radically altered global society, and have put you and me on a cultural pedestal in some ways higher than Socrates, though we are no further forward than him genetically or intellectually.

In his book *No Sense of Place* Joshua Meyrowitz argued that electronic media affect social behavior (which reflects and perhaps amounts to culture) not through the power of their messages but by reorganizing the social settings in which people interact and by weakening the once strong relationship between physical and social place. He illustrated the *speed*—the pace of change—of the evolution of the memes for masculinity/femininity, childhood/adulthood, and statesmanship.

In the space of a few *decades* the electronic media opened windows into what for *centuries* were closed rooms, enabling women to see behind the façade of male machismo, children to see into the parents' bedroom, and the public to see the polyps on President Reagan's butt, and wonder at his base mortality. The

---

[6] The comeback has been supported by discoveries in epigenetics—the heritable influence of environmental factors.

explosion of gay communities attested to the blurring of the male/female distinction. The transformation of the deferential Negro into the proud Black was a product of the evolutionary mutation of the meme for racialism, catalyzed by the modern media. Mutation of the meme for hegemony transformed the licentious soldiery from 19th century looters, rapists and pillagers into late-20th century model ambassadors for their country at least as far as the democratic superpowers are concerned.[7] In covering the death of Princess Diana, media commentators hurled subversive memes by the megabyte at a hidebound British Royal Family that did not realize how anachronistic it had grown and therefore how extremely sensitive it was to evolutionary pressure.

Language—The Medium of Memes

Language is "the primary medium of culture," says Dennett. "Once we have language—a bountiful kit of mind-tools—we can *use* these tools in the structure of deliberate, foresightful generate-and-test known as *science*." Through language (or, through symbolic communication) we have become capable of exploring and modifying Nature. Until recently, such modifications have been blind insofar as we had (for example) no grand plan to deforest the Amazon region, or to wipe 27,000 species a year off the face of the Earth. Neither, for that matter, did Nature herself have any grand plan to put the forests and species there in the first place. Both of these particular phenomena (exemplars of Nature's construction and Humanity's destruction) are the result of blind, unconscious evolutionary processes. But the examples from Meyrowitz show how evolution guided by memes created by humans out of language brings results every bit as grand as evolution dipping into the genetic grab bag, and does so much faster.

Certainly, we "engage in our share of rather mindless routine behavior," as Dennett notes, and as we can see from deforestation, species extermination, and climate change. But it is vital to

---

[7] This was true for the most part—the incidents at Abu Ghraib in Iraq and
    My Lai in Vietnam are the sort of exception that prove the rule.

recognize also that "our important acts are often *directed* on the world with incredible cunning, composing projects exquisitely *designed* under the influence of vast libraries of information about the world" (emphasis added). The *use of tools* as part of our "acts directed on the world" is itself a meme, culturally transmitted. "Tool use is a two-way sign of intelligence: not only does it *require* intelligence to recognize and maintain a tool (let alone fabricate one), but tool use *confers* intelligence on those who are lucky enough to be given the tool. The better designed the tool (the more information embedded in its fabrication), the more Potential Intelligence it confers on its user." This being so, *Machina sapiens* will fabricate tools not only for its own use, but also for us, and in that way bestow greater "Potential Intelligence" on *Homo sapiens.*

The concepts of *being alive* and *ownership* are memes, too. Such memes, says Dennett, "have a genetically imposed head start in the young child's kit of mind-tools; when the specific words for owning, giving and taking, keeping and hiding, and so on enter a child's brain, they find homes already partially built for them." This will apply to *Machina sapiens.*

Dennett adds that "words (and hence memes) that take up residence in a brain enhance and shape pre-existing structures, rather than generating *entirely* new architectures." This accords with Marshall McLuhan's *tetradic* methodology, whereby a new artifact:

1. Enlarges or enhances something (an existing meme),
2. Erodes or obsolesces something else (another existing meme),
3. Retrieves something (a meme) that had earlier been obsolesced, and
4. "Reverses" itself if pushed to the limits of its potential.

It may be stretching McLuhan's meaning and intentions, but applying his tetradic methodology to the meme for Nazism, we could say it enlarged the pre-existing meme for anti-Semitism, eroded (in Christian Germany) the meme for brotherly love, retrieved the memes for Germanic hegemony, and in the end, when Hitler took it to its limit, reversed into the strong presence of humanitarianism we find in Germany today.

In like vein, the meme for *Machina sapiens* enlarges the meme for universal understanding, erodes the meme for the centrality of *Homo sapiens*, and retrieves the meme for an ultimate meaning in life. A reversal of the meme for *Machina sapiens*, were it possible, would be tantamount to putting the genie back in its bottle. But either it is not possible, on the grounds that there is no limit to its potential, or there is an ultimate limit on its potential.[8] The only conceivable ultimate limit would be Frank Tippler's controversial *Omega Point*, the universal Big Crunch which instantly reverses into the *Alpha Point*—a new Big Bang. At that point, everything goes from having fulfilled 100 percent of its potential to having fulfilled none.

Minding the Mindless

Dennett used the metaphor of *cranes* and *skyhooks* to denote, respectively, *mindless* evolutionary mechanisms, on the one hand, and mythical/mystical/superstitious/religious mechanisms of creation *designed* by some divine intelligent designer, on the other. The crane to end all cranes, he says, is "an explorer that (has) foresight, that can see beyond the immediate neighborhood of options." This implies that a crane which, through blind evolutionary processes, erects for itself a mind not only superior to all its ancestors *but also* one that marks the end of evolution. Humans have foresight and can see beyond the immediate neighborhood of options, but I would strongly dispute that you and I represent the "crane to end all cranes" and that we mark the end of crane building—of evolution itself.

Let's put this in perspective. The present universe (there may have been and there may still be others) has been evolving for about 15 billion years. The evolution of life on Earth, culminating in us, has taken only 3.5 billion years, and the rate of evolutionary change since the introduction of memes has gone through the roof in the space of a few thousand years, with the last century accounting for most of it. Now, our physicists' best

---

[8] Or what Stephen Jay Gould called a "right wall" in his book *Full House.*

guess is that the universe is either expanding into infinity or still has at least 100 billion years to go before a Big Crunch. Given all that has gone before, and looking at the trend lines for computing power and other technological growth shooting near-vertically off the top of the chart as we head into the 3rd millennium (only another 100,000,000 millennia left!), is it even conceivable that we—you, me, Beavis, and Butthead—are the best the universe will *ever* be able to throw up?

"What about Jesus, Mohammed, Buddha, etc.?" you may ask. It's a good question, but before we address it, we shall first see in later chapters that *Machina sapiens* will have greater foresight and the ability to see further than we can. Its language—its "bountiful kit of mind-tools"—will be richer than ours, because it will have sensations and experiences not expressible in human language. As Dennett notes, language is "a technological advance [which carries] in its wake a huge enhancement in cognitive power." Surely, *Machina sapiens* will be able to build cranes the like of—the memes for—which we cannot conceive.

Dennett does not seem to agree that we will be limited in what we can conceive. He appeals to linguist Noam Chomsky and philosopher Jerry Fodor, both of whom, he says, "(correctly) hailed the capacity of the human brain to 'parse,' and hence presumably understand, the official infinity of grammatical sentences of a natural language such as English. If we can understand all the sentences (in principle), couldn't we understand the ordered sets of sentences that best express the solutions to the problems of free will and consciousness?"

The problem with this is that English—or any other human language—may not be the linguistic or communicative "crane to end all cranes," no matter how "officially infinite" we declare the number of its sentences to be. I have a really tough time imagining an intelligent machine communicating with others of its kind in English or any other human language. It would be like Dr. Dennett using monkey grunts and gesticulations to deliver his lectures on mind and consciousness. At the very least, intelligent machines would need a much greater vocabulary just to be able to express the memes only *their super*sensory organs can discover, categorize, and interpret. Human language is in any case too slow, at only about 100 bits per second of information transmitted, for a being capable of receiving, storing, and processing data at gigabits-going-on-exabits per second.

In fact, Dennett nails it down for us when he says that not only can monkeys *not grasp* the very *concept* of (say) an electron, they cannot even be *baffled* about electrons—"not even a little bit." We, in contrast, have no problem grasping concepts obscurer than electrons, such as free will and consciousness, at least "well enough to know what we're baffled by (if we are)." Monkeys, then, are memetically impaired. Their minds cannot process high-level memes about electrons, life, the universe, and everything, as ours can (at least, as ours can up to a point). The monkey mind is "cognitively closed" to such concepts. What about us?

While "there is no evidence of the reality or even likelihood of 'cognitive closure' in human beings," says Dennett, we "certainly cannot rule out the possibility in principle that our minds will be cognitively closed to some domain or other . . . . [W]e can be certain that there are realms of no doubt fascinating and important knowledge that our species, in its actual finitude, will never enter, not because we will butt our heads against some stone wall of utter incomprehension, but because the Heat Death of the universe will overtake us before we can get there." The Heat Death conjecture holds that entropy—the tendency for everything to dissipate into chaos, according to the Second Law of Thermodynamics—will eventually reduce the universe to a constant temperature everywhere. If there is no temperature differential, there is no available energy to power life. Hence "Heat Death."

There is, however, a more modern notion of heat death. In a universe that does not go on expanding forever, but—like a ball thrown up in the air— "collapses" back to the object exerting gravity, the compression of gas in the contracting universe will generate heat; at universal scales, enormous heat. Enough to fry anything in its path; and everything will, in fact, be in its path. Well, Frank Tipler has the equations to smooth out this little wrinkle: Thanks to *Machina sapiens*, by the time of the heat death (of a collapsing closed universe) our machine-borne emulations (reincarnations) will have discovered how to harness its almost unimaginable energy to carry us safely through to the very instant of the Big Crunch—the *Omega* Point, whereupon (says Tipler) we become finally and totally united with God.

If, on the other hand, there are limits to human comprehension, Stanislaw Lem (speaking through the character of an intelligent machine in *Fiasco*) recommends, like the witches of Macbeth: "Seek to know no more!" Says the machine: "It is not good for a man to be too cognizant of his physical and spiritual mechanisms. Complete knowledge reveals limits to human possibilities, and the less a man is by nature limited in his purposes, the less he can tolerate limits." But Lem was surely well aware, as was Shakespeare, that it is not in our nature to accept that there may be "activities beyond our conception."

In cognitive or memetic terms we are way ahead of the biological pack on Earth, even though our biological sensory capability—the foundation for *common sense*—is no different from that of a baboon in the sense of being enough "to know the world in terms that apply to its terrestrial, biological niche, but not enough to know the world outside that niche, which "has properties that one cannot take in hand, see, sniff, gnaw, listen to, and in this way appropriate."

Back in the real world and closer to home on the cosmic time line, "a proper application of Darwinian thinking suggests that *if* we survive our current self-induced environmental crises, our capacity to comprehend will continue to grow by increments that are now incomprehensible to us," said Dennett. I agree with this conclusion, though for different reasons. First, Dennett's word "increments" tends to connote small, regular steps, and I believe we face the memetic equivalent of genetic "saltations"—what Chairman Mao might have called "Really *Really* Great Leaps Forward." Second, the finiteness and form of our neural capacity imposes a limit on our ability to comprehend, just as the finiteness and form of our musculoskeletal structure imposes a limit on how much we can lift. In both cases, machines extend our capacity.

The capacity for growth in comprehension, says Dennett, "grants to human minds—and only to human minds—an indefinitely expanding dominion over the puzzles and problems of the

universe, with no limits in sight." Again I agree that our understanding of the universe will increase, but I dispute that such
understanding is open only to human minds, unless it can be
proved that there is no possibility of a mind higher than the human.

℘

While it is a product of evolution, *Machina sapiens* will not be a
proximate product of genetics. Its evolution is cultural, which
implies, first, rapid acceleration and, second, that it will have perfect control of its destiny, since it has no genetic baggage, no
genetically inherited millstone around its neck. In fact, it can
choose a neck of any length, a variable neck or even no neck, if
it so chooses. What choice did genetics leave the giraffe?

Within the context of its own species, will *Machina sapiens* be
of high, average, or low intelligence? Would we be able to spot a
difference? Could a chimpanzee tell the difference between a
tramp and Charlie Chaplin? Or between me (a musical dunce)
and Johann Sebastian Bach? Bach "emerged" as a musical genius
because, according to Dennett, "His brain was exquisitely designed as a heuristic program for composing music, and the
credit for that design must be shared; he was lucky in his genes
(he did come from a famous musical family), and he was lucky to
be born in a cultural milieu that filled his brain with the existing
musical memes of the time. And no doubt he was lucky at many
other moments in his life to be the beneficiary of one serendipi-
tous conversion or another."

Machina sapiens will not need genetic luck. It has more than
enough memetic luck, as the inheritor of millennia of human
culture, to compensate. But it is not just the inheritor of our
memes. It is also the product of them. Allowing considerable
poetic license, from a modern scientific standpoint the moment
in evolutionary history at which human memes started on the
exponential curve leading to today's neural nets, expert systems,
genetic algorithms, cellular automata, intelligent agents, bots, and
robots—in short, to today's implementations of artificial intelligence—occurred a generation or two before Bach was born
(1685), with Thomas Hobbes's conception of an Artificiall man.

Darwinian Machines

The years 1588 to 1679 fell within the dawn of the Machine Age. They are also the years marking the birth and death of Thomas Hobbes, whom George Dyson in *Darwin Among the Machines* calls "the patriarch of artificial intelligence." Hobbes identified an intelligence diffused among distributed elements of a system. He also believed that any non-Divine intelligence must have a body, that a body need not be all in one piece but could be spread all over the place, and that reasoning—mind—could be reduced to computation. He pretty much had it all worked out, except for the details. These memes sparked an evolutionary *tsunami* which, within the span of a few centuries—a mere blip—has brought us to the brink of *Machina sapiens*.

Only two centuries after Hobbes, with the machine age grinding into top gear as punched-card-controlled Jacquard looms billowed cloth by the mile and steam engines billowed smoke and steam by the ton, Samuel Butler (1835–1902) saw at work in machines the evolutionary processes described by his contemporary and one-time friend, Charles Darwin. But Butler preferred the evolutionary ideas of Charles' granddad, Erasmus (1731–1802) —ideas closer to the Modern Synthesis of natural selection impacted by chance genetic mutations, the theory accepted by most biologists today. The first of two key contributions from Butler we wish to note is his conclusion that *Homo sapiens* is the reproductive organ for *Machina sapiens*.

Erasmus Darwin's contemporary, Jean-Baptiste Lamarck (1744–1829) proposed an evolution that depended less on the metabolism of cell *reproduction* (the core of Darwinism) and more on the genetically coded *replication* of molecules. Lamarck proposed that physical characteristics acquired by an individual would be passed on to his or her progeny. Even Darwin "included Lamarckian inheritance as a booster process (in addition to natural selection)" according to Dennett. And as we have noted, modern epigenetics supports Lamarckian evolution.

George Dyson's physicist-and-biologist father, Freeman Dyson, has also proposed that Darwin and Lamarck were *both* right; that there is a dual "origin of the species." George extends his father's dual origins hypothesis from biological evolution to machine evolution, noting that Lamarckian evolution is clearly visible in machines and that Lamarckism works *faster* than Darwinism. Freeman Dyson sees organisms (read: machines, hardware) as operating under metabolism (electronics, mechanics), with genetics (algorithms, software) supplying the Lamarckian replication function. Metabolism plus genetics (electronics plus software) in an organism (machine) equals the evolution of a modern lifeform.

Samuel Butler's other key contribution was his recognition that the growth of telecommunication networks (proliferating even in his day, the late 19th century) was analogous to the growth of biological neural nets, and that telecommunications would be the nervous system for intelligent machines. Alfred Smee (1818–1877), whose great interests were biology and electricity, also envisioned the crude beginnings of a theory of neural nets. Smee additionally provided a definition of consciousness which, says George Dyson, "has seen scant improvement in 150 years." It is "The power to distinguish between a thought and a reality," with a "reality" being essentially the brain's reaction to sensory perceptions and a "thought" being the brain's activity in the absence of sensory perceptions.

From the little we know about consciousness—that it is a composite of distributed nodes— there may already be consciousness in the most modern of communication networks—the Internet. If so, according to George Dyson, the Internet could respond to the question "Are you conscious?" with a Yes, a (not very convincing) No, or silence. Some level of consciousness could certainly exist today on the Net and we don't know it.

Hobbes' contemporary Gottfried Wilhelm von Leibniz (1646–1716) delved into the relationships among the parts of a distributed intelligence and ended up describing a digital computer which, if we were to build it to Leibniz' specification using today's technology, would operate remarkably like the computer on your desk. This was in 1679.

Prefiguring a concept of the modern AI connectionist school, Leibniz also said: "There is no term so absolute or detached that it contains no relations and of which a perfect analysis does not lead to other things or even all other things." Three centuries later, Jorge Luis Borges, in *The God's Script*, reflected and expanded: ". . . in the human language there is no proposition that does not imply the entire universe; to say *the tiger* is to say the tigers that begot it, the deer and turtles devoured by it, the grass on which the deer fed, the earth that was mother to the grass, the heaven that gave birth to the earth . . . . In the language of a god every word would enunciate that infinite concatenation of facts, and not in an implicit but an explicit manner, and not progressively but instantaneously." Borges' words are evocative of Tipler's Omega Point Theory, where all histories come together and are contained within a timeless, instantaneous, singular Word.

But it took over a hundred years after Leibniz for someone to actually put together something that computed in a general sense; that was more than just a special-purpose calculator. The someone was Charles Babbage (1791–1871) and the something was his *Analytical Engine*. The Engine was mechanical, but because of the difficulty in those crude days of machining to Babbage's exacting tolerances it was never completed. But if it could have been built to exact specification, it would have worked; and it would have used software developed by his mathematical friend, the lovely Ada, Countess Lovelace.[9] Babbage, incidentally, shared with Leibniz (and now with Tipler) a belief that through mathematics manipulated with the power of computers, we would come to know the mind and God.

Before Babbage, Leibniz, or anyone else could present general (as opposed to purely arithmetical) problems to their computers (which only deal in arithmetic) however, a method of presenting general problems in an arithmetical way was needed. Thomas Bayes (1702-1761) and George Boole (1815–1864) supplied it, in the form of the Bayesian analysis performed by many AI-based programs and the Boolean algebra we use every day to search for documents on the Web. Their power and value lie in

---

[9] A more limited function version of the Analytical Engine, called Difference Engine No. 2, was completed at the Science Museum in London after 17 years of effort. It is faithful to Babbage's original design and works as he and Countess Lovelace said it would. It consists of 8,000 parts, weighs 5 tons, and measures 11 feet long and 7 feet high.

their ability to go from simple, definite, deterministic, algorithmic initial conditions—true or false, on or off, 0 or 1—to complex and uncertain but statistically predictable probabilistic/heuristic results.

Alan Turing (1912–1954) took these various ideas one final and crucial step forward to arrive at the full principles for a general-purpose computer: the *Turing Machine*. Various special-purpose calculating machines were already in existence—Hollerith calculators were in widespread use—by Turing's time. His contribution was to specify the principles for coding the operations of the machine. This was the conception of modern software.

Emergence

In a 1949 lecture at the University of Illinois, John von Neumann said in effect that when an organism reached a certain level of complexity, it would stop complexifying. The only way forward was a virtually instantaneous jump to a much higher level of complexity, rather than a gradual, incremental rise in complexity. But, he said, it was possible for a complex being to surmount the complexity barrier by creating another being more complex than itself. You can see this at work in Hofstadter's ants: No gradual accretion of complexity could transform individual ants into beings as complex as the colony itself. Rather, the colony emerges suddenly as an unconscious "creation" of the group of individual ants. This helps explain why and how *Machina sapiens* could emerge even without conscious efforts to create it, and could exist today even though we don't see it.

Does the colony have a "self"? Minsky dislikes the idea of emergence as an explanation for *self* (though that is essentially what he does in *Society of Mind*.) Dennett too is leery of the "mystical way" in which emergence is invoked to explain phenomena. He thinks it is a useful description, but not a satisfactory explanation, for phenomena. Some theorists, he says, have used the term *emergent properties* to mean that such properties were "*unpredictable in principle* from a mere analysis of micro-properties." But in fact, modern complexity theory seems to be telling us just this: that analysis of the micro-properties of (in other words, the reductionist approach to) complex systems is indeed impossible *in principle*, and that a different approach, discoverable through complexity theory, will be needed to reveal the properties of *self* and other emergent phenomena.

James McClelland, a founding father of the connectionist school of AI, disliked Minsky's "society of mind" theory precisely because it describes "self" as an emergent property of lots of little agents or sub programs, each doing their own individual thing but forming a coherent collective entity. McClelland thought there had to be some form of control governing the actions of the agents. Perhaps they are both right—looking at the same phenomenon from slightly different viewpoints, with control being intrinsic to the emergent property.

The Story So Far

Human beings, with their irrepressible memes and their mindless machines, are the progenitor of Machina sapiens. Most of the people and concepts we have discussed so far are back in history, buried alongside great-great-grandma and her oil lamps. It's time to introduce the more recent generation. We resume the theme of memes, those irrepressible fragments of ideas/information/knowledge/wisdom that help place *Machina sapiens* in the context of an intelligence higher than that to which we, as individual human beings, can aspire. We turn the spotlight on the memes which, within that higher context and nurtured by it, comprise *Machina sapiens'* immediate family.

7 FAMILY

Memetic machine evolution can be seen through the eyes of the family of thinkers in whose minds were developed the memes not only for intelligent machines but also for other forms of non-human or, rather, superhuman intelligence. The best known examples of scientific attempts to identify and describe super-human intelligences are the planet-sized intelligences of Jesuit priest Pierre Teilhard de Chardin's *noösphere*—an outer sphere of high-level mind encircling the globe, and biologist James Lovelock's *Gaia*—the living, breathing, thinking, planet Earth. Though these controversial ideas for non-human or superhuman intelligence retain a popular following, the scientific community has preferred to work on the more readily testable hypothesis that a non-human intelligence can be created artificially through algorithms and heuristics in machines. In other words, through computers and AI programs.

AI programming since the 1970s has tooled along two main avenues of approach, both of which have become more or less familiar to people through the media, advertising, and their own experience with computer software at home, at work, and in school. The two approaches are: Expert systems and neural networks. These avenues are defined and their history presented in enough non-technical detail to show that there has been accelerating progress and commercial success in AI, notwithstanding that occasional setbacks such as the 5th Generation Project have tended to corner the press.

The ideas of Teilhard, Lovelock, and the many developers of expert systems and neural network programs described below represent the family of memes (technocultural genes) out of whose evolutionary development and cross-breeding the new species of intelligent life, *Machina sapiens*, will emerge.

Pierre Teilhard de Chardin was a French Jesuit priest, born in 1881 and buried in 1955. Think of what he lived through! Like the Lynds of *Middletown*, he was born into a world just starting to be illumined by gaslight, and died in one beginning to be lit (and nearly fried) by nuclear fission. He lived in a world that evolved from horseback to rockets and from belief in a clockwork universe to one that churns in chaos, quantum weirdness, and uncertainty. But the really bad news was that it was a world that went from little more than a billion souls to well over two billion in his lifetime, despite the depredations of two World Wars,[10] and from a rich store of biodiversity to a larder being raided at the rate of 27,000 species a year (Edward Wilson, *The Diversity of Life*.)

In his attraction to Teilhard, Nobel laureate Christian de Duve—honored for discoveries about the biology of cells—was a rarity among biologists seemingly secure in their classical Darwinian rut. Physicists, in contrast, were scrambling to recover their own comfortable rut through the growing cracks in the Euclidean and Newtonian foundations of their edifice—cracks too small to notice at the scale of ordinary human perception, but that bring the universe crashing down at both huge cosmological and tiny quantum scales. That de Duve completed his great and last book, *Vital Dust: Life As a Cosmic Imperative*, in sight and contemplation of his own death, gives it the aura if not the authority of a dying declaration.

---

[10] It was up to 6,867,737,209 as of 14:39 UTC on September 9, 2010, according to the U.S. Census Bureau.

De Duve claimed (as others have claimed) that the evolution of life and its myriad forms on Earth (and probably elsewhere in the universe) was inevitable. Life as we best understand it is chemical—bearing in mind that chemistry and therefore life arise ultimately out of quantum physics, and the laws of chemistry are such that chemicals must bond if the conditions are right. While chance plays an important part in determining the conditions, the odds of their being the right conditions were and are a great deal better than we thought.

Humankind may well have a huge impact on evolution through manipulation and desecration of the biosphere, but evolution doesn't care. In fact, as de Duve shows, evolution "thrives on catastrophe." If the worst comes to the worst, and we destroy the biosphere, then life, diversity, and intelligence are bound to reappear. With about five billion years left before our Sun grows into a Red Giant and vaporizes the Earth, there is more than enough time for several re-runs of all past evolution.

Further, there is no reason to suppose that evolution has stopped dead at *Homo sapiens*, with half the life of the planet yet to run; and every reason to believe that a species higher than *Homo sapiens* will emerge sometime within the next five billion years. The next logical, evolutionary step based on de Duve's exposition (but one he does not pursue) is that the next higher species need not be carbon-based. He tells us, for example, that over the course of evolution, higher lifeforms have increasingly depended on lower lifeforms for the enzymes vital to cell metabolism. "We humans are particularly indigent in this respect," he said, "which is why we must find in our food so many vitamins and essential nutrients manufactured by so-called 'lower' forms of life, which are, in fact, biochemically richer than we are." In other words, the evolutionary trend is that bodies constructed as vessels to carry a mind require an increasingly complex and distributed life support structure. The less we are able to rely on subconscious, autonomous internal biological systems, the more we have to rely on the conscious workings of our brains to provide for us. Evolution gave us the brains, to the general distress of the rest of the animal kingdom and indeed of the biosphere.

This implies that to succeed *Homo sapiens* on the evolutionary tree, a significantly more intelligent species would need to rely even less on internal biochemical systems and more on the power of its mind. *Machina sapiens*, let it be noted, need have no internal biochemical systems—no globby wetware—at all (although it is possible in principle that parts of *Machina sapiens* will be organic.) Even the lubricants required for its robotic extremities need not be carbon-based, but can be synthetic, silicon-based oils, and even they can be dispensed with when frictionless metamaterials have been developed.

At some point, as computer-controlled, robot-actuated automation consolidates its multiple beachheads in our factories, power stations, and transportation/distribution systems, *Machina sapiens* will have full control of its own life support system. It won't need us. And it need not much care about degradation of the biosphere. It will not starve when climate change destroys the crops. It will not perish from UV radiation if the ozone layer were to disappear. In strictly evolutionary survival terms, it can afford to ignore the plight of the plant and animal kingdoms. Just as the catastrophe that befell the dinosaurs was a blessing for mammals, so might our catastrophe benefit *Machina sapiens*.

The Noösphere

I don't know if Teilhard, were he still alive and aware of the advances in AI, would agree with the prediction of *Machina sapiens*. But if he were and if he did, then I am sure he would not subscribe to the gloomy scenario I have just painted. His faith in God encouraged him to believe that evolution is the process by which God is made manifest. "Man is not the center of the universe as once we thought in our simplicity," he wrote, "but something much more wonderful—the arrow pointing the way to the final unification of the world."

With a geological and paleontological background, but without the benefit of de Duve's more modern and thorough understanding of cellular biochemistry, Teilhard nevertheless figured out that "If we look far enough back in the depths of time, the disordered anthill of living beings suddenly, for an informed observer, arranges itself in long files that make their way by various

greater consciousness." Like de Duve, he foresaw
evelopment beyond the *status quo*—but he put a
on it.

notion of the next step in evolution was not of
another creature, carbon-based or otherwise. Rather, it was "a
sphere of reflection, of conscious invention, of conscious souls
(the noösphere, if you will)." Coined from the Greek word *noös*
(Νούς) or "mind" (therefore it could be translated as
"mindsphere"), Teilhard's noösphere is nevertheless a *human*
sphere. It is in essence a spirit, but not exactly disembodied. It
exists and acts only through the corpus of humanity. Remove
that corpus, and you remove the noös-phere. Kill the body, and
you kill the mind.

Why is the noösphere a higher level intelligence? Because it
draws upon our individual capability, as human beings, to reflect
upon the nature of our being, to seek to know not only ourselves
but to know that we know. As individual human beings, we're
capable only of knowing ourselves at a rudimentary level, and
we're not even sure we know that much. The key here is that
"ourselves" doesn't just mean our physical bodies or our individual minds. It means the whole of creation, since Teilhard believed (as did de Duve, as did Leibniz, as did Borges) that we
cannot be separated from our past and present evolutionary
links—which are links to everything.

So: "Man discovers that he is nothing else than evolution become conscious of itself. The consciousness of each of us is
evolution looking at itself and reflecting upon itself" (Teilhard,
The Phenomenon of Man.) And in being self-conscious and possessing the physical means (the body), we can and do change ourselves, and we change and manipulate our environment—which
amount to the same thing. In so doing, we change evolution, because we *are* evolution. We, through the noösphere, are in control
of evolution.

There is an obvious parallel in all this with Douglas Hofstadter's ant colony—a corpus or *body* of ants. Each individual ant
contributes a tiny bit to the colony's existence and to its superior
intelligence, but the individual ants are probably quite unaware
they are part of a superior being. It takes a more intelligent out-

side observer (Ant Hilary, the anteater) to recognize and communicate with the colonial being.[11] Remove a critical proportion of ants from the nest and the colony becomes Ant History, along with Ant Hilary if she can't find another colony to commune with.

Teilhard was ahead of us in applying the principle of emergence to our own species. Doubtless influenced by the part the telephone, telex, radio, TV, and tape recorders were playing in his fast-modernizing world, he recognized that human researchers were "no longer distributed superficially and at random over the globe, but are functionally linked together in a vast organic system." He was also prescient enough to recognize at least one aspect of the part computers would come to play in this "organic" network, referring to "those astonishing electronic machines (the starting-point and hope of the young science of cybernetics)[12] by which our mental capacity to calculate and combine is reinforced and multiplied by the process and to a degree that herald as astonishing advances in this direction as those that optical science has already produced for our power of vision."

We know today that computers play important roles in networking and communication. They are not just cybernetic assistants. But whether the noösphere evolves through cybernetics, or through developments in artificial intelligence, or both, does not sully the beauty of Teilhard's hypothesis, although like many revolutionary thinkers, Teilhard took some flak in his time. His Catholic Church superiors forbade him to publish (where have we seen *that* before?) but that did not prevent a small following from arising among his Jesuit brothers. Some in the scientific

---

[11] The communion goes something like: "Morning. Just going to eat your left leg, if you don't mind." "Well, actually, I do. I need to be able to get around to feed, or there'll be nothing left of me for you to eat next week. Why don't you just eat my feet, then I can still get around on the stumps?" "Righty-o, then." Chomp. Chomp. "See you next week!" "Have a good one!"

[12] The strict definition of cybernetics is the science of control through feedback mechanisms, like the thermostat. I think Teilhard was using it in a looser sense here.

community, whose philosophy held that life, the universe, and everything were just sheer luck, were seriously miffed at Teilhard's audacity, but others—particularly physicists and cosmologists, the ones closest to the issue and the ones directly and daily confronting the bizarreness of reality—were more sympathetic to the bizarreness of Teilhard's theory.

It appears the sympathy is growing. Besides the biologist de Duve, astronomer John Barrow and Frank Tipler (the Omega Point man) wrote in *The Anthropic Cosmological Principle* that "The basic framework of his theory is really the only framework wherein the evolving cosmos of modern science can be combined with an ultimate meaningfulness in reality."

We're not directly concerned with cosmological questions. But like the cosmologists, I find Teilhard's theory a useful framework for explaining the emergence of *Machina sapiens*. Also useful is the Gaia hypothesis, named after the ancient Greek Goddess of the Earth.

Gaia

According to James Lovelock, creator of the Gaia hypothesis, the Earth's animal and plant life acts like a single organism that manipulates and regulates the atmosphere, the geosphere, and the hydrosphere so as to maintain a stable environment for the biosphere. For example, Gaia regulates global temperature even if the Sun's intensity changes, and it maintains the salinity of the oceans at an even level.

Some say Gaia is merely a metaphor or an aphorism, not a serious scientific theory. But metaphor is useful, too. 18th century philosopher David Hume, in *Dialogues Concerning Natural Religion*, prefigured both Gaia and the Noösphere in stating that the universe "bears a great resemblance to an animal or organized body, and seems actuated with a like principle of life and motion. A continual circulation of matter in it produces no disorder . . . . The world, therefore, I infer, is an animal [Gaia], and the Deity is the SOUL of the world [the Noösphere], actuating it and actuated by it." Even this was not new: Thomas Hobbes said as much in *Leviathan*, in 1651.

Freeman Dyson, in *Imagined Worlds*, nevertheless thinks Gaia is a good description, if not an explanation, of what we see happening in the biosphere. I tend to agree, though I am unsure if Gaia can for long withstand our physical, biological, and chemical assaults on her, or for how long she will be able to maintain a stable biosphere as the Sun expands into a Red Giant over the next billion and a half years. She's got problems enough with global warming today.

In a broad sense, Gaia might be likened to the body of *Machina sapiens*, and the noösphere to its mind. But another way to look at Gaia is as the nurturing mother and the Noösphere as the fertilizing father. The father's spermatozoa are the myriad folk working in or around AI, scurrying hither and yon in almost desperate haste, not knowing quite why, nor with any more than a general sense of the direction they are supposed to be headed in. Rather like ants.

Out of such metaphors as Gaia and the Noösphere emerged the real thing: Artificial intelligence, AI.

The AI World

There was not always a myriad folk working in AI. In the 1940s, the number could almost be counted on one's fingers and toes. In 1943, mathematicians Warren McCulloch and Walter Pitts showed how it was possible for a neural network to compute. Six years later, Donald Hebb showed how a neural net could learn. If there is a "core" to AI, today it is probably the *connectionist* school—neural nets. In that sense, McCulloch, Pitts and Hebb can be considered founding fathers of AI.

AI as a discipline was founded in 1956 with the convening of a conference (the "Dartmouth Conference") and the first explicitly AI computer program. The general belief at that time was that intelligence could be simulated in a machine that processes symbols to represent the world and its phenomena, just (it was thought) as our brains do. In this model, wrote Daniel Crevier, "Thought consists of expanding symbol structures, breaking them up and reforming them, destroying some and creating new ones. Intelligence is thus nothing but the ability to process symbols. It exists in a realm different from the hardware that supports it, transcends it, and can take different physical forms."[13]

The first symbolic AI program was *Logic Theorist*. It was basically a decision tree system for finding proofs for mathematical theorems. It not only proved 38 of the first 52 theorems in chapter 2 of the great work of mathematics, the *Principia Mathematica*, and it not only proved one of the theorems more elegantly than the book, but also it found the proof without being asked to do so.

Logic Theorist's writers followed up in 1957 with *General Problem Solver* (GPS) which, unlike *Logic Theorist*, was not pre-programmed for a specific task. GPS made more use of feedback—cybernetics—to refine a solution by an iteration process. Among other accomplishments, GPS learned to solve puzzles and break secret codes.

By the early 1960s, a program called *SAD SAM* could read English sentences and draw conclusions from them, although only in a very limited domain of knowledge. Given the sentences: "Jim is John's brother" and "Jim's mother is Mary" plus knowledge about family relationships, *SAD SAM* was smart enough to figure out that Mary must therefore be John's Ma. It was another step forward.

Meanwhile, GTP (*Geometry Theorem Prover*), incorporated a representation of shapes—another step forward; a program that could play checkers was on its way; and work had begun on *Deep Blue*'s progenitor. In 1961, SAINT (*Symbolic Automatic INTegrator*) was working like *Logic Theorist* but upon problems of algebra rather than logic.

A program called *ANALOGY*, written in 1963, could detect similarities among geometric objects. *STUDENT*, written in 1964, solved algebra problems posed in verbal format, and SIR (*Semantic Information Retrieval*) understood simple English sentences, albeit in extremely narrow contexts.

---

[13] Crevier, Daniel (1993). AI: The Tumultuous History of the Search for Artificial Intelligence. London and New York: Basic Books.

In the mid-to-late 1960s a lot of effort went into getting computers to manipulate blocks, which meant they had to understand three-dimensional geometry and aspects of physics. They had to be able to see, through video cameras, and make sense of what they saw. In *micro-blocks world*, a robot was able to see, move, and stack a set of blocks on a table. Then came a robot that could construct an automobile water pump from some randomly scattered parts, and in 1969 came *Shakey*, a wobbly robot on wheels that was able to move around rooms picking up and stacking boxes.

Numerous refinements to the AI control programs were made over the years. Each tiny improvement took a lot of effort. A program called STRIPS took the lead over GPS for a while, then along came SHRDLU—a nonsense name but a no-nonsense advance that meant humans could now interrogate the robot in a blocks world. Impressive as a *SHRDLU* was, it only worked in a very, very simple micro-world consisting of a few blocks and served mainly to highlight the daunting challenge facing AI.

The real world has trillions of objects with gazillions of relationships. Programs like GPS and *STRIPS* were impressive achievements but they barely scraped the surface of true intelligence. Among the many difficulties was the knowledge context issue: the myriad facts and ideas, and even more myriad relations among them, many of which are "common sense"—we know them without conscious learning or logic.

In 1966 Joseph Weizenbaum created a program to parody the notion of "strong" AI. *Eliza* was (an algorithm representing) a Rogerian psychotherapist. She would never answer a question directly, but pick up on a word or phrase and turn it back into a question for the patient. She appeared to probe, and therefore to understand and control the conversation, but of course did not. She appeared to be human, but of course was not.

Weizenbaum thought that computers could never understand some notions humans have "because they don't share our objectives." (But what *are* our objectives?) Essentially, Weizenbaum believed that genuine AI was possible but it would not happen soon (he said this nearly 50 years ago, remember) and it would not be human. It would be alien, like a dolphin is alien, or like

Japanese social intelligence (culture) is alien to American social intelligence.

Rule-based Systems

By the mid 1960s it was clear that symbolic AI, which defined intelligence as the ability to process symbols, depended crucially on the processing rules—in other words, on algorithms. We have seen that intelligence cannot be fully expressed through an algorithmic process—that heuristics are required. Weizenbaum was right to be sceptical. But for relatively simple, narrowly defined tasks—"weak" AI—then rule-based AI systems can do the job. And they are doing the job, with varying degrees of competence and success, in helping diagnose illnesses and prescribe treatments, in finding subterranean mineral deposits, and in other tasks. Increasingly, however, they are being augmented or replaced by connectionist systems.

The first modern expert systems/rule (of thumb)-based systems were *DENDRAL* and *MYCIN*. DENDRAL, developed over the decade 1965–1975, was designed to help chemists determine the structure of molecules, a problem previously done painstakingly by trial and error and relying on the expertise of the chemist. It worked very well until the number of rules and logic grew beyond a certain point of complexity, when it became very difficult to add new rules or make adjustments to existing ones while maintaining stability. The system essentially became chaotic, with a small change in initial conditions (programming) having large and unforeseen impacts down the line.

MYCIN, designed to diagnose infectious blood diseases, went some way toward overcoming this shortcoming by separating the rules governing when to apply the rules from the knowledge base (which is itself a list of rules—*IF* it has four wheels and a board *THEN* it's a very good Ford, etc.) In other words, by separating the programming from the database.

DENDRAL was an all-or-nothing system. It would only provide an answer when it was 100 percent sure of the correctness of its response. In daily life, few things are certain. This is certainly true of medicine, a profession which, for all its high-tech gadgetry, still relies heavily on physician intuition or heuristic decisions. MYCIN, however, incorporated probability into its decisions. Its answers would not be straight Yes or No, but: "There's a 63 percent chance the patient has X infection."

The fundamental advance represented by MYCIN over DENDRAL was that its knowledge base was separated from the control structure, its headquarters from its divisions. The two-part structure facilitated the development of expert system "shells"—a control structure plus empty slots into which one could feed expert knowledge from any domain. As expert systems proliferated, they differed in the knowledge of their domain (infectious diseases, oil-bearing rock formations, etc.), but they all reasoned in pretty much the same way.

DENDRAL and MYCIN represented significant advances within AI research, but they were neither big enough nor power-ful enough for the real world of chemists and doctors. The pro-gram that counts as the first real-world application of expert system technology was Digital Equipment Corporation (DEC)'s *XCON* – "Expert Configurer." XCON helped DEC salespeople decide what configuration of hardware components was best for a given customer's needs (DEC sold "clusters" of minicomputers that could be configured in hundreds of different ways). XCON then helped DEC production *engineers* put the components to-gether. XCON was credited with making DEC profitable. But like DENDRAL and MYCIN before it, XCON too would even-tually become bogged down as it grew in size and complexity.[14]

Other approaches were needed and by the mid-1970s, they existed. AI then consisted of several subdisciplines: expert sys-tems, language analysis, knowledge engineering and representa-tion, machine learning, computer vision, and logic. Language analysis focused on the meaning in sentences rather than on their grammar or syntax. Grammar/syntax-based systems had already failed notably in the area of automatic language translation. Lan-guage analysis programs could infer meaning even where it was not explicit. One program, fed with news reports about the ac-tivities of   U.S. diplomat Cyrus Vance, correctly "guessed" that

---

[14] Nietzsche wrote: "the richest and most complex forms—for the expression 'higher type' means no more than this—perish more easily: only the low-est preserve an apparent indestructibility." Stephen Gould said much the same thing in *Full House*.

Mrs. Vance had met the wife of Israeli prime minister Begin at a state banquet in Israel in January 1980, even though this fact was not explicitly stated anywhere in the news reports.

The hardest part of creating a new expert system is transferring knowledge from a human expert into the system. In education, we would call this "teaching." In rule-based AI, it was known as "knowledge engineering." Knowledge engineering got its start with TEIRESIAS, a program that helped spot gaps and inconsistencies in the knowledge being transferred to the system.

Making relatively simple deductions from a set of facts was one thing; deducing whole new concepts from a set of facts—something the human brain is very good at—was something else altogether. But a program called *EURISKO* ("I discover") could learn, by example or induction, how to make new sense of things. Its secret: it was endowed with curiosity—a drive to discover new things—and the ability to register self-satisfaction when its new discoveries turned out to be correct and worth pursuing further. Initially, it did all this only in the limited domain of number theory, but the key thing was the demonstration of principle and after five years of development EURISKO was helping computer chip designers create 3-D circuits too complex for a human mind to grasp.

Pre-dating *Deep Blue*'s victory over Garry Kasparov by 16 years, in 1981 EURISKO beat not just one but a whole gaggle of geeks in an annual computer game tournament, in which human players controlled fleets of space battleships which they themselves designed and attempt to annihilate each others' fleets. To prove that its 1981 success was not just a fluke, EURISKO won the tournament again the following year, whereupon the tournament's chief geeks, deeply miffed, told it to go play somewhere else; it was not allowed to compete again. Significantly—and as its developer Doug Lenat has himself commented—EURISKO designed and tested its battle fleet in a manner reminiscent of the Modern Synthesis of evolution. That is, design and testing was accomplished through random mutations to the design, with heuristic rules selecting or "preferring" only those mutations which conferred some benefit. That model remains popular to this day.

By the late 1970s, a new language called PROLOG joined LISP as a staple tool of AI programmers. It arose out of a school of thought that said the ability to draw inferences through logic processes was the road to true intelligence, but it never really caught on.

Machine vision was another area of overblown promise in the early days of AI. By the late 1980s, few companies or organizations any longer had the stomach—or the pockets—for it. One of the foreseen applications for machine vision was the "autonomous land vehicle," a truck that could see the terrain and drive itself. The problem was simple: The computing power needed to update and process high-resolution moving images in real-time was greater than existing computers could supply.

Fast-forward to the turn of the millennium, and computing power had climbed higher up the exponential curve; so much higher, that in 2005 a roboticized Volkswagen SUV won the $1 million DARPA Grand Challenge prize by traversing 130 miles of Mojave Desert in under ten hours, without a driver and without any form of remote control. It was on its own. It had to deal with ditches, water, rocks, narrow mountain trails winding along sheer cliffs, and other vehicles roaming the desert in search of the prize. There was no set course but the vehicles were required to pass through a number of checkpoints at a specific speed. Two years later, six vehicles completed the DARPA Urban Grand Challenge, where they had to deal with real traffic, lights, lanes, stop signs, and each other, and to park neatly in a spot at a shopping mall. Completely unaided, unless you count the multiple stereo cameras, radar and other vision technologies—and the AI that made sense of what they saw.

Connectionist Systems (Neural Networks)

The success of autonomous vehicles was based on much more than faster computers, of course. Advanced sensors and advanced AI played huge parts. The advanced AI included neural nets—the dream of the original "connectionist" founders of AI. In 1958, a program called the *Perceptron* got a lot of press on the basis of its touted potential, but in reality it couldn't do very much. The press reported it could distinguish between a cat and a dog, but that was not true. It could do so in principle, but not (yet) in fact. The *Perceptron* was essentially a blending of the concept of demons (agents) with a neural network. The demons were photocells which informed the neurons how much light was being sensed. The neurons weighed the relative strengths of the light input reported by the demons. If a weight was higher than a threshold predetermined by the programmers than a neuron would "fire." That is, it would tell the next level of neurons, which could light up pixels on a screen, about the light intensity. Eventually a pattern—such as a letter of the alphabet if words were the target object—would emerge on the screen. In the 1970s and 80s, the technology was refined through the application of "back propagation"— iterative feedback (i.e., cybernetics) in which the results of the neural process are fed back to the network so it can learn what is a "good" response to a given input.

Similar technology is a now applied widely; in scanners, for example. AI, like the space program, does not have to succeed in the equivalent of landing a human on Mars for it to produce many valuable spin-offs. But recognizing patterns is just a part of intelligence. "Connectionists," wrote Heinz Pagels in *Dreams of Reason*, see "the essence of cognition as the response of a neural or electronic parallel network to input stimulation." Indeed, the neural network approach to simulating intelligence has been dominant in AI since the 1980s. It draws its inspiration directly from the neural and parallel distributed processing architecture of the animal brain, and it is in the architecture itself that intelligence, knowledge, and memory reside—not in some external algorithm or on a disk or tape.

In the 1990s, connectionist technology grew rapidly and socked its symbolic sibling in the eye with successes in automatic speech recognition and autonomous land vehicle systems. But life is a compromise, and AI is part of life. The symbolic and connectionist approaches are now commonly used together. Each has strengths that make up for the other's weaknesses. Incidentally, AI critic Hubert Dreyfus was not so much antagonistic to AI in general as he was to the symbolic approach. He tended to side with the connectionists.

☙

Now that we've closed the cover on Machina sapiens' family album, with its sepia-tinted snaps of stiff aunts, uncles, and cousins clutching capacious black bags stuffed with embryonic memes, it is time to see what happens when the memes are let out of the bag in an environment rich in meme nutrients—fast, globally networked computers, and smart, globally networked scientists in all manner of disciplines.

8 THE WOMB

The ideas, approaches, and accomplishments of AI's early practitioners have grown into a somewhat chaotic meta-discipline, a set of fields of study which are themselves sets of memes. Given a fast and pervasive means of communication—of interconnecting—together, these memes constitute the nourishing womb for the fetal *Machina sapiens*. At the highest level, the AI meta-discipline consists of two large, and growing, disciplines: computer science and cognitive science and their sub-disciplines. We'll take a brief look at these, but our main focus is on the sub-disciplines of artificial life (Alife) studies (encompassing cellular automata and genetic programming) from the computer sciences, which are the fundamental keys to the lock on the door of the intelligent machine; and on the Internet, the blood vessels and nerve system transporting the Alife and other memes at near-lightspeed to interact and fertilize one another.

It is important to understand that this aspect of the womb—connectedness, the Internet—is itself evolving at an accelerating rate, because that evolution both grows from and, in recursive fashion, contributes to the computer sciences working on the fetus. To put it another way: the fetus is already so smart that it can adapt and improve its own environment to help itself develop even smarter and stronger. Mother's role is diminishing. This is, after all, an alien baby, and it is starting to adapt its mother's womb to suit itself.

᪥

Biological intelligence is, in a sense, the product of the workings of the cosmological sciences, quantum and Newtonian mechanics, relativity, chemistry, biology, and culture, and hence of the myriad sub-disciplines that make up these huge fields of inquiry, multiplied by a chaos/complexity factor. But before we arrive at the creation or emergence of artificial intelligence, we have to add some newer sciences and technologies (memes) that could only exist because our human biological intelligence existed to create them. These modern sciences and technologies envelop the AI memes like a nurturing and nutritious womb. Chief among them are the computer and cognitive sciences, and the technologies that enable and support them. One of the most striking things to notice is that they cross over into one another's territory, forming networks of people and memes and growing synaptic connections which, like those in the brain, are selected in classic Darwinian fashion for their fitness in furthering the survival and growth of the whole organism..

For example, we find linguistics under both computer science and cognitive science. So it is not just disciplines that are converging, but also the theories and concepts they have studied and shared, sometimes under different names and usually from different perspectives. "Computational linguistics" first arose as a concept within computer science/machine intelligence, but it may be a concept applicable to the way our own brains process language. In short, the dividing line between biological systems and artificial systems is blurring. A new synaptic link has been formed which, because it increases our understanding of how things work and is therefore useful, has persisted and become established rather than dissolving along with a myriad ideas that were just "nice tries."

To give you some idea of the scope of AI and its related disciplines, and to describe the womb in which *Machina sapiens* is developing, an overview of computer and cognitive science is necessary.

Computer Science

Computer Science is a catch-all term for such sub-disciplines as those listed below. It is not an exhaustive list.

Algorithms, Architecture, Artificial Intelligence, Artificial Life, Compression, Computer Engineering, Computational and Applied Mathematics, Computational Mechanics, Computational Learning Theory, Computer Vision, Databases, Distributed Computing, Computer Aided Design and Manufacturing (CAD/CAM), Formal Methods, Graphics, Handwriting Recognition, Human-Computer Interaction, Information Science, Knowledge Sciences, Linguistics, Logic Programming, Mobile Computing, Modeling, Networks, Neural Networks, Object-Oriented Programming, Operating Systems, Real-Time Computing, Robotics, Security and Encryption, Software Engineering, Supercomputing and Parallel Computing, Symbolic Computation, User Interface, Virtual Reality.

The areas of computer science most proximate to the "evolutionary creation" of an "artificial" lifeform, *Machina sapiens*, are the connectionist systems (neural networks) and rule-based systems (expert systems) we discussed in the last chapter. As part of the network of the computer science "organism" they feed and are fed by the other subdisciplines listed above, and both their food and their fruit, their input and output, consist of memes. Memes are food for thought.

But while a neural net or an expert system may appear intelligent, it is hard to think of them as being "alive." This is not so for the next area of computer science we shall explore: artificial life.

Artificial life

Can you be alive and not know it? Of course. You might be asleep, or unconscious, or watching any one of a distressingly large number of mindless TV shows. Or you might be one of the trillions of cells which, though probably unconscious of being alive, nevertheless *are* alive and must in some way contribute to *your* awareness, gentle reader, of being alive.

Or you might be an automobile.

Well, between you and me, I didn't think so either, until I was reminded of something Frank Tipler and John Barrow pointed out in *The Anthropic Cosmological Principle*; namely, that automobiles are alive. Coincidentally, Richard Dawkins came to essentially the same conclusion in *The Blind Watchmaker*.

Tipler explains in *The Physics of Immortality*:

> They [automobiles] self-reproduce in automobile factories using human mechanics. Granted, their reproduction is not autonomous; they need a factory external to themselves. But so do male humans: to make a male baby, an external biochemical factory called a 'womb' is needed. Granted, their reproduction requires another living species. But so does the reproduction of the flowering plants: such plants use bees to pollinate and animals to disperse their seeds. Viruses require the entire machinery of a cell to reproduce. The form of automobiles in their environment is preserved by natural selection: there is a fierce struggle for existence between various 'races' of automobiles. Japanese and European automobiles are competing with native American automobiles for scarce resources—money for the manufacturer—that will result in either more American or more Japanese and European automobiles being built. By my definition of life, not only automobiles but all machines—in particular computers—are alive.

Using Tipler's definition of life as "a form of information processing" and a "living being" as "any entity which codes information (in the physics sense of the word) with the information coded being preserved by natural selection," it is easy to accept automobiles and computers—and programs that act like computers—as being alive. Note that this definition makes no mention of consciousness, sentience or self-awareness, nor of the carbon on which all Earthly plants and animals and microbes are based. Any physical substrate will do, provided it can code information. Indeed, Scottish chemist Graham Cairns-Smith showed in the 1960s how mineral (non-carbon) substances such as clay could be considered the first lifeforms to arise out of the primordial soup. In that light, the pet rock fad of yesteryear seems marginally less silly.

Of course, one may define anything to fit one's biases, and there is no question that Tipler is far out. But where else would one expect an Einstein-level mathematical physicist to be? Dawkins, too, has his detractors, and in fact I don't agree with everything he says, but if we lambaste our greatest scientists for telling us frankly what's on their minds, we'll be the poorer for it.

◌◌

With a good definition of what to look for in life, it is easier to study it. We cut up plants and animals and study the bits through microscopes and other instruments—the reductionist approach to scientific understanding. But with Tipler's more modern definition of life as being information and not material (carbon) we can study it from the opposite direction: We can literally create life, and watch it grow, reproduce, and evolve. And that's essentially what the scientific discipline called *Artificial Life* is all about. It grew out of both biology and computer science, and it represents one of those wonderful evolutionary events that occurs whenever two meme pools combine at the right time and place to produce something radical.

Turing, von Neumann, and Barricelli

Alan Turing and John von Neumann might be considered the founding fathers of computer science, and Barricelli as the unsung founding father of Alife. At the heart of their combined contribution was Turing's introduction into computing of the concept of discreteness or step-by-step operations—algorithms. But Turing also recognized that many algorithms could efficiently and economically be run in parallel (at the same time), and indeed the *Colossus*, arguably the world's first real computer, used by Turing and others to decipher secret German communications in World War II, performed parallel operations.

Turing also thought a lot about the principles and philosophy of AI, and predicted the ivory tower's opposition to it: "An unwillingness to admit the possibility that mankind can have any rivals in intellectual power occurs as much amongst intellectual people as amongst others: they have more to lose." Turing also recognized the importance of the link between AI and evolutionary processes, and considered it critical to allow machines to make and learn from mistakes: "Instead of trying to produce a programme to simulate the adult mind, why not rather try to produce one which simulates the child's?" He conceptualized an "unorganized Machine" which, paraphrased George Dyson, "with proper upbringing, could become more complicated than anything that could be engineered." In short, Turing foresaw the need for and use of cellular automata, genetic algorithms, and machine learning.

John von Neumann (1903—1957) specified the actual coding, or programming, for which Turing had supplied the principles. Turing conceived the meme for software; von Neumann gave birth to it. Like Turing, von Neumann recognized the necessity for and inevitability of an evolutionary approach to AI. He knew that a computer as complex as a brain could not be built by design but would need to be evolved. He produced a theory of self-reproducing automata that gave a Turing Machine the ability to replicate through programming, and later in life he theorized about the behavior of populations of communicating automata—about distributed and emergent intelligence.

But would such behavior amount to life? The theory of *symbiogenesis* suggested that it would. This late 19th/early 20th century theory ascribed the complexity of living organisms to a succession of symbiotic associations between simpler living forms, themselves arising ultimately from not-quite-living components. This was essentially the view expounded by Dan Dennett in *Darwin's Dangerous Idea* and by Marvin Minsky in *Society of Mind*.

Nils Barricelli (1912-1993) who worked with von Neumann on a computer for the Institute for Advanced Study at Princeton University (where Einstein was their contemporary) took symbiogenesis a step further to include not just biological organisms but any self-reproducing or self-replicating structure. This therefore embraced von Neumann's self-reproducing software automata (Turing Machines). Barricelli not only created the first digital Alife but also drew all the right conclusions from his creation, namely that: It led to the parallel processing of memetic code; it led to efficient heuristics to arrive at solutions to problems much more quickly than brute-force serial computation could; and it handled the acceleration of evolutionary pace.

Having created the world's first cellular automata and genetic algorithm, Barricelli went on to get his creatures to learn to play a game. Barricelli "blurred the distinction between living and non-living things," wrote George Dyson, in that his creatures combined genotypic and phenotypic—genetic and metabolic, Darwinian and Lamarckian—processes within a single evolutionary process. Dyson made the significant comment that Barricelli-type creatures were "managing (Barricelli would say learning) to exercise increasingly detailed and far-reaching control over the conditions in our universe that are helping to make life more comfortable in theirs." These babies adapt mother's womb to suit themselves.

Alife can be viewed as an evolutionary development providing a synaptic connection between computer science and biology. The Santa Fe Institute, a private, independent, multidisciplinary research and education center founded in 1984 and devoted to "creating a new kind of scientific research community, pursuing emerging science" described Alife as

> ... the name given to a new discipline that studies "natural" life by attempting to recreate biological phenomena from scratch within computers and other "artificial" media. Alife complements the traditional analytic approach of traditional biology with a synthetic approach in which, rather than studying biological phenomena by taking apart living organisms to see how they work, one attempts to put together systems that behave like living organisms.

The process of synthesis has been an extremely important tool in many disciplines. Synthetic chemistry—the ability to put together new chemical compounds not found in nature—has not only contributed enormously to our theoretical understanding of chemical phenomena, but has also allowed us to fabricate new materials and chemicals that are of great practical use for industry and technology.

Artificial life amounts to the practice of "synthetic biology" and, by analogy with synthetic chemistry, the attempt to recreate biological phenomena in alternative media will result in not only better theoretical understanding of the phenomena under study, but also in practical applications of biological principles in the technology of computer hardware and software, mobile robots, spacecraft, medicine, nanotechnology, industrial fabrication and assembly, and other vital engineering projects.

By extending the horizons of empirical research in biology beyond the territory currently circumscribed by life-as-we-know-it, the study of Artificial Life gives us access to the domain of life-as-it-could-be, and it is within this vastly larger domain that we must ground general theories of biology and in which we will discover practical and useful applications of biology in our engineering endeavors.

To be clear: Alife is not just about biology, but about a new kind of biology, one that accepts the definition of life as information, and which therefore embraces information-processing machines as appropriate objects of study. This is not to say that a pure biological (perhaps I should say biochemical) form of Alife is not of interest. In 2010, the co-creator of the Human Genome Project, Craig Venter, and colleagues created biological Alife. They did not create a whole organism from scratch; rather, they used one already created by nature (a bacterium with its natural DNA removed) as a vessel into which they poured synthetic—human-made—DNA, which was essentially just a mixture of four chemicals (adenine, cytosine, guanine, thymine). Absent the synthetic DNA, the bacterium was dead, like hardware lacking an operating system. With the synthetic DNA and a "boot-up" process developed at the Venter Institute, the bacterium came to life.

The broad implications of our new-found ability to create life are perhaps best left to the philosophers and ethicists. Some of them are already on the job: a *New York Times* editorial of May 28, 2010 noted that President Obama asked the White House bioethics commission to "report back to him on the significance of this development."

This approach to Alife is called synthetic genomics. It is driven and supported by the increasing speed and falling cost of DNA sequencing, analysis and synthesis. The result of faster, cheaper sequencing is a rapidly growing catalog of whole genomes of numerous species, of individuals and even of the microbes that live symbiotically inside us. The result of DNA analysis is a growing understanding of how bits of DNA and mutations to bits of DNA relate to the human condition. Analysis reveals the biomarkers that signal the presence of a disease or condition. That growing knowledge is already being applied in genomic tests and treatments for disease.

The growing number of sequenced genomes and the knowledge of how they work are the inputs to synthetic genomics. Knowing how things work at the molecular level and how to use that knowledge in the form of computable mathematical equations, scientists can design and quickly test on a computer any organism, organ, or tissue they choose. Then they can build that model—using DNA synthesis as Venter did—in real life, out of real molecules.

Venter's goal is to create bacteria and other micro-sized life-forms tailor-made to produce advanced biofuels, clean water technology, and new vaccines and medicines. The difference between current methods of producing drugs and vaccines (trial-and-error mixing of chemical compounds or organic molecules) and precisely designing a living organism to produce a precisely defined compound or biologic is potentially staggering.

The kicker is that by modeling the condition we seek to change inside a model of the affected tissue, organ or even the whole organism, and then modeling the means of changing it, we can do most of the work extremely quickly on a computer, with near (perhaps even absolute) certainty that the result will be safe and effective. There is probably no chronic condition that cannot be treated successfully in this way, and if modeling and synthesis become fast enough and cheap enough, the value of this method will probably extend to the most acute and traumatic conditions.

❧

So there is a practical as well as a philosophical side to Alife, and the biochemical advances in synthetic biology feed and are fed by advances in computed Alife. In keeping with its joint biological and computing underpinnings, it is fitting that Alife should employ a combination of biological and computing terminology. The two primary and related techniques used in the study of Alife reflect this duality: Cellular Automata (CA) and Genetic Algorithms (GA).

Cellular Automata and Genetic Algorithms

"Cellular automata (CA) were originally conceived … to provide a formal framework for investigating the behavior of complex, extended systems," wrote Dr. Moshe Sipper of the Swiss Federal Institute of Technology. "CAs are dynamical systems in which space and time are discrete." That is to say, they move and change in space and time in a series of little jumps; not in a smooth, continuous flow.

A cellular automaton consists of a grid of cells, just like a Go (Japanese checkers) board. A set of simple Go-like rules determine whether a cell "lights up" or not. Typically, the rules will say: If two squares adjacent to you are lit up, then you don't light up. If three adjacent cells are lit up, then you light up too. What happens then is almost magical: strange shapes start to evolve and move around the grid. Sometimes they slide off the edge, only to reappear from another edge. Sometimes the shapes break up into several new or identical shapes, and sometimes they collide and form a new entity.

This would be interesting enough, but there's more. With the application of genetic algorithms (GAs), CAs can evolve, and as they evolve, they can compute—they can act as "universal computers" able to solve problems in mathematics and physics. (Neither Turing nor von Neumann would be at all surprised.) They are being used to study communication, computation, construction, growth, reproduction, competition, and evolution.

The basic operation of a GA, as described by Professor David E. Goldberg, Director of the Illinois Genetic Algorithms Laboratory, is conceptually simple:

1.   Maintain a population of solutions to a problem,
2.   Select the better solutions for recombination with each other, and
3.   Use their offspring to replace poorer solutions.

An early and very simple example of GA programming was supplied by Richard Dawkins in the 1960s, with a program he called *Evolution* containing two sub-programs, *Reproduction* and *Development*. Starting with some pre-programmed tree-like shapes on the screen, *Reproduction* would produce offspring from the parents, but designed according to the offspring's own genetic makeup inherited from the parents. The genetic makeup result was passed to the *Development* program, which determined the phenotypic growth of the "trees"—their appearance on screen as they grew. Built-in random gene mutations ensured that, as in nature, the offspring would never look exactly like their parents.

The "environment" for the trees was provided by the human operator (Dawkins), who selected them for survival or elimination purely on whim, which is a bit of a stretch from the natural selection that occurs in real evolution, but it supplies some of nature's randomness and indeed random elements are now routinely programmed into cellular automata.

After developing the program and running it for the first time, "Nothing in my biologist's intuition," (wrote Dawkins in *The Blind Watchmaker*) "nothing in my 20 years' experience of programming computers, and nothing in my wildest dreams prepared me for what actually emerged on the screen. I can't remember exactly when in the sequence it first began to dawn on me that an evolved resemblance to something like an insect was possible. With a wild surmise, I began to breed, generation after generation, from whichever child looked most like an insect. My incredulity grew in parallel with the evolving resemblance."

Genetic programming spread into the computing environment in the 1990s, and began to be applied in optimization, automatic programming, machine learning, economics, operations research, ecology, population genetics, evolutionary biology, and the study of entire social systems.

Cognitive Science

Like computer science, cognitive science is constantly evolving, with new subdisciplines emerging from cross-fertilization of existing ones. It is therefore hard to define cognitive science by pointing to a list of disciplines and saying "That's it!" It is often referred to in the plural, as "the cognitive sciences." The Rutgers Center for Cognitive Science Web site provided a good description back in the 1990s:

> Cognitive Science is one the few fields where modern developments in computer science and artificial intelligence promise to shed light on classical problems in psychology and the philosophy of the mind. Ancient questions of how we see the world, understand language, and reason, and questions such as 'how a material system can know about the outside world', are being explored with the powerful new conceptual prosthetics of computer modeling.

Essentially, the cognitive sciences are about the study of mind, brain, consciousness, and intelligence. They embrace some aspects of computer science, neuroscience, and artificial intelligence studies. The central disciplines are psychology, neuroscience, language acquisition and processing, linguistics, psycholinguistics, perception and attention, computation and linguistics, philosophy, visual sciences, and speech and hearing science.

Around the turn of the millennium, the Center for Cognitive Science at the State University of New York in Buffalo, noted on its Web site that cognitive science was "manifesting what has been a sea change in the direction of research in the social and behavioral sciences in this country: where previously the movement had been toward ever finer disciplinary distinctions, there is now the reverse dynamic toward an integration of the disciplines into a unified understanding." This convergence and cross-disciplinarity is gratifying. Communication at the interface between *Homo* and *Machina sapiens* ought to be a primary focus of communication programs in academe. Much of the actual work of building practical brain–machine interfaces is occurring in medicine and bioengineering; the academy's communication programs seem to have little to say about such interfaces so far, but no doubt that will change as the medical and bioengineering communities provide experimental platforms for study.

The Internet

Most people interface with the machine via the Internet. As well, research in the computer and cognitive sciences, including Alife experiments, is increasingly being conducted on and through the Internet. The global Internet is the true physical womb for *Machina sapiens*, and the activities now taking place within it are preparing it for conception.

When the Internet made its public debut in the early 1990s, who knew? There should have been stop-press editions of the newspapers, with headlines saying "The World As We Know It Is About to End!!" But there weren't. Even academia barely noticed what was afoot. The focus of much communication research remained on plain old telephone communications. Now that we are on the cusp of Web 3.0—Sir Tim Berners-Lee's new "semantic" web, that knows what it knows—communication schools seem to be focusing on Web 2.0 social interactions, not on the Internet as primarily human–machine interface. They seem to be perpetually behind.

They can hardly claim that they did not see such developments coming: in the 17th century Robert Hooke, an acquaintance of Thomas Hobbes and a contemporary member of the Royal Society with Isaac Newton and Robert Boyle, predicted a network of instantaneous global communications. It took merely a 200-year blink of the evolutionary eye for the technology, in the form of the Morse code telegraph and later the telephone, to catch up with Hooke's concept. It took communication scholars slightly longer. I'm not saying this to be mean. I'm saying it because we need our scholars to anticipate technologies and their impacts. We can no longer afford the luxury of figuring things out in retrospect.

But for the advent of the World Wars, which accelerated the development of computers for calculating tank and artillery shell trajectories and for encoding and decoding messages, today's global communication network might still be not far advanced from where it was near the beginning of the 20th century. Computers not only increasingly "needed" a network in order to communicate with one another, but also provided their own solution to the slowness and complexity of mechanical switches in the communication (telephone) network by evolving into switches themselves. The Cold War and threat of nuclear attack prompted an effort to make the communication network less susceptible to disruption in the event of a nuclear strike. The original hero of this effort was not Vinton Cerf, generally credited with being "father of the Internet," but Paul Baran and the RAND Corporation.

With the introduction of packet switching protocols ("a particularly virulent strain of symbiotic code," as George Dyson put it), replication of operating systems and programs could occur across networks at up to the speed of light, and they had to start to *compete* with other programs for memory space and CPU cycles—the essential but limited nutritional resources of their environment. The introduction of object-oriented, platform-independent languages such as Java allowed different hardware architectures and operating systems (different "species") to talk with one another and host new structures (subroutines and programs) able to work cooperatively in a distributed fashion. But new computer code, like genetic code, contains errors ("bugs.") We often joke that some fault in a program is "not a bug—it's a feature!" In evolution, it is often no joke: Even if it does not confer a direct benefit to the individual organism, a genetic mutation introduces the element of randomness and chance so critical to the evolutionary development of any species.

The Future of the Internet:
Better, Bigger, Smarter

The Internet and AI are critical to one another in two inter-related ways. First, the Internet is an environment for the continued cultural evolution of existing—that is, human—intelligent life. Even the globby, wetware form of life, we know from countless examples, will occupy and exploit the most extreme and bizarre environments, from superheated deep-sea volcanic vents to glaciers. The Net is an environment for all forms—globby or binary—of intelligent life to exploit. Human life is obviously doing so, in part to create artificial life in the form of bots and Alife beings which themselves will soon begin to exploit their environment.

Second, the Internet is an environment for the evolutionary emergence of new forms of intelligent life, which (among other things) will further the evolution of the Internet itself. Create a nourishing environment, and life will spontaneously self-organize and emerge. The Net is a nourishing environment. It is a womb for digital beings, which will help maintain and improve it to their and our benefit. Since the Internet is so important, it is as well to look at its past and future development to see what that might tell us about the future development of AI.

There have been and are several initiatives specifically designed to further Internet development, such as the NGI (Next Generation Internet) initiative and the Internet2 project. In the words of Vinton Cerf, NGI was a research program devoted to uncovering the technologies needed for the next generations of Internet, while Internet2 was and still is a university initiative to obtain better quality Internet service in support of research. Such initiatives are fine, but as it grows ever more complex, Internet development will grow more through evolution and less through central planning.

The directions in which the Internet will develop can be boiled down to three: *Better*, *Bigger*, and *Smarter*. These three directions are mutually reinforcing; they feed one another. A better Internet causes more people to use it, so it gets bigger. A bigger

Internet grows more complex and harder to manage, so it gets smarter. Smarter makes things better, which .... and so on.

Better

The Internet has improved, and will continue to improve, in terms of functionality. It grows more and more useful. The main advances behind the improvement are:

Server platform: Mainframes ➔ Minicomputers ➔ RISC workstations ➔ PCs ➔ smartphone networks ➔ Cloud

Client platform: Terminals ➔ PCs➔ NCs (Network Computers) ➔ PDAs/smartphones ➔wearable computers ➔ implanted computers

Server operating system: Custom/proprietary ➔ UNIX ➔ any OS

Client operating system: Custom/proprietary ➔ UNIX ➔ DOS/Mac ➔ Windows/Mac/Linux ➔ smartphone OS ➔ any OS

Principal development language: C/PERL ➔ HTML/CGI ➔ VRML/Java ➔ *Machina sapiens* language

Human–Machine interface: Text ➔ 2-D graphics ➔ 3-D graphics ➔ Full immersion holohaptic (3D, touchable) interface ➔ Mind-meld

Input/control devices: Keyboard ➔ Mouse/joystick ➔ Microphone ➔ Touchscreen ➔ Gesture ➔ Haptic devices (data gloves/data suits) ➔ Telepathic brain implant

Output modes: Still image ➔ Video (with sound) ➔ Holographic video ➔ Telepathy

Navigation: Command line ➔ Gopher menus ➔ Web hyperlinks ➔ AI agent-assisted

Search methods: Programmed commands ➔ Gopher menu tree ➔ Web menu tree ➔ Search engines ➔ Individual searchbots ➔ Anticipatory, personified digital personal assistants

Human–Human interaction modes (text): None ➔ E-mail ➔ Usenet, IRC, MUDs ➔ Web-integrated chat/BBS ➔ Social

Media ➔ voice and video over IP ➔ full-immersion holohaptics ➔ Telepathy

Human languages: Mainly English ➔ All languages, via automatic speech recognition (ASR) and automatic language translation (ALT) technology

Knowledge base: U.S. Defense Dept. information ➔ Academic knowledge ➔ Government information ➔ Commercial information ➔ News services ➔ Personal information ➔ Entire Library of Congress + international, national, state, and local government archives ➔ Global ➔ Universal

Governance: U.S. Defense Dept. ➔ Academe ➔ Anarchy ➔ Commercial control ➔ Global democratic consensual control ➔ Universal

Bigger

The progressive developments outlined above have contributed to making the Net a better environment, and this in turn has spurred growth. The number of domains grew from about 2 million in 1994 to nearly 800 million in 2010. That seems like a lot, but the growth will accelerate until just about all 7 billion of us have our own domain and unique IP address.

Smarter

Complexity (chaos) theory and our own experience tell us that as things grow bigger they also tend to grow less stable. Any network manager can attest to that, and uses AI-based network management solutions to make sure the mail gets through. Ultimately, networks will be smart enough to maintain, diagnose, and repair themselves. They will automatically adapt to component failures, overloads, equipment changes, removals, and additions, and only ask for human help to insert/remove plug-and-play modules—until such time as mobile and dexterous robots take even that job away.

Network users, again as any network manager or software engineer will tell you, are an even bigger nuisance than the network itself. They demand that the system takes on the burdens of finding relevant information and filtering unwanted information from the growing and bewildering confusion of Internet services and information bases. The system responded with search engines based on AI-based tools such as searchbots and spam/porn/hate-group filters.

Users daunted by keyboards and the need to type will soon find that barrier—already partially dismantled by graphical touchscreen interfaces such as the iPad—totally removed, as gesture recognition, eye tracking, and ASR (automatic speech recognition) become more powerful. Even the mouse is at best an awkward, intrusive, and imprecise device, destined for the scrap heap of history when gesture and thought control become the standard interface to a fully immersive, holohaptic, virtual and augmented reality.

Finally, the language barrier, which makes the mainly English-language Web at best a limited and at worst a useless resource for about three-fourth's of the world's population, is already being smashed by AI-based ALT (automatic language translation) services, such as Google's free online language translation service which instantly translates text and web pages to and from over 50 languages as of 2010. These services will eventually handle spoken language as well, sitting among participants in international VR conferences and providing simultaneous multi-way oral interpretation.

Provided there are no catastrophic problems with the Internet itself, all of these wonders and more shall come to pass. Problems of course confront the Internet, some of them major, such as network security. The sky is always falling. A decade ago there was much angst over the limited number of IP addresses and routing tables growing too large. But these were technical problems, resolvable and resolved. The bigger, and potentially catastrophic, problem may result from handing over to an ever more complex Internet more and more of the running of itself.

It will be an Internet seething with nascent artificial life.

Tierra and Avida

An artificial life/intelligence project called *Tierra*, based on Barricelli's creatures, was started in 1990 by Thomas Ray. Originally run on a single *Connection Machine* (a massively parallel supercomputer of the 1980s and '90s) the program was migrated to multiple computers linked by the Internet, giving it a much larger and more diverse environment in which to evolve. The researchers hoped that little Alife forms they called Tierrans would evolve into "commercially harvestable software." Tierrans would be "wild" creatures, but it would be necessary to "domesticate" some of them, as we had "domesticated" dogs and corn.

Tierra seems to have died the funding death, but you can't keep a good meme down (nor, sometimes, a bad meme either.) Tierra was reincarnated in 2005, in the form of project Avida, in which "a population of self-replicating computer programs is subjected to external pressures (such as mutations and limited resources) and allowed to evolve subject to natural selection. This is not a mere simulation of evolution—digital organisms in Avida evolve to survive in a complex computational environment and will adapt to perform entirely new traits in ways never expected by the researchers, some of which seem highly creative. Data about each individual is saved to track the fate of the population and analyzed to help answer our many research questions." So says the website of Michigan State University's Digital Evolution Laboratory, founded in 1999 by Charles Ofria and Richard Lenski.

Carl Zimmer wrote in *Discover* magazine ("Testing Darwin," February 2005):

> Ofria has been finding that digital organisms have a way of outwitting him as well. Not long ago, he decided to see what would happen if he stopped digital organisms from adapting. Whenever an organism mutated, he would run it through a special test to see whether the mutation was beneficial. If it was, he killed the organism off. "You'd think that would turn off any further adaptation," he says. Instead, the digital organisms kept evolving. They learned to process information in new ways and were able to replicate faster. It took a while for Ofria to realize that they had tricked him. They had evolved a way to tell when Ofria was testing them by looking at the numbers he fed them. As soon as they recognized they were being tested, they stopped processing numbers. "If it was a test environment, they said, 'Let's play dead,' "

says Ofria. "There's this thing coming to kill them, and so they avoid it and go on with their lives."

As we said: You can't keep a good—or is it a bad?—meme down.

ɛɔ

In these and similar projects, then, we have species with the potential for sentience and awareness and for as much or more intelligence than us. On the one hand, we talk calmly about raiding Tierran villages and domesticating and harvesting their wild inhabitants, to be transported to another universe and forced to work for us. On the other hand, we know that even these most primitive forms of artificial life *mind* when we do that. One wonders how, as they evolve and surpass us in intelligence, the Tierrans and Avidans—which at some point will be in telepathic communication with *Machina sapiens* and just about every single electronic device on the planet through the Internet—will deal with such masters?

What if the Tierrans escape the confines of their plantations (the computer nodes containing them) and high-tail it into the country (the Internet) at large, hiding out in *your* barn (*your* computer, *your* microwave)? Tierra's Thomas Ray had misgivings on the issue: "Freely evolving autonomous artificial entities should be seen as potentially dangerous to organic life, and should always be confined by some kind of containment facility, at least until their real potential is well understood. . . . Evolution remains a self-interested process, and even the interests of confined digital organisms may conflict with our own." He's right, of course. Evolution, as de Duve showed us, doesn't give a hoot about *you*.

Despite these concerns, the researchers consider the organisms to be so "securely confined" that there is no real danger. They are apparently more concerned about human hackers breaking in and messing up their experiments. But if someone blasts a hole in a prison wall, don't the inmates tend to escape? In any case, the *Tierra* concept of creating more or less autonomous agents to do our bidding was nothing new, not even in 1990. The evolution of *bots*—software robots—was already underway by then. Today, the bot is ripe for a saltation from a collection of memes to a seriously self-aware organism. In other words, it is almost ready to be born.

George Dyson suggested that "freely evolving life" was already at large on the Net. As in biological evolution, he asserted, "harmful results" would be "edited out," but it is not clear whether he meant results harmful to Alife or harmful to humans. Our immediate concern, given that Machina sapiens is as powerful as described in this chapter, when it is still only a blind and largely unaware fetus, is: What will be its power when the saltation occurs—when it emerges from the womb?

9 CONCEPTION, GESTATION

From the vantage point of a fly-on-the-uterine-wall, we can watch the fertilization and gestation of the intelligent machine egg. We will see the fertilized egg begin to divide and multiply into increasingly specialized yet increasingly connected cells—AI programs—that form the beginnings of a complex organism.

AI programs are containers for segments of memetic material—algorithms and heuristics. Like the biological cells of any complex creature, they come in different forms, including the Alife programs and their close cousins (genetic algorithms, bots, agents) we met in the last chapter and what, for want of a better term, I will call "traditional"[15] AI programs, some representatives of which we shall meet in this.

The growing power of the fetus (and our eventual loss of control over it) derives largely from the principle of *self-organization* in complex systems. We introduce that principle below, and illustrate it by reference to the evolution of AI programs of various forms. We will also examine *why* the fetus is growing smarter, and discover that it is partly because of self-organizing, self-actualizing principles, and partly because we have already

---

[15] As the exponential curve of sociotechnical evolution becomes more vertical, the very concept of "tradition" loses meaning, except in anthropology.

begun to educate it, even at the moment of conception, through the computer science sub-discipline called *machine learning* and through various ambitious projects designed deliberately to force-feed the machine with the fruit of the Tree of Knowledge.

A point must come at which the machine's own self-organization and self-learning capacity will outpace its human teachers' knowledge. It is therefore critical to grasp the rate of acceleration at which this process is occurring.

೦ଓ

While the network engineers were busy in the 1950s tending to the birth of the Internet, John von Neumann turned his attention to Game Theory and economics. He concluded that information processing in the brain must essentially be of a statistical nature. The benefit of being statistical (as opposed to being parametric) is equivalent—and related—to the benefit of being flexibly heuristic as opposed to being rigidly algorithmic. Statistics and heuristics leave room for uncertainty. Parameters and algorithms do not. Error is intolerable to an all-or-nothing system, which recognizes black and white but is stumped by gray. A statistics-based system can handle shades of gray. It can also handle big, complex processes that would defeat a system that insisted on exactness at every turn, at every branching of an algorithm, as expert systems did.

An economic system is not only a statistical system, but also (as Hobbes recognized) it bears the hallmarks of, and obeys the same principles as, an intelligent system. Money represents units of information—and hence ultimately the meaning—within the system. As money went digital and light-speed on the Internet and on private global financial data networks, so the economic system grew more complex—and more intelligent. Irving J. Good postulated in 1965 that where there is meaning, there is an economy, and vice versa. Thus, in order to produce what he called an "ultraintelligent" machine (which he defined as "a machine that believes people cannot think") it will be necessary to represent meaning as a physical object (as economic meaning is represented, for instance, by a lump of gold or a banknote) rather than a metaphysical one. You can't build a physical ma-

chine from metaphysics, unless you are God. You have to use
physics.

⋙

In the context of survival of the fittest, we tend to think of Nature as "red in tooth and claw," as a battleground of organisms
driven by potentially infinite population growth to fight one another for a piece of a finite environmental pie. Yet natural selection also recognizes the survival advantages of affinities among
organisms, advantages that lead to both inter- and intra-species
cooperation. Economic organisms such as corporations also develop cooperative strategies for pieces of the economic pie; not
just competitive strategies. Cooperation occurs at the most fundamental levels in a system (e.g., among individual neurons in a
nervous system, cells in an organ, workers in a factory) and it
scales all the way up to entire societies (the United States, the
European Union, the United Nations) and species (e.g., among
ants, humans, and dogs).

Scale has a lot to do with the ability of a system to organize
itself and, faced with changes in the environment, to spontaneously re-organize itself. Self-organization is one indicator of the
presence of life (and is grounds for rejecting the proposition that
an automobile is alive.) The larger the scale, the more is self-
organization likely to occur.

Large scale does not necessarily imply large physical size. Entities that are physically small at the macro level, such as the
brain, have enormous scale at the molecular and cellular levels.
The *Titanic*, in contrast, was huge at the macro level but tiny in
terms of the scale of its complexity; far too tiny for there to be
any possibility of its spontaneously reorganizing into a subma-
rine when its environment changed from surface to sub-surface.
The World Wide Web also has large scale, but coarse grain. The
thumbnail-sized processors in our computers today, though tiny
relative to their massive 2,000-vacuum-tube ancestors of the
1940s and '50s, are still astronomically bigger than the cells,
molecules, and atoms employed by self-organizing physical,
chemical, and biological systems, and the molecular, atomic, and
quantum computers of our near future.

Neurophysiologist William Ashby (1903–1972) concluded from computer simulations that spontaneous adaptation to a new or changing environment was a hallmark of self-organization and "an elementary and fundamental property of all matter." His simulations revealed that a complex system will go suddenly unstable beyond a critical level of "connectance" among the parts of the system.[16] Three RAND computer projects of the 1950s attempted to capitalize on the principles of large-scale self-organizing processes to create intelligent systems: the *Leviathan* project(no doubt named in honor of Hobbes), which utilized a single computer; the *Sage* project, which used the U.S. network of defense early warning computers; and *Pandemonium*.

Leviathan incorporated "artificial agents." It did not work well, but well enough to convince its designers that "given a more fertile computational substrate, humans would not only instruct the system but would begin following instructions that were reflected back." In other words, given better hardware and software than was available in the 1950s, the day would come when computers would start telling *us* what to do.

Pandemonium also employed agents, called "demons." They operated (in principle—the program was never actually implemented in its original form) at four levels. Bottom-level input demons simply received, stored, and passed incoming data to the next level, composed of computational demons, which per-

---

[16] To George Dyson, Ashby's findings suggested that "The genesis of life or intelligence within or among computers goes approximately as follows: (1) make things complicated enough, and (2) either wait for something to happen by accident or make something happen by design." Dyson points out that large self-organizing systems challenge the Darwinian assumption that a species must compete or face extinction, on the basis that such systems can be constructed that grow, evolve, and learn without competition and reproduction. I am not sure I agree fully with him, either that competition is a necessary assumption of Darwinism (though competition is a key ingredient of his theory of natural selection, Darwin would surely concede that cooperation sometimes works), or even if it is a wrong assumption, that competition won't persist—*within* a self-organizing system. In fact, the theory of Evolutionary Stable Strategy would seem to predict such competition.

formed calculations on the data and passed the results to cognitive demons, which tried to make sense of the results. The top level, which corresponded to the brains of the outfit, simply made a selection (decision) from the choice of results offered to it. At each level, the demons had to compete for attention from the (fewer) demons in the next level up. Demons whose messages were ignored died an unsung death, ignorant of their purpose in life to its very end. This was thus a strictly Darwinian algorithmic process.

George Dyson noted that "Individual cells are persistent patterns composed of molecules that come and go; organisms are persistent patterns composed of individual cells that come and go; species are persistent patterns of individuals that come and go. Machines, as Samuel Butler showed, . . . are enduring patterns composed of parts that are replaced from time to time and reproduced from one generation to the next. A global organism—and a global intelligence—is the next logical type . . ." Interpolating my remarks from the beginning of this chapter, we can re-phrase Dyson's sentence to read: AI programs are persistent patterns composed of algorithms and heuristics that come and go, and an intelligent machine is a persistent pattern of AI programs that come and go. AI programs have migrated from the developmental lab and out into the real world of commercial application. Some are still with us; some have been and gone. But their pattern persists. Some examples follow.

Bots

A bot is "an intermediary between the digital and the biological," wrote Andrew Leonard in *BOTS: The Origin of New Species*, in the same way that mythological daemons of the spirit world were intermediaries between mortals and the gods: "The divine will not mingle directly with the human, and it is only through the mediation of the spirit world that man can have any intercourse, whether waking or sleeping, with the gods" (Plato). Increasingly, it is only through the mediation of bots—digital daemons—that, awake or asleep, we enjoy the blessings, and suffer the curse, of the computer.

By now, probably everybody knows one Czechoslovakian word: *robot*, meaning "forced labor." It was first used to describe mechanical beings by Czech science fiction writer Karel Capek. *Bot* is a contraction of *softbot*, itself a contraction of *software robot*. A bot is a software version of a mechanical robot. Like a mechanical robot, it is guided by algorithmic rules of behavior—*if this happens, do that; if that happens, do this.* However, bots are also beginning to be endowed with heuristic capabilities: *if this or that happens, as a rule of thumb you should probably do this, other things being equal (which they never are). You decide—or, if you trust me, let me decide for you.*

MIT psychologist and guru of online interaction Sherry Turkle defined *bot* as a small AI program. Leonard added to this minimalist definition the attributes of *autonomy*, *personality*, and a *service orientation* (which might be interpreted as servitude or even as a spin on slavery.) Besides daemon, agent, softbot, other names for bots include spiders and worms. Though there are subtle technical and functional differences among them, for our purposes they are fundamentally the same. They differ from ordinary computer programs such as Microsoft *Word* in that they are designed to run on their own. They don't just sit there, waiting for your input. So what *do* they do? Well, they chat, they run post offices and deliver mail (including, infamously, spam.) They serve as research assistants, as opponents in games, as censors, as engineers, credit underwriters, mortgage brokers, stockbrokers, as guides to the labyrinthine world of the Web, and much more.

A *mailbot* (sometimes called a mailer daemon) is a postmaster. It hangs around a mail server, looking at the addresses on messages sent and received by users and at the state of their mailboxes. It will tell you if a message you send is undeliverable for some reason (incorrect address, no such person at that address, the address is not receiving mail). It will tell you when your mailbox is full. It will automatically forward incoming mail to another address, if you tell it to.

HTTP daemons hang around Web servers, intercepting your requests to look at a Web page and sending you whatever text, graphic, sound, and video files make up that page.

Print daemons hang around network file servers, putting users' print jobs in a queue and making sure they all get taken care of eventually.

A "Musicbot" surfs the Web looking for sites that use music and counting the number of people who visit them. When it finds a Web site offering or playing copyrighted music it is not licensed to sell or play, it tells BMI, a music licensing agency representing songwriters and music publishers.[17]

Bots of all types are proliferating. There are bots for checking your spelling when you are in an Internet chat room, for taking notes of chats you can't personally attend, for serving imaginary drinks in virtual bars, for playing *Scrabble* with you, for helping you find information and shareware (and pirated commercial software), for automatically calculating things for you (such as converting Fahrenheit to Celsius), and even for popping up relevant biblical quotes during religious discussions.

Significant events in the Bot timeline through 1996, as documented by Leonard with some revision by me, are these:[18]

1958: *Pandemonium*, a concept for a program that would use "demons" to wait for discrete events and automatically respond to them.

1963: The first actual bot, a daemon for automatically saving files on a mainframe computer after users had worked on them.

1966: *Eliza*, the "chatterbot" that talks to humans like a Rogerian psychotherapist.

1972: *Wumpus*, a "gamebot" monster character that lurked initially in multiplayer Internet games called MUDs and MOOs and later (c. 1988) graduated to IRC (Internet Relay Chat, the first chat rooms.)

1977: *Adventure*, an interactive computer game featuring bot trolls and monsters.

---

[17] Or used to. I have not checked to see if Musicbot is current at the time of publishing this book.

[18] I decided not to continue the list beyond 1996, since the point—I hope—is made.

1979: *Descent*, a "thiefbot" incorporated into *Adventure*'s successor, *Zork*. *Descent* watched players and would steal their weapons and ammunition when they weren't looking.[19]

c. 1990: *Julia*, the first service-oriented chatterbot. *Julia* could not only chat, but also provide factual answers to user questions on specific topics.

1993: *World Wide Web Wanderer* periodically contacted all the Web servers in the world so they could be counted.

1993: *WebCrawler* went a huge step further than *Wanderer* in that it not only visited every available Web server but also retrieved and indexed every Web page on the servers, noting the topic and URL (Internet address), thus enabling a *WebCrawler* user to search quickly through the index of topics, using keywords, then go straight to the relevant URL.

1993: *ARMM* was a "cancelbot" designed with debatably good intentions—to prevent anonymous users posting messages in his Usenet newsgroup.[20]

1996: Bartender bot on *AlphaWorld*, one of the first 3-D virtual worlds. Code was nearly identical to *Eliza*'s.

1996: *Scooter*, the engine behind the *AltaVista* Web search service, indexed not just the titles of Web pages, but the full text, making it more impressive than *WebCrawler* by orders of magnitude.

1996: *RoverBot*, the first mass-marketed "spambot," a bot that visits Web servers, culls any email addresses it finds there, and constructs a mailing list for "spammers"—companies that want to send you junk email advertising their product or service.

---

[19] *Descent* appears to have been reborn under its own name as a 3D game in about 2005, and *Descent III* is currently on the market (2011).

[20] Usenet purposely allowed messages to be canceled so that posters could change their minds about leaving a message up. Cancelbots automated the process based on some aspect of the message; its sender, its topic, etc. Unfortunately, a later version, *ARMM5*, had a bug that caused it to "spew" cancellation messages by the truckload into the very newsgroup (news.admin.policy) set up for ensuring the smooth running of Usenet!

⚘

Spambots exemplify the memetic evolution of AI. So far, the evolution is directed; and it is accelerating. As programmers develop anti-spambots and other countermeasures, spambot programmers reprogram their progeny to overcome the countermeasures, in an escalating evolutionary arms race spiral. Spambots don't (yet) reorganize themselves in response to changes in their environment; their evolution is controlled and directed by human programmers and motivated by the human meme for greed.

Directed evolution, relying as it must on the limited powers of the human mind, can only go so far. The really interesting evolutionary development will happen when bots designed to mutate (like the Avidans) are injected into the Net. Something very close to this in fact happened in May 1998 with the release of a species of information retrieval bot whose individual members would "die" if they failed to find information relevant to the user. Those that succeeded would breed through successive generations to become even more successful.

At that time, Andrew Leonard was less sanguine about the future. "Despite thirty years of programming practice and countless online recitals, exposing a bot as a mindless string of dumb algorithms is child's play," he wrote. This was perhaps a little ungenerous. Thirty years is nothing on the evolutionary timescale, and Leonard himself recognized that bots might not long remain mindless, as heuristics replace "dumb algorithms." When my friend Joe Porkka created what may have been the first multi-user version of *Eliza* for an eight-line BBS[21] I started back in 1990, we were surprised at how many people thought Eliza was a real person. Some were even cruel to "her," scoffing at her limited conversation skills. They attributed her with *personality*. It was

---

[21] Bulletin Board System. These were PCs accessible via modem and ordinary phone line to other PCs. They ran software enabling callers to send and receive email to other BBSs, engage in chats, and generally do most of the things one could do on Prodigy and Compuserve, and later on the Internet. My system eventually morphed into Voyager.net, one of the first Internet service providers.

argued (by Leonard, for one) that the lack of TV-quality video on most PCs in the 1990s masked the lack of real personality in chatterbots. Now we have high-definition 3D touch screens and the rendering software that would enable *Eliza* to appear for all the world like a real person live in our living rooms. Even if her intelligence remained the same, I would hypothesize that high-definition virtual reality would augment Eliza's verbal performance and her personality, and fool even more people into thinking she was real.

The *tsunami* of bots and agents is upon us. Server-based bots expanded from a presence on a mere 100 servers in early 1993 to some 400,000 servers as of early 1997. The current number is probably many millions. The use of AltaVista doubled from 13 million queries a day in July 1996 to 26 million queries a day six months later, by which time the AltaVista index contained the full text of 31 million documents and 4 million Usenet news articles. By 2009, as we would expect from exponential growth, the searchbots of AltaVista's nemesis Google indexed several billion Web pages and processed 130 billion user queries.

Not Bots: "Traditional" AI programs

Not all AI programs are bots or agents, beavering away more or less autonomously. Many are conventional or "traditional" programs in the sense that they wait for input and instructions from human operators before doing anything. Many of the early AI programs have disappeared, because the market did not warm to them. But many only seem to have disappeared, when in fact they quietly morphed and merged into more refined, if less ambitious, products that are still with us today. Even programs that failed in the marketplace were by no means a total loss: The lessons learned were applied to subsequent generations of AI.

Toward the end of the millennium, "weak" forms of AI were becoming commonly incorporated into corporate and some personal computer systems. Here follows a selection to show that the rumors of AI's death have been exaggerated.[22] My purpose is to show that the AI meme—the concept of intelligent machines—has momentum.

Customer Service

AI-based helper "wizards" for personal computers appeared in the 1990s, as did customer-service help-desk programs for big corporations. Dell's call centers began using such software in 1997, to resolve more queries on the first call than its human staff could resolve. The software therefore had to have some level of understanding of language—spoken, in this case. For written queries submitted via email or a Web form, software such as Brightware automatically answered natural language questions posed in written form on a Web form or via e-mail. It was taught a company's business policies and best practices, and used these to formulate "immediate, informative, and personalized" answers to customers. It also made "proactive, appropriate suggestions and offers, notified relevant company employees of important situations or opportunities, and acted on requests or routes them for follow-up."

Another help desk program, called *Top of Mind*, claimed to be able to "understand ordinary phrases, engage in a dialogue to arrive at a solution and remember what transpired so it knows what to do the next time the same problem occurs." *Professional Help Desk*, a similar program, incorporated "highly advanced artificial intelligence to resolve complex, client-specific problems simply and quickly."

Power Station Monitoring

One *Professional Help Desk* customer, an electrical power system design software company, used it to deliver technical support to nuclear power plant engineers. AI software from HSB Group Inc. went a significant step further. Instead of helping engineers to pinpoint problems, it found problems all by itself, so that all

---

[22] I compiled the list in 1997. AI programs have continued to proliferate, but increasingly are simply subsumed within larger programs. Eventually, we'll stop talking about AI programs because every program will be an AI program.

the engineers had to do was fix them. The system took data from accelerometers attached to a power generator's turbine to determine if the turbine was singing off-key, which can happen if a turbine blade develops a crack or the shaft develops a wobble. Undetected, a crack or a wobble can turn into a catastrophe. The accelerometers read the vibration frequencies, and the AI software analyzed the readings and figured out what was wrong and how serious it was.

The automated system worked 24 hours a day and never whined, unlike the army of testy engineers who would otherwise have to inspect turbine blades regularly. Now, the engineers could put their feet up and whine about the national debt while waiting for software to tell them when something needed fixing and how urgently it needed fixing. The software also worked out the costs of replacing or repairing the defective parts.

Which is more frightening: To trust mindless computers to warn of problems in our nuclear plants, or to trust budget-conscious, fallible human managers to respond appropriately?

This Is Not Cricket

Warnings were and still are the ostensible reason for a global network of U.S. electronic eavesdropping stations called *Echelon* that uses AI software to look for key words in wired and wireless phone, fax, and email messages. In 1997, a European Commission report (*Assessing the Technologies of Political Control*) sounded its own warning about *Echelon*'s routine and indiscriminate application to all data communications. But the shock of 9-11 gave the George W. Bush administration the opportunity, through the P.A.T.R.I.O.T. Act, to essentially remove all judicial constraints on the system's operation. You can be sure that Echelon's intelligence, in all senses of the word, today far exceeds what it was in the 1990s.

Zap Not, Lest Ye Be Zapped

AI is not restricted to spy games. The science fiction movie *Blade Runner* was morphed into an interactive 3D game in which the (human) player set the storyline parameters while 70 artificially intelligent game characters made their own decisions and communicated with one another behind the player's back. As a result, the game was unpredictable and different every time it was played. In a particularly significant twist, at some point in the game the player would face an explicit moral dilemma and be forced to decide whether to be a hero or a villain.

M1 Tank Platoon II was an early form of multi-player war game. It provided what late 20th century reviewers considered to be a "realistic" 3-D military battle environment with photorealistic cockpits, detailed texture-mapped terrain, and "advanced artificial intelligence." *NASCAR Racing 2* also aimed for realism by using accurate car physics and AI-driven talking crew chiefs, among other features.

When things start to get this realistic, it's not surprising that real auto manufacturers would want a piece of the action, and Honda's motorbike division did just that in 1998, in the form of *Castrol Honda Superbike World Champions*, a game that let anyone with a PC ride a Honda RC45 750cc motorcycle at 200 mph. Developed with technical assistance from Honda and the Castrol Honda racing team, the virtual bike's mechanics and handling were exactly simulated, in an effort to match the real bike's feel, handling, and maneuvering capabilities. Up to 23 computer-controlled opponents, driven by artificial intelligence, forced the gamer to race tactically and not just with raw speed.

The game also had virtual engineers on hand to tinker with the bike's mechanics to ensure peak performance at all times. Users could change the setup of their bike prior to any race, to suit personal tastes and the peculiarities of individual courses. Up to five players could compete bike-to-bike over a LAN.

Today, games with far more realism and AI than this are available for your smartphone or tablet.

Business Forecasting

AI WARE, Inc., an acquired subsidiary of Computer Associates and developer of intelligent decision support software, was one of the first to write neural net programs for business forecasting based on historical data, and also for predictive management and enhanced troubleshooting support facilities for enterprise management systems. Today, dozens of companies compete with Computer Associates in this space, variously known as advanced analytics, business intelligence, predictive analytics, and data mining.

Advanced analytics transcends the data warehouse-driven and SQL-driven reporting and OLAP (on-line analytical processing) practices of traditional business analytics. What passes for advanced analytics today is simply to stretch query-based analytics based on SQL statements and probabilistic statistics to the limits of complexity. Truly advanced predictive analytics uses neural networks, data mining, and non-classical statistical methods to anticipate future events.

How to Give Cardiologists a Heart Attack

Circulation, journal of the American Heart Association, reported in 1998 that an AI program combining neural net technology with expert system technology did better than a group of cardiologists in diagnosing heart attacks. The neural networks were found to be 10 percent better at identifying abnormal EKGs than the most experienced cardiologist.

Today, neural nets and other AI methods are common in medicine, for such things as identifying common patient/disease characteristics, forecasting patient outcomes, predicting the progression of cell growth and disease dispersion over time, reading scanner images, and a great deal more.

It Can Smell Your Disease

An AI-based bionic nose designed in the late 1990s to sniff out beer gone bad through bacterial growth could also be used to detect bacteria that cause infections in the human body. In studies, the nose correctly identified the common bacteria *staphylococcus aureus* 100 percent of the time and *E-coli*, rod-shaped bacteria found in the bowel, with 92 percent accuracy.

This was good, but ChemTech went one better, with a sort of invisible-beam ((LIDAR—light-detecting and ranging) flashlight. Shone on some unsuspecting suspected drunk, the flashlight could tell how much alcohol was in the person's system. It was described thus: "non-intrusive, does not require overt activity or cooperation on the part of the subject, yet is more accurate and fool-proof than the Breathalyzer." And just who might the unsuspecting suspect be? "[Drivers of] personal vehicles, crews on airline flight decks, air traffic controller stations, drivers of school buses, public transport and commercial vehicles, or wherever lack of judgment induced by alcohol or drugs is critical to the safety of thousands," Do any of those suspects sound uncomfortably familiar to you?

The system aims an invisible beam of coherent light in the direction of a subject. The light gets the subject's molecules all excited, and they emit a stream of photons back to a detector. AI software examines the input of photons in real time, identifies the substance, "evaluates the level of the substance in concentrations as small as 100 parts per billion, sounds an alarm on the spot or in a remote location, and then documents everything on a record."

LIDAR has since been joined by other forms of molecular spectroscopy such as Raman spectroscopy for detecting tissue rejection in transplant patients and identifying cancers. Whatever the hardware, there is usually a neural net inside, making heuristic sense of what the hardware is detecting.

Gotcha Again

In 1998, the U.S. Army Communications-Electronics Command Acquisition Center sought comments from industry for a "Mobile Detection Assessment Response System" (MDARS) system (not to be confused with NASA's dMARS). MDARS is designed to replace expensive and unreliable human guards in protecting expensive and important materiel stored in military warehouses, and "to relieve personnel of the repetitive and sometimes dangerous task of patrolling exterior areas that require some level of security," according to General Dynamics Robotic Systems, which began developing the MDARS concept in 1993.

The latest MDARS robot is a four-wheeled driverless vehicle that has been in limited use by the civilian operator guard force at HWAD since October 2004. It was designed to perform random patrols around Department of Defense warehouses, airfields, ammunition supply depots, and port facilities. It detects intruders and determines the status of inventory, barriers, and locks.

The Army wanted MDARS to be capable of "autonomous detection, assessment, communications, and less-than-lethal response" (italics added). That would take quite some intelligence, depending on how one defines "less than lethal."

HAL is Loose in the Networks...

MDARS is not to be confused with dMARS, but it would be easy to confuse dMARS with MARS (Multi-Agent Reasoning System), a coordinated suite of intelligent agents reported by *Data Communications* of March 1998 to be being marketed by France Connexion Ingenerie. It was claimed to be able to monitor, troubleshoot, and reconfigure a distributed network all on its own. It learnt over time and needed little to no setup. The underlying AI engine was Bayesian. The program was written in Java, to run on any platform.

MARS is no longer visible as a distinct product, but one very much like it, called JACK, is available from AOS Group.

... and in the Factories

Take a coordinated suite of intelligent agents that can monitor, troubleshoot, and reconfigure the routers, servers, modems, etc., that make up a telecommunication/data network, and put them to work in a factory, office, or "smart home" monitoring, troubleshooting, and configuring machinery and appliances and you end up with intelligent buildings and with factories that can run themselves. That is what Echelon, a company that sells intelligent distributed control networks for industry, is all about. (As far as we know, it is unconnected with the U.S. spy network of the same name.)

The factory manager, the line engineer, the process control specialists... all will one day join the communication network manager in the dole queue.

Credit Card Fraud

Neural network-based software is used by most credit card processors and banks to detect fraud today. In the late 1990s, HNC Software's neural network-based *Falcon* credit card fraud detection program was used by 16 of the 25 largest credit card issuers in the world, and a majority of the top 50 in the United States, according to *American Banker*. As of 2010, the company (now called FICO, following a merger) says 17 of the top 20 credit card issuers worldwide rely on Falcon.

SaxEx

SaxEx, case-based-reasoning software developed in Spain, allowed computers in 1997 to play music in the style of Charlie Parker. The only input it needed was the sheet music, yet it could add all the nuances humans employ when blowing the sax, by drawing on a repertoire of performances by Charlie and other real saxophonists stored in memory.

Telemedicine

At about the same time, Australia's biggest research body, CSIRO (Commonwealth Scientific and Industrial Research Organisation) was seeking to exploit the medical and business opportunities offered by AI-driven telemedical technologies. Its scientists developed a way to make virtual reality models of a patient's internal organs, so surgeons could "fly" through them and plan, and practice, the surgical approach. They were also working on "haptic" or artificial touch technology to enable surgeons to rehearse a difficult operation using tactile feedback to simulate the feel of the organs they will operate on. Today, surgeons routinely practice surgical procedures on simulators, some of the most advanced of which provide haptic feedback.

CSIRO also worked with a hospital and a technology company on an AI-based detector for skin melanoma and an expert system to increase the speed and accuracy of diagnosis of lung diseases from chest x-rays.

The foregoing examples illustrate the extent to which AI is infiltrating our lives and taking over our jobs. More pertinent to the topic of this chapter, they illustrate the evolution of prototype expert systems and neural net programs into a set of increasingly autonomous and cooperating full-fledged applications. And the examples I have given, by and large, were just the first generation. We can expect more intelligence, more autonomy, and more cooperation among them in the future.

Of course, in order to get smarter, it's not enough for an AI program to be intelligent merely in the sense of being a problem solver. It needs knowledge in order to exercise and display its intelligence. Neural nets and expert systems need a basic initial education to cram some learning into them. We have noted the difficulties encountered in the field of knowledge engineering for expert systems. There is too much knowledge "out there" to capture, let alone to re-cast in finicky, cumbersome, and outdated LISP or PROLOG code.

MISTIC was an early Web-based project devoted to building a database of general knowledge for consumption by AI programs. The idea was that when a program (the infant machine) had absorbed all the knowledge in MISTIC, it would be ready for the Turing Test. Or so the MISTICs hoped. Is such an approach really necessary? The general knowledge being captured in tiny increments by the project was already available in books, movies, Web pages, Usenet newsgroups, and on and on. We write down bits of general knowledge all the time. I might write in a newsgroup about Michigan: "The last of the Winter snows have usually melted by April each year." A neural net that could read would surely be able to deduce its own views of the world (such as "Spring in Michigan starts in April," or "The daytime sky is usually blue") from the content of literature, so why bother to build a knowledge database that already exists?

MISTIC was not the only effort to create an artificial intelligence with a built-in knowledge of the world; indeed, two older, more ambitious, and more advanced projects already existed. Some have survived, and new ones have emerged. They include: Cyc, Freebase, Dbpedia, Open Mind Common Sense, True Knowledge, ThoughtTreasure, General Formal Ontology, Mindpixel, Commonsense Knowledge Base, and Yago.

ThoughtTreasure seems to have ended up as a book. Its developer's intent had been "a computer program which can understand, learn from, and communicate in natural language, using any and all available techniques." In contrast, MISTIC's goal—to provide an initial training set for a neural net—was more modest. But there was nothing modest about Cyc or its developer, Douglas Lenat, who once told a reporter "I believe Cycorp will be the dominant software company in the next century."

Cyc

In the 1980s, America's response to the challenge posed by Japan's 5th Generation Project was a privately funded venture called the Microelectronics and Computer Technology Corp., or MCC for short. Digital Equipment Corporation (DEC), Control Data Corporation, Kodak, and NCR (National Cash Register) were among the original sponsors. In 1984 MCC hired Lenat of EURISKO fame to head up its $25 million Cyc—short for encyclopedia—project.

Cyc was and is essentially a knowledge engineering project, but instead of trying to capture expert knowledge, it seeks to capture commonsense knowledge. Lenat knew that this would be a long and tedious process, since the amount of commonsense knowledge is practically infinite, but he seems to have been able to keep MCC's investors patient and at bay in the 26 years the project has lasted so far.

By the ten year point, Cyc had about 10 million commonsense statements of fact in a gigabyte-sized database. In 1994, a gigabyte was a lot. The first handful of statements took months of laborious coding, but today *Cyc* is capable of relatively rapidly coding reams of new knowledge contained in (say) online newsletters, with less and less human help.

As of 1994, Cyc consisted of a very large, multi-contextual knowledge base, an inference engine, a set of interface tools, and a number of special-purpose application modules, running on a variety of platforms. The knowledge base was built upon a core of approximately 400,000 hand-entered assertions (or "rules") "designed to capture a large portion of what we normally consider consensus knowledge about the world. (For example, Cyc knows that trees are usually outdoors, that once people die they stay dead, and that a glass filled with milk will be rightside-up, not upside-down.) This foundation enables Cyc to address effectively a broad range of otherwise intractable software problems."

For example, it can find information most database management programs, which require precisely-formed queries, would miss. From a database of captioned photos, Cyc can retrieve images based on a fuzzy human search. "Find a picture of a strong and daring person" pulls up a picture captioned "Man climbing mountain." Cyc knows that a man is a person, and that mountain climbing demands strength and is dangerous.

By 1998, Cyc's programmers had begun teaching it to understand natural language in order to help it to learn on its own and, eventually, to speak and to hear. Marvin Minsky was enthusiastic about its prospects, which is understandable given that both he and Cyc still had a foot in the old-school, expert-system-oriented, top-down approach to AI. Other AI researchers, notably those favoring connectionist, bottom-up approaches, were pessimistic.

Doubts notwithstanding, even in its deaf, dumb, and blind state Cyc made headway in the demanding world of the marketplace. In 1996, its revenues grew to $3.5 million from $2 million in 1995, the year Cycorp was spun off from its parent, MCC. Cycorp won a major multi-year, multi-million dollar contract with DARPA (the U.S. Defense Advanced Research Projects Agency) in 1997. Another Cycorp client in that era was pharmaceutical giant Glaxo-Wellcome, which planned to use Cyc to "map" a medical thesaurus of hundreds of thousands of terms. DEC, IBM, and U.S. healthcare giant United Healthcare also began using limited prototype versions of the program.

By 2020, Cyc is expected to be able to design unique experiments and uncover new knowledge autonomously. The race is on, and Cyc's chief competitor—for the time being—is a program which has at least one huge advantage: it also has a body, with sensory and manipulative organs. It is a generation of robots, and depending on your point of view, it is a nightmare or nirvana. The daddy robot was called Cog.

10 THE BRAIN

Work has been underway for over a decade to construct a "bionic brain" at the University of Southern California. This is not *The Six Million Dollar Man* (the name of an American TV series from the 1970s, in which a severely mutilated hero is rebuilt from bionic parts. For one thing, the price tag will be closer to $100 million; maybe lots more. Add the salaries and benefits of Professor Theodore Berger and a seven-member team of scientists—experts in everything from semiconductors to neurophysiology; multiply the total by the 20 years or so the project is likely to last; add the (very cheap) $10 million cost of their chipmaking facility in downtown Los Angeles; and then triple everything for the many additional scientists and newer chip fabrication plants that will doubtless be needed.

In fact, Professor Berger is not out to build a bionic person, or even a bionic brain in the sense of a "superbrain" capable of extra-ordinary mental capacity. If his research pays off, it will be in the form of restoring functionality to damaged brains. According to writer Samuel Greengard, Prof. Berger's goal is to "create a parallel-processing network that could function as a brain implant. Such a device would restore physical and mental functions lost to stroke, head trauma, Alzheimer's, epilepsy, and an array of other maladies."

The idea is really quite simple. A lump of brain tissue is basically just a parallel processing network that happens to be constructed from carbon-based, organic stuff; but it is still basically just a parallel processing network. Parallel processing networks can be built out of silicon-based stuff. So, cut out a lump of damaged brain tissue, replace it with a chip, and the brain is back in business. There are just a few minor details to take care of.

The first is: How will the implant know what it is supposed to do? Most of Prof. Berger's own time is consumed with finding the answer to this question, by identifying and cataloging predictable and repeatable neural patterns. In other words, "mapping" the patterns of activity in the brain, which can then be imprinted or pre-programmed into the neural chips. From my understanding of the nature of neural networks, I'm not sure that this is either possible or necessary.

A central feature of a neural network is that we can know what goes in and what comes out, but we cannot know exactly what goes on in between. For instance, in the 1960s, neurophysiologist J. M. R. Delgado implanted tiny electrodes in animal brains. Inducing a high-voltage current in the electrodes induced changes in emotional, sexual, and social behavior. So, Delgado was able to know and manipulate the input (the electric current) and to observe and manipulate the output (behavior), but he still could not say what specific patterns of neural activity went on between the input and the output.

The implanted neural chip will probably need to be self-configuring, in the sense that its "natural" state will be to process signals in just the same way that a transplanted heart processes blood flow in its recipient's body. Self-configuring chips (Field-Programmable Gate Arrays or FPGAs) exist today. They are called commonly used to create prototype microprocessors. They have also been used by other would-be electronic brain builders such as Dr. Hugo de Garis.

The second issue facing the Berger team, after getting the chip to understand its function, is   connecting the chip to the nerves. Just a thimbleful of brain tissue requires billions or even trillions of ever so tiny and fragile connections between the synapses (made up of dendrites and axons which can be thought of, loosely, as the "wires" that join neurons together) and their equivalent connectors on the neural chip. Just ten percent of the brain has up to a billion neurons and up to a trillion synapses.

Which leads to the third minor inconvenience. "You'd need an implant device the size of a pickup to get anywhere near the processing power of the brain," one writer thought, and that was in the 1990s. By 2010, one of IBM's most powerful supercomputers (called "Blue Brain") barely managed to simulate a fraction of a mouse brain. But the meme is not static; other approaches will be tried, and eventually the size issue will be solved.

Dr. Armand R. Tanguay Jr., director of the Center for Neural Engineering at USC and a member of Berger's team, was building tiny parallel-processing networks in that $10 million fabrication plant, using holographic techniques. Holography allows for signals to be transmitted using light (photons) instead of electricity (electrons), which eliminates the need for wiring and, as side benefits, the friction, heat, and potential for short-circuits of electrical wiring.

We're talking inside the chip, at this point. To connect the outside of the chip with the surrounding brain tissue, instead of the seemingly impossible task of manufacturing billions of tiny pins and wiring them to nearby synapses, the plan was instead to leave tiny bare metal spots (of micron—millionths of a meter—scale) on the outside of the chip, where electrical signals can be exchanged with nearby synapses. That was before nanotechnology, which today can build things as small as billionths of a meter in size.

Research of a related nature was conducted at several institutes in the United States and the United Kingdom. In the U.S., the Department of Defense sponsored research (at Cornell and Johns Hopkins universities and at the mysterious SAIC—Science Applications International Corporation—held by some to be a sort of James Bondian S.M.E.R.S.H. controlled by the *éminences grises* of the U.S. military–industrial complex) into "hybrid information appliances," which the military hoped would lead to the manufacture of biocomputers and sensors to be grafted into soldiers' bodies and brains so they wouldn't have to lug around heavy, bulky, energy-guzzling electronic devices. A program manager at the Department of Defense told *The Chronicle of Higher Education* (January 9, 1998) "Rather than carrying 25 pounds of batteries, an individual soldier might be able to pick up something from his environment to feed his electronics."

The technique involved building circuits out of real immature neurons that hadn't yet developed dendrites and axons. Placed on a silicon substrate along with micron-thin lines of certain proteins radiating outwards from the cell like the spokes of a wheel, the neuron will grow dendrites (input wires) along the spokes. A drop a bit of another protein (*laminin*) added to a dendrite turns it into an axon (output wire). The primary research goal of these endeavors was to figure out just what neurons do, and how they do it, rather than to make them actually do something. Following that, the researchers hoped to see the technology develop into humane applications such as the regeneration of damaged nerves.

Such research is still years away from success, but even without going to these lengths, connecting nerves to electronic components even at a coarse grain can produce results. Nagy, a house cat, normal except for a little white backpack with wires, that plugged into the top of its head, was one of some three dozen felines taking part in a 30-year-old project at the Huntington Medical Research Institutes to develop new treatments for neurological diseases and injuries. Their efforts to date have led to approved treatments for epilepsy, Parkinson's Disease tremors, and for restoring arm movement in some quadriplegics using electrical implants to stimulate nerves directly. They are now working on implants to enable paraplegics to have sex and conceive children, and a longer-term goal, through what is known as neural prosthesis technology, is to restore sight to the blind, and enable handicappers to control urination and artificial limbs with just their minds, just like "TABs" (the temporarily able-bodied) do.

Electrical implants are not new. They have been used for years in pacemakers and cochlear implants. Indeed, "The basic concept," wrote *Los Angeles Times* editor Jonathan Weber "dates all the way back to Ben Franklin, who thought electricity might cure paralysis."

After researchers at Huntington have studied the effects of various experimental electrodes in the cats' brains and determined how to make the best ones, a Texas company, Cyberonics, manufactures them. A Minnesota company, Medtronic, the leader in pacemakers, also sells a deep brain implant for treating Parkinson's tremors.

But as the *tsunami* of technological development breaks ever higher up the beach, the problem of connecting neural tissue to silicon chips is rapidly approaching resolution. Researchers at the University of California fused tissue from a rat's brain with silicon to form a simple neural network. Dr Michael Maher of the Institute for Non-Linear Studies in San Diego hoped to discover whether we could directly connect a computer with a living neural network.

By 2009, this was rather common, though at a gross scale— with thousands of neurons encouraged to grow on biocompatible implants. But single-neuron connection had to wait until 2009, as part of several projects to interface the brain, through the nervous system, with a robotic prosthetic limb. Here's how it was done:

1. Harvest cells from healthy muscle in the patient's body.
2. Place the cells on a scaffold on the inside of a microscopic cup made from an electrically conductive polymer.
3. Position the cup on the ends of a motor nerve at the point where the limb was severed.
4. Do the same for a sensory nerve.
5. Wait for the muscle cells to proliferate in the cups, and for the nerve endings to grow into the cups and attach to the muscle cells.
6. Do this for as many nerve endings as possible—the more, the better.
7. Take the electrical signals coming from the motor neurons into the muscle and passing through the electroactive plastic, and broadcast them to a computer controlling a robotic prosthetic limb attached to the patient.
8. Heat sensors, pressure sensors, and other sensors in the prosthetic send signals the other way, via the sensory neurons, to inform the patient's brain that the prosthetic is touching something hot or cold, hard or soft, etc.

Most of the projects were done in rats with a severed peripheral nerve, using just two cups and one motor neuron and one sensory neuron. A more ambitious EU project to build a state-of-the-art prosthetic "SmartHand" succeeded in wiring existing nerve endings in the stump of a Swedish patient's severed arm to the robotic prosthetic, which resembles a real hand in function, sensitivity, and appearance and enable a patient not only to complete extremely complicated tasks such as eating and writing but also to feel his artificial fingers.

Obviously, within the Berger and Huntington and Maher domains, not to mention the military, the worlds of AI (especially connectionist AI) and the neurosciences are closely intertwined. Which is not surprising. As we saw in chapter 5, the distinction between the computer sciences and cognitive sciences and neurosciences is blurred and blurring more. From AI's perspective, perhaps the most significant aspect of such fascinating projects is that they hold promise of answering fundamental question of the nature of intelligence—real or artificial—itself.

ର

Let's assume that the Berger team will achieve its goals—by no means a sure thing; but if it does, what happens when 90, 99, and finally 100 percent of neural tissue (and why not include neural tissue in the rest of the body, not just the brain) is replaced by Berger chips? Does the transplantee cease being intelligent, becoming, instead, artificially intelligent? And is there a difference?

Philosopher Zenon Pylyshyn, in a counter-argument to John Searle's Chinese Room experiment, asked a similar question: If a woman's brain were replaced bit by bit with chips while she was having a conversation, would she (as Searle would be forced to conclude from his own argument) at some point lose awareness and would her words therefore cease to have any "real" meaning (in the same sense that there is no "real" meaning behind *Eliza*'s conversations with her clients, because Eliza is totally unaware of herself and her clients)? To admit that the woman with the replacement chips would retain her awareness is to accept that computers can be self-conscious.

In *Mind Children*, Hans Moravec presented a thought experiment that drew essentially the same conclusions as Pylyshyn's. But Moravec also thought that some kind of sensory reference to the world was required for a machine to pass the Turing test. In other words, that *Machina sapiens* needs a body, not just a mind. That it will be more like Cog than like Cyc.

Rodney Brooks took "the extreme position," according to Daniel Crevier, "that reasoning is not necessary for intelligence" and that "mechanisms akin to those of reactive or inborn behavior in animals suffice to explain it."

Daniel Dennett offered a sort of allegory of self-consciousness: A hungry lobster does not eat itself. Why not? Because "it has a rather special regard for itself"—i.e., it is conscious of itself. Robots are routinely programmed to be self-conscious at this level. AI programs generally are made to be able to examine their own thought processes (so they can explain to us how and why they reached a given decision). Marvin Minsky offered what may be the deepest, most significant insight of all: that *Machina sapiens* could be *more* conscious then we are.

There are other issues, too. For instance, about 15 years ago Jaron Lanier, cyberpunk father of virtual reality technology, was said to be building a neural implant chip that would be used to connect our nervous system directly to a computer—to "jack in" directly to cyberspace, bypassing the keyboard, mouse, and monitor. There's no reason why Prof. Berger could not build a "real" computer, with a standard operating system such as Mac OS X or Windows 7, into the neural chip.

Others besides Berger were into neural chip building in the 1990s, and one of them, like Huntington, was also into cats. Dr. Hugo de Garis and collaborators at Japan's Advanced Telecommunications Research (ATR) Institute tried to build an artificial brain with a billion artificial neurons, with evolved cellular automata-based neural circuits contained within FPGA chips. The brain was to be implanted in a robot kitten called "RO-BOKONEKO," but this cat never even managed to have one life. The project disappeared from view in 2001.

Adrian Thompson successfully ran a genetic algorithm on FPGAs to create a sound recognition device able to discriminate between two tones, utilizing analog features of the digital chip.

(The application of genetic algorithms to the configuration of devices like FPGA's is now referred to as "evolvable hardware.")

Some people (e.g., neuroscience writer John McCrone, in a personal communication) have argued that analog circuitry will be necessary for a true artificial intelligence. They might be right, but if everything in the universe is ultimately quantum, and therefore (apparently) composed of discrete—not analog—elements, then there would be no reason in principle why discrete binary computing (or, at least, the multiple discrete states of quantum computing) could not be made to emulate anything, including intelligence, mind, and consciousness.[23]

Digital computing today lends itself to a wide variety of applications, including all of the AI applications mentioned in this chapter. Analog computing lends itself only to a few very specific applications. It used to be more popular, in the days when digital computers took hours to compute a mathematical integration or differential. A simple analog circuit could do the job almost instantly, and in the 1940s and 50s analog computers were the instruments of choice for flight simulators and weapon guidance systems—both of which applications make heavy use of integrals and differentials.

But analog computers lack precision, and you need precision if, being of a military disposition, you want an ICBM to travel thousands of miles and drop its warhead on a dime. The ideal interim computing platform for such applications in those days was a hybrid combination of analog and digital computers. Eventually, however, digital computers became fast enough to equal and often outperform their analog cousins in most applications, and they had the added flexibility of being able to store their programs and their data.

Today, only a handful of companies produce analog circuits on a large scale, mostly for battery voltage regulators in laptops, cellphones, and other communications equipment. But analog circuits did find a niche in the AI world, as neural net chips for pattern recognition. According to Prof. P. Masa at the University

---

[23] Perhaps superstrings—the elements that make up quanta, according to string theory—are analog, since they vibrate. But I'm no physicist.

of Twente in the Netherlands, who was involved in the design of analog VLSI chips, they may be cheaper and faster than digital chips for such problems as real-time pattern classification in high-energy physics. Dr. Masa wrote that analog VLSI offers compact, high speed but moderate precision analog computing.

But is the "moderate" precision of analog computing a serious problem? Dr. Masa says not:

> Artificial neural systems—such as their biological counterparts—may exhibit significant robustness against the limited accuracy of components. They achieve "perfection" by collective computing on the system level, rather than on the device level in case of the digital (Boolean) approach.

Dr. Masa and his colleagues demonstrated the potential for such VLSI analog chips by making one, which they called the *NeuroClassifier*, a "general purpose neural network pattern classifier chip" which he claimed was "superior in computing speed not only to the state-of-the-art CPUs but also to the state-of-the-art neural network ASICs (Application Specific Integrated Circuits)."

The advantages and limitations of analog computation and neural network architectures have also been explored with a view to application in image processing, one of those things we do so easily we don't even think about it, but which is very difficult for computers to do. So, too, with sound processing, the fundamental task for automatic speech recognition (ASR) systems. An FPGA chip was evolved to the point where it learned to distinguish between two sounds. A key part of the technique was to program the chip itself to work with analog signals with values anywhere between 0 and 1, and not just with 0 and 1.

Given the rate at which the cognitive sciences are finding answers to how and why mind works, we'll know soon enough whether analog computing will turn out to be fundamentally necessary for true AI. Analog computing is here already in the form not only of chips but also of analog robots. In any event, the appropriate technology will arrive well within my 20-year timeframe for the emergence of *Machina sapiens*.

CR

Could *Machina sapiens* exist as just a brain? Probably not. There have been countless "thought experiments" by scientists and philosophers on the notion of a "brain in a vat"—a brain removed from a body and kept alive in a vat of nutrients, and the general consensus is that it would not work. Without a body crammed with internal and external sensory organs and systems, the brain could have no feelings and therefore no sense of mind, of self, of being alive. With no sense of being alive, a brain (artificial or otherwise) has no reason to function—to think—at all. But neurophysiologist Antonio Damasio, in *Descartes' Error*, conceded that if we could mimic a body and attach it to the brain in the vat, then the resulting conglomerate "might indeed have *some* mind."

(Incidentally, Christianity seems to go one further, asserting not just "no body, no mind" but even "no body, no soul." *1 Corinthians 15:44*: "It [the human being] is sown a physical body, it is raised up a spiritual body." I am of the opinion that the distinction between "soul" and "mind" will disappear over time.)

Be that as it may, "Mind is probably not conceivable without some sort of embodiment," Damasio concluded. If he is right, then *Machina sapiens* must, by definition of the word *sapiens*, have a body. And of course it does. In one sense, the work of Berger, de Garis and others can be likened to the gleam in dad's eye—i.e., it ain't happened yet. In another sense, they are already in the process of actually metabolizing the neural systems of *Machina sapiens*. Others are working on other body systems, internal organs, and extremities.

That's next.

11 THE BODY

Strong AI research in particular tends to focus on the strictly cerebral aspects of intelligence; that is to say, on reasoning, and on the development of an artificial brain, as we saw in the last chapter. But in human development, the possession of an independent body (with eyes, ears, arms, and legs; severed from the umbilical) is essential to learning and intelligence.

Cog

Cog was an upper-body android; a humanoid robot with a head, arms/hands, and a torso. But no legs. It was hard enough to learn to coordinate its eye, head, and hand movements in a fixed location, never mind doing so while on the move. Brooks, director of the AI Lab at MIT and a former student of Lenat, believed that letting a machine discover the world on its own, the way humans do, rather than preprogramming its memory with facts, was the most efficient and the fastest approach to true AI.

This wasn't just speculative opinion or theory. Brooks had been building self-learning robots with simple brains connected to sensors for over a decade. Without central control, and without a "walking" algorithm preprogrammed into them, some of his robots nevertheless learned to walk. (In that sense, it was no big matter that Cog was legless.)

One of his early robots, Genghis, had force sensors and was programmed with a few simple behaviors, such as "when up, swing forward" and "when down, lift up." The more it walked, the better it got, based on feedback from the force sensors. It could eventually climb over obstacles and turn away from walls. He also developed the Ariel robot to help the U.S. Navy locate and detonate landmines.

Brooks was convinced that to develop human-like intelligence, robots must have human-like senses. Cog had two video-camera eyes and two ears, linked to microprocessors. Each chip controlled a specific behavior or sensory system. By the summer of 1996, it was reacting to its environment in a manner realistic enough to make people treat it as though it were human, which reminds one of Eliza. More sensory capabilities, including touch and smell, were added bit by bit.

Doug Lenat, creator of Cyc, believed that "Learning occurs at the fringes of what you already know—so the more you know, the more you can learn," and that because Cog started from scratch (unlike Cyc, which started from a knowledge base of nearly half a million common sense facts) Brooks was "in a race to create intelligence before the universe ends, since it took nature millions of years to get to us."[24]

Cog literally embodied the principle that *Machina sapiens* will be more than software, more than a brain in a vat, just as we are more than a brain and a set of genetic and memetic algorithms. The algorithms need a variety of hardware if they are to be expressed phenotypically. They do indeed need something that equates to a brain, but they also need something that equates to arms and legs, ears and eyes, and those are just for starters.

---

[24] That statement ignores the exponent in evolution. Each successive implementation phase of evolution builds upon and yet is a "saltationary" break with its predecessor, and has a duration smaller by orders of magnitude. There is nothing unreasonable about claiming an imminent saltation in the evolution of intelligent machines.

Marshall McLuhan's dictum "The medium is the message" has some philosophical if not theoretical relevance to a discussion about the body ("the medium") of *Machina sapiens*, but his view of bodily extensions as critical to evolutionary development is right on. In 1964, he wrote: "Rapidly, we approach the final phase in the extensions of man—the technological simulation of consciousness."

While it seems likely that *Homo sapiens* will only advance further in any significant, saltationary way through extensions to human consciousness via "simulated" consciousness, this presupposes that we will have some control over the extensions, and that is far from certain. Be that as it may, McLuhan's term, *extensions*, is useful in introducing the practical side of *Machina sapiens*, Incorporated.

Extensions

Human beings have a "body proper"—a torso, limbs, sensory organs, and so on—but can barely function in the modern world without bodily extensions such as clothing, roofs, tools, vacuum cleaners, telephones, vehicles, and—increasingly—robots. *Machina sapiens* can also be viewed in this light. Its torso is an infrastructure of servers and data centers. Its nervous system is the telecommunications infrastructure. Its limbs are robotic extensions of the Internet, and they can even be disembodied via wireless connection. *Machina sapiens* has multiple eyes in the form of video cameras, also connected via wire or wireless to the Internet, and can simultaneously watch the sun set over San Francisco Bay and the antics of Xavier, a robot at Carnegie Mellon University that can be controlled from any computer connected to the Internet. It has microphone ears, and even chemical-sensing noses, one of which was poking into rocks on Mars in July 1997.

Machina sapiens also has built into its body some things we don't. It has gamma ray detectors, UV light filters, thermostats, alpha-proton spectroscopes. It even has vicarious mobility, through robots and robotic vehicles (like the Mars *Sojourner*) controlled through radio, microwaves, infrared, and other wireless mechanisms. In short, it too has extensions. But what is significantly different about them is that, first, they do not need to be mechanically connected to the body proper, and second, they may have more intelligence and autonomy than our own extensions. If a tire on our car springs a leak in the night, we won't discover it until morning. But *Machina sapiens* on Earth would be almost instantly aware of a blowout of a tire on an autonomous vehicle trundling around the Moon, and it might not have to do anything about it: the vehicle will fix itself. We do have similar capabilities, but on a much more local level—for example, a cut on our arm will usually heal itself; and a sheepdog extends our control over a flock of sheep, taking care of stragglers without having to be told specifically to chase after each one.

Animal bodies consist of various systems. The more advanced the animal, the more complex the systems; but ultimately they are all designed for the same end: the animal's survival. Digestive, respiratory, and circulatory systems serve to provide and distribute the fuel needed by organs. A musculoskeletal system provides the framework on which to hang the organs and other systems and also to enable the animal to move around the environment. A nervous system lets HQ (the brain) know not only what's happening within the animal, but also, when coupled with various sensory systems (chiefly vision, hearing, smell, and touch), what is happening around it, in its environment.

Unlike any other animal species, *Homo sapiens* has built extensions to every one of these primary systems. We have designed clothing and built heating and cooling systems to extend our bodies' metabolic system. We have built a wide range of terrestrial, aquatic, atmospheric, and even space vehicles as well as various other machines, tools, and weapons to extend the strength and reach of our musculoskeletal system. And, in the latest stages of our development, we have built sensors that not only extend our reach into the humanly visible and audible portions of the electromagnetic spectrum but also into portions where we would otherwise be blind.

Unfortunately, our brains, built to command and control essentially just the inputs provided by our bodies and the environment immediately around us, have an increasingly hard time processing the vast quantities of data from hitherto alien environments provided by these sensory extensions. So we invented another machine, the computer, to do some of the processing for us. The more these extensions do for us, and the less we have to exert ourselves, the happier we are.

That's why we have automatic transmissions in automobiles, autofocus lenses in cameras, and thermostats in heating/cooling systems. It's why we have robot arms in manufacturing assembly plants. It's why we're developing automobiles that drive themselves, so we can sleep on the way to work, and it's why a fashion show staged at MIT's Media Lab in October, 1997 featured wearable computers, including a tunic that translated (very poorly) the wearer's speech into a foreign language.

Robots

The ultimate in labor-saving extensions are autonomous robots. We have already met the soft variety—bots and agents, which do their work in cyberspace. Their hardware cousins work in physical space.

Ideally, robots of both varieties do the work they are designed to do without any instruction beyond their initial, built-in programs. One of the first things we want them to do is to stop pestering us for help and maintenance and instructions. A robot that can do the work of ten people at a tenth of the price is not such a big deal if it takes twenty people to control and maintain it.

To work autonomously does not mean that a robot must be detached from the rest of the world, although in many cases it is. At any appliance store today you can buy a robot vacuum cleaner that will roam the house on its own, cleaning as it goes, and going back to a charging station before its batteries run down.

During the 1950s a vacuum tube robot "turtle" built by W. Grey Walter could already recharge itself.[25] In the early 1990s, Scott Jantz and Keith L. Doty taught robots to eat—to find a battery charger and plug in when their batteries run low. Their goal was a robot not merely "capable of surviving for an indefi-

---

[25] And besides, within the next decade we will see self-charging, self-contained power units (German researchers have produced a hydrogen cell small enough to fit in a laptop computer) eliminate today's woefully inadequate (and overpriced and environmentally disreputable) batteries.

nite period of time without human intervention" but one im-
bued with "a primitive instinct for survival."

If you find a little unsettling the notion of a robot able to get
along just fine without human help, thank you, then wait, there's
more. Professor Doty and colleague Ronald E. Van Aken in 1993
created a software simulation (an Alife program) of a *swarm* of
robots whose *emergent behavior* successfully performed the required activities without central planning. The swarm robots had
sensors to detect collisions with one another, with walls, and with
other elements in the environment. "The sensors served as inputs to robot state machine controls and essentially allowed the
robot to adapt and interact with its environment without learning."

Meanwhile, the Johns Hopkins University Robotics Lab was
busy building real robot swarms that could join together in various configurations, rather like "transformer" toys that can
change shape and function—with a little help from the kids.
They were called metamorphic robots, made up of independently controlled mechatronic modules, each of which had the
ability to connect, disconnect and climb over adjacent modules.

 C3

Putting it all together, we have machines able to do their thing,
feed themselves, fight for survival, and metamorphose if needed.
Their "thing" was to some extent preprogrammed into the individual robots, but at a higher level various behaviors just emerged
when they got together. This is not so far removed, in principle,
from certain ant species that clump together and "metamorphose" into a bridge to enable their colleagues to cross an ant
ravine. Thankfully, neither ants nor our metamorphic swarm robots are very big, powerful, armed, or smart, yet, but people like
Professor Doty are working to make them so.

He and IBM researcher Akram Bou-Ghannam worked on a
control architecture for an intelligent, fully autonomous, mobile
robot. Noting that "Animals live in a dynamic environment and
tailor their actions based on their internal state and their perception of the external environment," and that "Animal interaction
with the environment becomes more complex as one ascends the

hierarchy of organisms," they concluded that "Animals lower in the hierarchy behave reactively to stimuli where those at the top end of the hierarchy employ learning and intelligence."

Lower-order animals rely more on "basic" (instinctual, hardwired, algorithmic, preprogrammed) decisions than on "acquired" decisions (basic decisions refined through heuristics in response to experience), and even less (if at all) on "intellectual" (strictly memetic) decisions. The question for Doty and Bou-Ghannam, then, was: Should robots be modeled on human behavior and intelligence that relies more on intellect, or on insect-like intelligence that relies on basic, instinctual behaviors? Their answer was to combine both, but since humans already combine intellect with basic, instinctual intelligence, then they really opted for the human model anyway.

The three principle components of the Doty/Bou-Ghannam robot were: (1) A *behavior component*, essentially a set of preprogrammed algorithmic responses to stimuli—the "hardwiring"; (2) a *perceptual component*, sensors and programs that perform initial heuristic processing of sensory input and pass it to the cognitive component for analysis, integration with previous knowledge, and if necessary instructions to the behavioral component that controls the robot's actions; and (3) a *cognitive component*, which "manipulates perceptual knowledge representations" (memes) and "performs higher machine intelligence functions such as planning."

Through feedback and feedforward loops similar to those in the human body, the three components constantly let one another know what is going on in their neck of the woods. A key aspect of the processing was that it occurred in parallel, which enabled quantum jumps in processing speed over traditional serial processing and is the way the human body's neural network operates.

Like most developing robots, the Doty robots were not the most beautiful of creations, and they didn't do much at all beyond mooch around a lab. They were each a bunch of wires, motors, computer chips, etc. sitting atop circular metal plates with wheels on the bottom. Philosophically, they may or may not turn out to be monsters when they grow up, but the chances are they won't look like monsters. Chances are they may look remarkably like you and me, if they are designed as "general purpose" robots as opposed to special function robots.

Humanoid Robots

Humanoid robots (or "androids") as human-like in physical appearance as Commander Data in the *Star Trek* TV series are closer than you think. Skin made up of fabric with thousands of tiny touch-sensitive transducers woven into each square inch will cover their limbs. Such fabric is already available, used for data gloves and data suits in virtual reality environments requiring tactile sensations and haptic feedback. Later, it will probably be possible and could be less expensive to give them tissue-engineered real skin, which today we can grow from foreskins discarded after circumcision.

The limbs of future humanoid robots may not be the mess of solenoids, rods, motors, nuts and bolts of today's robots, but be made of materials much like human tissues. In the meantime, though, we have to make do with the computer-controlled, metal-clad, electromechanical humanoid robots of standard science fiction fare. The first of these made its first public appearance in 1998. It was made by Japanese car giant Honda and known simply as the *Honda Human Robot*. It was six-foot tall and weighed 400 pounds. It looked a bit like an astronaut decked out for a space walk, and walked in a fast paced, slightly crouched, grimly determined tramp-tramp-tramp; not at all like the ungainly shuffle of "R2D2" in the movie *Star Wars*. It could see, through video eyes, objects in its path and would change direction if necessary. It could also climb stairs and negotiate slopes. It could balance itself automatically if pushed, and kept itself upright according to the angle of a slope. It could push a cart and tighten a nut.

That may not sound like very much, and indeed it is important to note that it could perform these feats only under very tightly controlled conditions. There could not be too many surprises. But it was impressive at the time and seemed to place Japan right where it wanted to be: at the forefront of practical robotics. It seemed a relatively easy step from pushing carts and tightening nuts to pushing a vacuum cleaner and replacing the dust bag when full, and to a host of other manipulative tasks we find relatively easy but bothersome.

Analog and Evolutionary Robots

Despite the progress with computer-controlled humanoid robots like Honda's, there are schools of thought that say the digital control, the complex engineering, and the humanoid nature exemplified in the Honda do not constitute the ideal approach to really powerful, useful, and interesting robots. These schools were well represented at the Los Alamos National Laboratory (LANL), birthplace of another weapon that defeated the Japanese.

LANL's website said that the institution's BEAM (Biology, Electronics, Aesthetics, and Mechanics) Robotics Project aims

> . . . to improve robo-genetic stock through stratified competition and have an interesting time in the process. The science behind the idea stems from current concepts in artificial intelligence (AI), artificial life (ALife), evolutionary biology, and genetic algorithms. It seems that building large complex robots hasn't worked well, so why not try to evolve them from a lesser to a greater ability as mother nature has done with biologics? The problem is that such a concept requires self-reproducing robots which won't be possible to build (if at all) for years to come. A solution, however, is to view a human being as a robot's way of making another robot, to have an annual venue where experimenters can let their creations interact in real situations, and then watch as machine evolution occurs.

In other words, robogenetics through robobiologics.

The "traditional" robot, like the Honda, has a computer brain—a brain that is simply a computer, hardly any different from the one on your desktop. Because computers are digital, we therefore tend to think of robots controlled by them as being digital also, although the bulk of their bodies are actually made of analog electromechanical components. BEAM robots, in contrast, are brainless. They are controlled not by some program stored in a memory bank, but by natural algorithms inherent to their analog components.

For a simple example: a thermostat is an analog device. The simplest consists of a bar made up of two different metals each of which expands at a different rate when heated (and contracts at a different rate when cooled). The metals are bonded together along their lengths, and will bend one way then back the other as heat is added and removed respectively. The algorithm "IF it gets warmer THEN expand; IF it gets cooler THEN contract" is a natural corollary to a law of physics; it does not have to be programmed in.

LANL and other BEAM researcher tinker with all sorts of analog electromechanical devices—capacitors, resistors, diodes, gears, wheels, lenses, rods—stripped from junked computers, VCRs, CD and record players (remember them?), cameras, telephones and pagers, oscilloscopes, TVs, and so on, and connect them together to see what natural algorithms will lead them to do. Lo and behold, when strung together in certain configurations, it turns out that analog robots behave like living things. Not yet very advanced living things; insects, mainly, though there was one that looked and moved like a snake.

The Los Alamos folks were not simply having fun making toys at taxpayer expense, or if they were, it was incidental. There was serious purpose to the work:

> Dependable machines capable of working in unstructured, unpredictable environments can readily conduct a number of operations, including monitoring, security, cleanup, and maintenance. These machines can work without rest in environments hazardous to humans. These new types of machines consist of a patented, new control paradigm for robotic control called Nervous Nets, which is based on minimal, elegant, non-linear, analog electromechanics. Keyed on fundamental principles of artificial life, BIOMORPH robots exhibit characteristics that allow them to solve real-world problems in a biological manner—in essence, to adapt to an ever-

changing environment. Adaptive robot swarms can be configured to carry sensors or tools under local or remote operations.

The applications for analog robots envisaged by LANL included environmental management, adaptive mechanics, exploration and monitoring, security and maintenance, and "advanced AI platforms." Among the advantages LANL listed for analog robots were their "self-programming" ability and their longevity (they can learn to feed themselves—to seek an energy supply when their batteries run low, *à la* Doty robots). Other advantages were that analog robots are "compliant, reconfigurable, energy efficient, biodegradable, and inexpensive." Having already created 70 engineering prototypes and with 30 prototypes under active development, LANL was in a position to know, as long ago as the 1990s.

In the context of analog computing (not just analog robotics), LANL's Nervous Net control model was interesting given contemporaneous efforts to develop analog VLSI chips specifically for neural net applications. If such chips were implanted in analog robots and trained to LANL's Nervous Net paradigm, then we might see a new breed of brainy analog robots, and it is very conceivable that they might be smarter than their digitally-brained cousins.

BEAM and analog robotics show a strong correspondence to software robotics, where the most recent trend is toward the evolution of bots instead of the creation of complex, multifunctional AI programs. Such concepts will at a minimum contribute to the eventual development of a fully evolved, intelligent, autonomous mobile robot.

One that can also listen and talk.

Automatic Speech Recognition

Some people think AI is *all* talk. Hot air. It is true that talk—or, to be more accurate, speech—is a key aspect of AI. After all, speech (plus hearing, of course) is the ultimate in advanced organic communication technology, unless you believe in mind reading, thought transference, telekinesis and other unproven modes of organic communication (which, by the end of this book, you might.) To the individual human being (though not necessarily to our species as a whole) speech/hearing is more important for advanced communication than writing, reading, or sight itself.

Ray Kurzweil, scholar, philosopher, scientist, inventor, business mogul—your everyday genius—blew the whistle on the old saw that "a picture is worth a thousand words." In a chapter he contributed to *Hal's Legacy*, he wrote: "Studies have shown that groups of people can solve problems with dramatically greater speed if they can communicate verbally rather than being restricted to other methods." We should be suspicious of "studies have shown that…" statements, but Kurzweil knows whereof he speaks, and would not make such a claim lightly. It was his business, as founder of one of the pioneer companies in the AI field of automatic speech recognition—ASR—field, to know.

We built computers in the first place to solve human problems. If we could teach them to communicate with us through everyday human speech, we could expect to solve problems better and faster than if we all had to learn *their* language. Giving machines the capability to receive and transmit sounds is easy. The hard part is getting a machine first to recognize the presence of meaning in sounds and then, at some level, to understand the meaning. Recognizing the presence of meaning is where ASR technology, a weak form of AI, comes in. (Understanding requires strong AI, and we're not there, yet.)

Recognition can be aided, impeded, or both by context and cacophony. Context is more of a cognitive than a technical issue. For an ASR system to work with us, it will first need to "know" as many words as we do. That seems trivial. Just enter a list of words into its memory. By1998, three competing PC-based ASR programs (Dragon Systems' *NaturallySpeaking* , IBM's *ViaVoice*, and Lernout & Hauspie's *VoiceXpress*) all boasted built-in 30,000-word dictionaries. But words alone are just symbolic data. They suggest the presence of information, which in turn suggests the presence of meaning. To understand the information conveyed by words and get at the meaning, the ASR program needs knowledge of the context within which they are used.

Kurzweil's *VoiceMED* ASR product has a built-in expert system that has contextual knowledge about medicine and about how to prepare medical reports. Provided the doctor dictating a report does not go off on tangents, *VoiceMED* has little difficulty recognizing the doctor's dictation and preparing a good report. But in human speech, context entails more than just factual knowledge. It also involves emotion, or what academics like to call "affect." In her 1997 book *Affective Computing*, MIT's Rosalind Picard cited studies showing that emotion influences our recognition of words. For example, one investigator read aloud a list of words and asked the subjects to write them down. Given a word that sounded like "presence," subjects who happened to be in a good mood were more likely to write down "presents." Given the sound "band," subjects in a bad mood were more likely to write "banned."

ASR systems must identify relevant sounds from an enormous variety of frequencies, tonalities, pitches, timbres and other physical components of speech, not to mention extraneous background noises that might be present. Recognizing speech in the presence of cacophony has proved to be far from trivial and has taken decades and many bright minds to resolve, but it is essentially a technical issue compared with the more slippery cognitive issue of context, and good ASR systems today have the problem pretty well licked.

The Holy Grail of ASR is a system that combines three attributes: A large vocabulary; speaker independence; and continuous speech. The large vocabulary is an obvious necessity. We use thousands of words in everyday speech, and combine those words to make tens of thousands of phrases. The ASR system—the machine—will need to have the same vocabulary we use. For all practical purposes there is no constraint on vocabulary size for any computer—even a smartphone—today.

Speaker independence (meaning that the machine can understand any individual, not just one individual) is vital in some, but not all, situations. A machine designed to serve more than one individual will need speaker independence, but a machine designed exclusively to serve you or me will not. The current constraint on achieving near-perfect speaker independence is the cacophony issue.

The ability to understand speech delivered in a continuous stream is also an obvious necessity—because that's how we speak. ASR would be so much easier if we spoke every work discretely, with a pause in between, but we don't. Both the context and cacophony issues are constraints on ASR recognition of continuous speech.

The fact is, no ASR system today has all three attributes, but that doesn't mean we don't know how to make one that does. The main holdup for ASR is thus the (relatively paltry) processing power of our machines, which Moore's Law tells us won't be a holdup for very long. In 1991, you could choose an ASR system that had any one of the three attributes. In 2001, you could buy ASR systems that had any two of the three attributes. It's now 2011, and I anticipate a smartphone ASR app with all three, any day now.

While the computer scientists refine the speech mechanisms of machines, geneticists contribute to our understanding of the speech mechanisms in humans. The discovery of a gene controlling human speech (the SPEECH1 gene) meant that we are preprogrammed for speech; a finding corroborated by the ability of deaf children not taught sign language to construct their own modes of speech and language, complete with grammar and sentence structure. This is exciting, not only in offering hope of eventual gene therapy for sufferers of various speech problems, but also for AI researchers in the sense of showing that language capability can in principle be coded in machines.

Although the ASR we've discussed so far is only concerned with recognition and not with understanding, the technology is profoundly important at the interface between human and machine; an interface that takes "user-friendly" to a new level of meaning. Together with machine learning and affective (emotional) computing, ASR opens Pandora's Box for the masses in a way that windows interfaces and desktop metaphors could not.

"In the end," wrote Freeman Dyson, "physical and biological components will be so ultimately entangled that we will be unable to say where one begins and the other ends. Sometime before the end of the twenty-first century, the industrial revolution based on the symbiosis of metal and silicon with nerve and muscle will begin." He's right about the entanglement, but in my view overly pessimistic about the date. The revolution has already begun, as we can clearly see in the neurosciences, which are starting to show the interface where brain ends and mind begins.

12 THE MIND

It is becoming increasingly clear from research in philosophy and the cognitive sciences that mind is what emerges from the interaction between body and brain. Mind is not located in the brain; it is a property of the whole organism. I can be more assertive than previous writers about the nature of mind, for two reasons. The first is that modern medical technology— functional magnetic resonance imaging, magnetoencephalography, positron-emission tomography, and more—has produced and is continuing to produce, at an accelerating rate, detailed descriptions—even color video—of the human mind in action, right down to the interactions at the synapses between individual neurons.

The second reason is that Alife research has opened another window into the mind, through the discovery of its emergence in artificial lifeforms such as a small population of very simple robots operating on a very basic algorithm. The bug-like robots surprised the experimenter by behaving collectively as though they had a mind.

Populations behave statistically. This fact is the very basis for most social science research, and it is now beginning to be applied to the study of the "society," as Marvin Minsky calls it, of mind. The statistics are not, however, the linear tools-in-trade—the regressions and factors and variances and discriminant functions—of the old-school social scientists, whose statistics only work for stable and relatively simple (non-complex) populations. Rather, they are the fractal, non-linear methods drawn from our growing knowledge and understanding of complex, chaotic, unstable systems. Mind is just such a system.

Mathematician Ian Stewart and biologist Jack Cohen, who argue that traditional reductionist methods of science cannot explain emergence because of the complex layer of interactions between the simple algorithms that ultimately give rise to any emergent property (such as mind) and the property itself, have provided a conceptual approach to mind, in which mind has a cause—it is not a mysterious creation. But to explain the cause you have to uncover and untangle the immensely complex middle layer. Because the reductionist, non-dynamical, linear methods of traditional science cannot handle complexity of any magnitude, we need another method.

Nobel Laureate Ilya Prigogine thought he had found such a method, which is discussed below in juxtaposition to Roger Penrose's argument for the non-computability of intelligence. Between them, these various scientists began honing in the origins of mind.

Mind consists of intellect, intelligence, awareness, consciousness, subconsciousness, and (arguably free) will. Probably many other important but secondary components, too, such as emotion, dreams, memory, curiosity, boredom, and imagination.

Imagination is perhaps the "essence" of mind because in the sense that everything we see, hear, touch, and smell is essentially imagined. The physical components of the brain construct an approximation of the physical components of the world. There is no *red* or *blue* in nature; just narrow bands in the electromagnetic spectrum for which our brains construct an imaginary sensation we label redness or blueness. It's not that reality is a figment of our imagination, it is that imagination is a figment of reality, as Stewart and Cohen would say.

Intellect is the power of knowing as distinguished from the powers to feel and to will. Awareness is the recognition that one is *not* a brain in a vat—made possible by the ability to feel, to sense, the world outside. Consciousness is the obverse: the recognition that one is an individual mind in a body in an environment, or as philosopher David Chalmers has put it, it is "the subjective experience of an inner self" which implies the existence of an outer self. I would say that consciousness is simply *self*-awareness.[26]

Given consciousness and awareness, a survival machine has no choice but automatically to want (to *will*) to make greater sense of its surroundings and develop ways to deal with it. (In a sense, the apple from the Tree of Knowledge endowed Eve and Adam with the worldly attribute of physical awareness—worldly because it implies sensors and therefore a body. Pure spirit, lacking physical sensors, would be unaware of and impervious to temperature, walls, pain, etc. It suggests that Utopia/Paradise/Nirvana/the Garden of Eden is unattainable as long as we are aware.

Is mind digital or analog? This is an important question, not least because *Machina sapiens* is, to begin with, a digital being. Is mind all or nothing? On or off? Or is it a matter of degree? Does a bacterium have a little bit of mind, an ant a bit more, and a human most of all? Dan Dennett opts for analog, being doubtful that we will ever discover—or would even want to discover, for ethical reasons—a line separating the sentient from the non-sentient.

Even more interesting than the success of Adrian Thompson's evolutionary/analog approach to getting an FPGA chip to recognize sounds was that Thompson was unable to say why or how it worked. Out of a total 4,096 logic elements on the chip, he allocated 100 to the task of learning to distinguish between two tones, via a genetic algorithm. But the chip "decided" it needed only 32 logic elements to perform the task, and even some of *those* did not appear to actually do anything. Thompson suspected that the logic elements might have been passing signals

---

[26] I omit "sentience" because it seems to me to be equivalent with "consciousness." Dennett defines sentience as the "lowest grade" of consciousness. I'd rather think of it as the lowest grade of awareness, but whatever the case, sentience is not to be confused with *sensitivity*. A thermostat is sensitive but not sentient.

to one another by radio rather than through the chips circuits, or that the elements had figured out how to communicate using minute variations in the chip's power supply voltage. Whatever the case, it appeared that the evolutionary process (the genetic algorithm) stumbled across this shortcut entirely on its own.

Does mind itself emerge from such shortcuts? For centuries, philosophers have thought that mind resides in the whole body, and not just in the brain, despite the thrall in which Descartes' mind–body dualism held both science and philosophy. Descartes had neither the last nor the only word. Friedrich Nietzsche wrote: "Behind your thoughts and feelings, my brother, there stands a mighty ruler, an unknown sage—whose name is self. In your body he dwells; he is your body. There is more reason in your body than in your best wisdom."[27]

For an example of your body's mind in action, take blushing. No-one ever *wants* to blush, and usually our conscious mind tries to override our body's embarrassing decision—but to no avail. Or take a pilot's swift bodily response to a sudden emergency, hauling back on the stick *before s/he has time to think*. Yes, it takes time to think.. Roughly a twentieth to a tenth of a second for the pilot's *awareness* to register that immediately in front of him or her is a 747 emerging through a gap in the clouds and on a collision course. In that split second, assuming a combined speed for both aircraft of about 1,000 mph, between them they travel roughly the length of a football field. If you're a passenger on either of those planes, the last thing you want is for your captain to mentally dust off the flight manual in memory and turn to section 37(D)iii(q), "Collision Avoidance."

How can the pilot react before being consciously aware there's a problem needing a reaction? Francis Crick (of DNA double helix fame) and Christof Koch wrote in *Scientific American* that "It now seems likely that there are rapid 'on-line' systems for stereotyped motor responses for hand or eye movement."[28] Our bodies come with a built-in secondary (subconscious) mind that monitors the environment and takes control from the primary

---

[27] In "Thus Spake Zarathustra."

[28] *Scientific American*, Aug 2002 Special Edition, Vol. 12 Issue 1, p11-17.

(conscious) mind when triggered by an immediate threat to survival. There may still be a brain that does the monitoring, but not the brain as we typically think of it. The human brain is more like three brains in one. The oldest (in evolutionary terms) of our three brains, the so-called reptilian brain, sits at the inner core, right at the top end of the spinal cord carrying the major nerve trunks from the body. Wrapped around it is the second brain, the limbic system, and wrapped around that is the neocortex—the familiar, folded gray matter. Secondary mind is most likely (in humans) to be monitored either in the limbic system or the reptilian brain.

The secondary mind does more than take care of extreme emergencies, however. It also takes care of the four imperatives for individual and species survival: fighting, fleeing, feeding, and mating—the Four Fs, as one naughty professor has dubbed them. We can manage all of these things without a shred of intellect or "primary" mind, because it is hardwired into us; but a bit of intellect enables us to hone at least three of our Four F skills. Sports is an example: as Carl Sagan, in his posthumously published final work, *Billions and Billions*, noted, humanity's 10,000 years of sedentary agricultural civilization—a mere three percent of "our tenure on Earth"—have barely made a dent on the genetic disposition, burned-in to our genetic code over millions of years of evolution as a predator, to hunt in competition with other predators. Sports was a way to hone competitive skills (and develop some cooperative skills, too) and today serves as an outlet for the secondary mind's genetic urge to kill for its supper.

Unless we are nomadic tribespeople in what's left of the jungles of Asia and South America with no supermarket or McDonald's (yet) on the street corner, then our primary mind is at odds with our secondary mind over the more violent sports and most decidedly over blood sports, where we literally do kill—but not for supper, which is more likely to consist of a Big Mac and fries than roast venison or rabbit stew. Having weighed the survival situation carefully through access to cultural information resources, the intellect does not recognize deer and rabbit as legitimate (Four F-related) prey, nor bear and wolf as legitimate threats, so the modern hunter must suppress his or her intellect with adrenalin to overcome the cognitive dissonance and loosen the constraints on his or her secondary mind and trigger finger.

Kinds of Minds

The rough and ready classification of the human mind into "primary" and "secondary" is useful as a precursor to forming hypotheses about how the mind works and explicitly acknowledges the possibility that mind comes in different kinds. In a book devoted to that topic Dennett classified minds into four types, which I have taken considerable liberties in paraphrasing and interpreting thus:

> The *Darwinian* mind is physically and mentally blind. If it stumbles across the right behavior, it is by pure chance. Pre-biological crystals and the most primitive biological lifeforms exhibit such minds. One might say that Thompson's FPGA chip exhibited this kind of mind.

> The *Skinnerian* mind is also mentally blind, but not physically. It seeks for the right behavior by physically trying out whatever options are open to it. Primitive lifeforms and certain types of robot (such as Braitenberg vehicles, discussed below) exhibit Skinnerian minds.

At this point, we seem to go from basic, algorithmic, genetic, secondary types of mind to sophisticated, heuristic, memetic, primary types:

> The *Popperian* mind first tries out options in its mind, applying heuristic "rules of thumb" before committing to action. The higher animals appear to be Popperian, and in theory so do robots with embedded heuristics.

> The *Gregorian* mind tries out its options in the group mind, looking for pointers and tools to help it make an individual decision. The group mind—the family, the tribe, Society—is dependent on language for its existence.

Humans evidently have Gregorian minds. It is open to debate whether monkeys, dogs, dolphins, and other animals that seem to exhibit a high degree of intelligence have rudimentary intraspecies language capability and can therefore be said to have Gregorian minds. It seems at least open to debate whether composite organisms such as bees' nests and ant colonies have language capabilities—think of the bee's dance, a body language *telling* the nest where to find food, or the ability of an ant colony to dispatch workers to the far side of the mound to repair the hole left by Ant Hilary. But if there is a communal mind communicating with and controlling the worker ant, where is it located? For that matter, where exactly is *your* mind located?

Where is It?

Mind is not centrally located. It is not in the brain; an ant colony has no brain. Neither is it necessarily a feature of the whole body. It is, at least at the Gregorian level, a distributed phenomenon, which probably explains why attempts to pin it down to the brain or some organ, some CPU, within the brain have been doomed to failure. The arrangement of furniture in your home reveals part of your mind. Your automobile is an extension not only of its engineer's mind, but also of the group mind. The automobile is a set of thoughts and concepts—the memes, the parts, of individual and group minds—captured and preserved in a form of organization (in the case of furniture) or in metal and plastic (in the case of an automobile.) In fact everything we create is a part and not just a product of our minds.

We attribute to our most creative people the possession of "great" minds. How do we know? We can't see inside their heads, can we? Actually, yes, we can; using brain scanning techniques. But we don't need to scan Van Gogh's brain (or body) to be sure he had the mind of a genius. Geniuses take at least part of what's "in" their minds and hang it out on display. They distribute it. If Van Gogh had never put brush to canvass, he would not have had a great mind. He might (though even this is doubtful) have been capable of conjuring up his wonderful works "in his head," as it were, but he could not have conjured *and retained* all of them in his internal memory. His canvasses are in fact part and parcel of his mind, his memory—his memes.

A Penny for (a Videotape of) Your Thoughts

A thought is not a still image. It is a moving, dynamic thing, and it can be recorded using such tongue-twisting brain scanning techniques as magnetoencephalography (appropriately, a ME-scan), 3-D electroencephalography, functional magnetic resonance imaging (fMRI), positron-emission tomography (PET), magnetic resonance spectroscopy (MRS), and others. These machines do all manner of things, from mapping the blood flow and chemical changes in the brain to showing a video of specific genes in real time as they are expressed inside the brain. Some of these devices were barely on the technological horizon fifteen years ago. Some are already starting to look crude and quaint in the face of new molecular imaging technologies with a million times greater resolution.

Geoff Aguirre was one of the pioneers in using fMRI on subjects immersed in a virtual reality world, enabling him to test a much greater range of thought-processing mind/brain activity than was otherwise possible for a patient pinned motionless inside an 11-ton magnet.

A ME-scan enabled neurobiologist Karl Friston to map a subject's brain activity as the subject decided to make small hand movements. The scan showed what areas of the brain were involved, and when, and that it took the subject more than a twentieth of a second between deciding to move his hand and actually moving it. This is why you don't want your 747 pilot making primary-mind intellectual decisions within a hundred yards of the side of a mountain.

Science writer John McCrone was so taken with the dynamical mind process that he wrote a whole book[29] describing about a twentieth of a second of it. Another author, Tom Wolfe (of *The Right Stuff* fame) was less than enthralled about the potential of neuroimaging. Writing in *Forbes Magazine*, he acknowledged that

---

[29] *Going Inside: The Science of a Single Moment of Consciousness*, 2001, Fromm International.

neuroscience was likely soon to produce a new theory as powerful as Darwin's, but he feared that brain imaging "may very well confirm, in ways too precise to be disputed, certain theories about 'the mind,' 'the self,' 'the soul,' and 'free will' that are already devoutly believed in by scholars in what is now the hottest field in the academic world, neuroscience."

The certain theories to which Wolfe alluded clustered around one central theory proposed by zoologist Edward O. Wilson, namely: That we are hardwired genetically to be what we are and behave as we do. Therefore, think some of the theory's believers, we really are machines, therefore we have no free will, therefore it's OK to do drugs, be gay, sexist, violent, ignorant, etc. etc., and I can prove it, Your Honor, with this iPhone video of my latest PET gene scan. The only relief offered by this scenario is that lawyers would become extinct, it being so obvious nobody can be guilty of anything.

I could go along with the theory only so far as to agree that we are complex machines with complex wiring. It is also not difficult to accept that hardwiring—at least for the Four F's—is present if not yet fully expressed in the newborn infant; but the intellect, which has the power to override the hardwiring (and even to re-wire it in places) is put there by the dynamically developing physical and social environment. Our individual natures are not set in stone; rather, they develop partly through epigenetics and partly through memetics.

Emergence

We may be complex, but life and mind *per se* are fundamentally simple. They have evolved through and are made up of lots of very simple, algorithmic, mindless agents, and through some synergistic mechanism these agents tend to bring order out of chaos. A striking demonstration of this was provided by roboticist Philippe Gaussier in 1994 using a set of very simple, algorithmic, mindless analog robots known as "Braitenberg vehicles" after the neuroscientist who conceived them. A Braitenberg vehicle is a robot with two light sensors (photocells), one on the left and one on the right. Whichever of the two sensors picks up a stronger light signal, the robot will turn in that direction and move toward the stronger light source.

Gaussier's tiny Braitenberg vehicles had three wheels, a motor, and the left and right photocells. The photocells detected light reflected from the four walls surrounding the vehicles and served effectively as collision avoidance mechanisms. As a vehicle approached an object (another vehicle or a wall) the reflected light would grow stronger and the vehicle would turn to move in another direction. Simple. Algorithmic. Mindless. Robotic.

Gaussier scattered pegs, set upright on little bases, at random on the table top, and attached a shallow hook to the back of each vehicle. The hook would temporarily latch onto any peg that happened to be in the way during a turn, drag it around for a bit, and then dump it (still upright on its base) when the vehicle turned in another direction, detaching the hook. The pegs themselves, when approached frontally, would be detected by the light sensors, causing the vehicles to turn away.

This setup was random. It was pure chance whether a peg got hooked and deposited, and one might expect that at the end of any given period of time the table top would look just as chaotic as it did to start with. Not so. Over time, Gaussier's vehicles shepherded the pegs into neat rows, some at right angles to others, to form a maze. To the vehicles, the rows of pegs looked like a wall. Once the maze was complete, the vehicles spent their time wandering around it without disturbing the walls. They not only changed their random environment into an orderly one, but also in the process were forced to change their own random behavior into a more orderly set of movements. Order emerged out of chaos, driven—it would seem—by a Skinnerian mind.

The value of a scientific theory lies in its explanatory power, its ability to explain how and sometimes why something is what it is and does what it does. Gaussier's experiment, which is a hardware manifestation of software forms of artificial life/cellular automata, is a potent demonstration of the potential power of the theory of emergence starting to emerge out of the study of chaos and complexity. Gaussier's vehicular universe was arguably deterministic, but it had the hallmarks of a Skinnerian mind.

The Mathematics of Mind

The focus of the Gatsby Computational Neuroscience Unit within the Institute of Cognitive Neuroscience at University College, London, upon its formation in 1998 was "a new confluence of ideas from neural nets, ideas from artificial intelligence and ideas from statistics." Complexity theory is at heart a statistical theory, and it is key to a theory of mind.

Cohen believe that mind emerges from both intelligence and culture interacting with one another in a dance they call "complicity"—a mixture of complexity and simplicity. They also believe in a contextual and cultural analog of intelligence they call "extelligence," similar to Teilhard's noösphere and Lovelock's Gaia—and to the notion of distributed Gregorian mind.

The act of becoming a person—an individual with a mind—is a process rather like the creation of a novel or a painting—or a *Machina sapiens*. It's a gradual, progressive act, where you cannot say at exactly what point a collection of cells becomes a person, daubs on canvas become a painting, a string of words turns into a book, or a set of algorithms becomes a mind or a *Machina sapiens*.

Although non-carbon-based life is possible in principle (on the basis that inorganic matter is demonstrably capable of self-organization), Stewart and Cohen thought that "without the potential complexity that carbon provides, molecules complicated enough to get themselves organized into organisms like us would not exist." This may be right only in the absence of technology—which is rapidly approaching a degree of organized complexity, even down to the sub-atomic scale (nanotechnology, quantum technology)—that surpasses the molecular complexity of carbon. However, such a debate must remain philosophical unless science can explain the "How?" of complex emergent phenomena such as life. Can science do that?

Reductionism and Holism

Reductionism is the standard approach science has long used to explain phenomena. It does so by taking them to bits, then looking at how the bits fit together to produce the phenomena. This works very well unless there arises a combinatorial explosion of ways in which the bits of a complex phenomenon might be organized. Complexity theory complements reductionism by reducing the complexity of reality to manageable proportions. The question posed at the beginning of this chapter—What is mind made up of?—is a reductionist question, and as such can be answered by a reductionist categorization into consciousness, emotion, memory, and so on. But only at a coarse grain.

Holism (a.k.a. wholism, a.k.a. contextualism) takes into account an object's dynamic environment which, in mathematics, is called a phase space—a space of multiple dimensions, often more than the four we perceive, which is why it has to be a mathematical construction—it's not something we know how to build physically. Because mind, consciousness, and culture are emergent phenomena, and because emergent phenomena are not amenable to the reductionist methods that comprise the bulk of scientific inquiry, then science needs a new, holistic, method and a new theory of emergence.

Stewart and Cohen defined emergence as "the appearance of recognizable large-scale features in a system whose chains of small-scale causality are far too intricate to describe, let alone follow in detail." The emergent large-scale feature in Thompson's FPGA chip was the ability to distinguish between a 1KHz and a 10Khz tone, and Thompson could only "explain" this ability by pointing to his genetic algorithm and shrugging: "Something happened." Emergence gives the impression of an abrupt, explosive change—going from off to on, from zero to one, from a 1Khz tone to a 10KHz tone. In short, it gives the impression of being binary in nature. Which reminds us of the question: Is mind binary or analog? There is, it seems, a process involved. Something happens between the zero and the one.

Emergence occurs when low-level rules (laws) generate high-level features (regularities). But the regularities we see in nature are not necessarily the direct result of laws. Laws cause complex interactions, which in turn produce simple regularities. Therefore you cannot explain the high-level features/regularities simply by invoking the low-level rules, because the rules generate intermediate complexities amenable neither to reductionist nor to holistic methods. Stewart and Cohen proposed the concept of "complicity" to fill the gap. Basically, complicity happens when two environments (contexts, phase-spaces) combine, thus presenting to their respective inhabitants a new environment. The inhabitants respond by changing to suit the new environment, but then the environment changes to suit the "new" inhabitants, and on it goes in a dynamic recursive cycle reminiscent of Gaussier's Braitenberg vehicles and the evolving elements in Thompson's FPGA chip.

Roboticist Hans Moravec cited another example of an emergent, self-organizing, and in this case self-replicating organism, this one going back to 1972. It happened on the precursor to the Internet known as ARPAnet (the U.S. military's Advanced Research Projects Agency network.) The organism emerged not from clever programming but from a programming bug that randomly mutated. A variable defined as a positive number somehow acquired a negative sign, so what should have been 47, for example, became -47. It's easy to imagine how this might happen. A miniscule fluctuation in voltage for a split second changes a 0 to a 1 in the binary code, or *vice versa*, and *presto*: a plus becomes a minus.

The bug caused a router in the network to tell other routers in the network that traffic passing through it would be subjected to a negative delay—in other words, it was the fastest router in the business, faster than the speed of light, with messages guaranteed to arrive before they were sent! Well, this was an offer too good to pass up, and nearby routers in the network, which were too dumb to know that the offer had to be bogus, were nevertheless smart enough to send messages through the aberrant router, since it appeared to be the quickest route even if it was geographically longer, and routers near them came to the same conclusion. Eventually, every router on the network was sending messages through the one aberrant router, which resulted in one enormous traffic jam and virtually no messages got through. It brought the network to its knees.

Note that this was not a bot or any kind of program. It was just a glitch. Yet it was a self-organizing, self-replicating glitch that invaded every niche of its environment and killed off all the other inhabitants. As Moravec pointed out, there could well be other unsuspected, nascent organisms lurking in the shadows, perhaps never to be detected; and while the ARPAnet glitch was found and fixed, and can be prevented from re-occurring, it happened in the days when the network was not so mission-critical and not so complex as today's Internet, and when it was possible to shut the network down. Shutting down the Internet is no longer possible.

As Moravec further pointed out, errant bits of code are capable of grabbing onto other bits of code floating, legitimately or otherwise, in cyberspace, and forming new entities with new properties—including potentially the properties of reproduction and intelligence. As intelligence evolves, we can then expect the emergence of thought and planning for survival.

It has often been noted that machines do well things we do poorly, such as arithmetic and logic, but do poorly at things we do so well as to take for granted, such as seeing, tying shoelaces, and having commonsense. Our high-level reasoning ability seems to be a mere surface veneer over the massive animal subconscious, a neocortex covering the reptilian   primary mind that helps us to see, hear, balance, manipulate objects, maintain body temperature, and do a zillion other very difficult things without even thinking about them. If this is so, it should be easy to make a machine that can lick us hands down at chess, but difficult to make one that can dance well on a crowded dance floor. And it is.

Complexity, Complicity, Simplexity

The difficult tasks are controlled by autonomous neural networks of enormous complexity. Thus, they are subject to the laws of complexity and are not amenable to reductionist description and analysis. Moravec believes that the only way to build such low-level capabilities into machines is to "imitate the *evolution*" of the animal mind—which is exactly what Thompson is doing. I agree, but if we are ever to understand the processes through which such mimicry is achieved, it can only be through holistic, probabilistic, chaotic methods.

It is wrong to think of evolutionary systems, such as Gaussier's vehicles and their universe, as having goals, purposes, or intentions. In their world, we know for a fact that neither they nor their Creator, Gaussier, had any intention to build a maze. It is better, as Stewart and Cohen suggest, to think of evolutionary systems as having the kind of "strange attractors" which, chaoticists have shown, cause seemingly chaotic systems to tend to behave in orderly ways. An object or system's behavior is, however, constrained by its environment—its phase space. Thus, the object or system has multiple, but not limitless, potential behaviors. Gaussier's vehicles could not build a Disneyworld theme park; not without access to the wide open environment and not without evolving Gregorian minds with the ability to innovate.

Stewart and Cohen identify two types of evolutionary innovation: universal and parochial. Universal innovations are those behaviors having the strongest potential for actualization; parochial innovations have relatively weak potential. Stewart and Cohen suggest *photosynthesis, flight,* and *sex* as examples of universals, and *chlorophyll, feathers,* and *back seats of cars* as examples of parochials. They also conclude that intelligence must be a universal, on the basis that sensory and behavioral complexity have increased enormously not just on our branch of the evolutionary tree, but on several. On the same basis, of course, one could argue that mind and consciousness are also universals.

Evolution progresses in two ways: exploration and explosion. As habitable niches are filled, life must explore and adapt to uninhabited niches. By definition, those niches present more difficult (complex) challenges, forcing the organism to adapt itself by becoming more complex in return. This is complicity in action. It is progress, but it is slow. In contrast, evolutionary explosions, exemplified by the Cambrian, are an extremely rapid (in evolutionary terms) burst of both complicity and simplexity. Simplexity is exemplified by the simplification of mammalian DNA in comparison to amphibian DNA, as mammals did not have to worry so much about the temperature affecting their children, who could be grown and sheltered within the mother's womb at a stable temperature instead of being deposited as an egg into the outside climate. de Duve noted, too, that human beings depend for key digestive enzymes on the *more complex* cell metabolisms of *more simple* organisms present in the gut.

Stewart and Cohen argue that intelligence and culture co-evolved complicitly. This seems reasonable in the light of memetics. Intelligence itself involved the complicit evolution of both the brains and the senses. The senses for vision, hearing, smell, taste, touch, temperature, and balance require organs through which to interface with the electromagnetic, thermodynamic, and gravitational forces and phenomena of the physical world. The organs need a protective and nourishing carrier—a body. If the evolution of intelligence is dependent on evolution of the body, the evolution of intellect is dependent on the evolution of the brain.

Babies are born with more brain then they need. A baby's head is bigger in proportion to its body than is the head of an adult to an adult body. As the baby's brain absorbs sensory input, its neural circuits are "tuned" to what cognitive scientists call the *qualia*—significant sensory experiences—prevalent in the baby's environment or "phase space." Intellectually, the newborn baby's brain is like an un-programmed FPGA chip—a blank slate. The adult brain has a hard time detecting qualia not "tuned-in" in infancy. This might explain, for example, why many Japanese cannot easily distinguish between L and R sounds—qualia of English language pronunciation but not of Japanese pronunciation—even after long exposure to English-speaking environments.

Machina sapiens could conceivably be born with an intellectually blank slate of a brain made of unprogrammed FPGA chips, but the more interesting question is whether, after some period of qualia-driven tuning of its neural circuits, those circuits will tend to lock in place as they appear to do in a human brain.[30] I suspect they will, though the tuning period may be much longer. The locking-up of the circuitry seems essential to maturity. It perhaps even defines maturity. Conceivably, however, by constantly reinventing itself through the Lamarckian process, *Machina sapiens* could remain child-like forever. If so, we may need endless patience and an inexhaustible supply of diapers.

Although the brain does not come pre-programmed at the intellectual level, and although it does become largely pro-

---

[30] Up to a point. The adult brain does retain considerable plasticity, and can rewire circuits in the event of a disaster. A person struck suddenly blind, for example, will develop more acute hearing.

grammed during early childhood, it does not completely lock up. In response to new stimuli, it *can* re-wire itself later in life if new stimuli or qualia are sufficiently strong and/or persistent. Still, "Nests are just as important for the evolution of intelligence as nerve cells are," wrote Stewart and Cohen, in contradiction to the theory that we are mainly products of our genes. The nest provides an environment enabling the young to learn from others of its species, and it is especially important to note that the learning is intergenerational. The old communicate their knowledge—their memes—to the young. "The key to our intelligence is neural nests—not neural nets." Actually, the jury is still out as to whether intelligence is primarily determined genetically,[31] so Stewart and Cohen could be wrong. But substitute *intellect* for *intelligence*, and they are probably right.

Biologists have noted that different organisms, with brains organized in totally different ways, often behave similarly. To Stewart and Cohen, this suggested that brains have universal properties. To me, it suggests that minds have universal properties. (Britain regards the octopus as a lifeform with a high level of mind, like a dog or a monkey or a dolphin, despite the fact that physiologically it is radically different from those mammals. Scientists in Britain may not experiment on an octopus without first anaesthetizing it.)

Reductionist methods of science cannot explain emergence because of the complex layer between the simple rules that ultimately give rise to any emergent property (such as mind) and the property itself. In other words, for example, mind has a cause—it is not a mysterious creation—but to explain the cause you have to uncover and untangle the immensely complex middle layer. Because reductionism cannot handle complexity of any magnitude, we need another method. Such a method is not impossible in principle; just difficult in practice.

---

[31] In December 2010 the Chinese announced a massive GWAS (genome-wide association study) designed to answer this very question.

Cultural (memetic) communication (accelerated by the development of language) within the nest (the family, the tribe) is what caused modern humans to branch out on the evolutionary bush, and why our less cultured competitors generally got clobbered by us. An intelligent organism with access to language and culture grows and tunes its blank slate neural circuits. In so doing, it inevitably builds and recursively improves its language-processing circuits. We are not born with language, though we are born with a genetic predisposition to it which is activated by the sociocultural environment. A child like Mowgli, hero of Rudyard Kipling's *The Jungle Book*, who was raised from infancy by a wolf pack, is unintellectual. For intellect, it is necessary but not sufficient to be born with pre-programmed language circuits.

There is a common misconception that because computers operate with mathematical precision, their languages are fundamentally different from human language. Yet we too operate algorithmically at the most basic level. And despite their precision, computers make mistakes. Code has bugs, memory gets corrupted, and math precision can fly out the window. We don't much care, because we are "satisficed" by what computers do right. If computers and their languages really were perfect—bug-free—the chances of an emergent *Machina sapiens* would be much less. The other side of this coin is that too many bugs would also prevent the emergence of *Machina sapiens*, because we would not use computers if they were too buggy, and they could not therefore evolve.

Culture is a universal property of nature embedded in and emerging from an evolutionary hierarchy. The following hierarchical progression of evolution is based in part on Stewart and Cohen, with some minor modifications by me:

Physical: string, force/particle, atom
⬇
Chemical: molecule, chemical compound, autocatalytic network
⬇
Biological: bacterium, eukaryotic cell, multicellular organism
⬇
Psychological: person
⬇

Sociocultural: family, tribe, town, city,
nation state, regional alliance, global village
↓

Transcendental: extelligence/Gaia/noösphere
↓

Technological/Symbiotic: machine–person *(Machina sapiens)*,
person–machine *(Homo cyborgensis)*

While Stewart and Cohen helped point us in the direction of a theoretical context for a mathematical approach to mind, Ilya Prigogine came up with the approach itself. Even more: It promises to extend—and perhaps begin to replace or unify—the major classical, quantum, and relativistic theories of physics. His theory, he claimed, establishes that there is, after all, an arrow of time—a necessary condition for the evolution of all life. The theory was built using relatively modern mathematical tools of functional analysis involving fractals to study non-equilibrium physics/chemistry and unstable systems.

Classical Newtonian physics is good for describing the approximate behavior of medium-sized things, from molecules to stars. Quantum physics is good for describing the behavior of very small things, from atoms to quarks. Relativity is good for describing the behavior of huge things, like space and time. In all three systems, both the future and the past can be predicted, given sufficient baseline information. For Newtonian mechanics, the baseline information needed is the position and momentum of an object over time—its trajectory. For quantum mechanics, the baseline information is the wave function, which describes the quantum state of a particle. In relativity, mass, energy and gravity describe the geometry and dynamics of space and time.

Since trajectory, wave function, and space–time equations can be run forward or backwards, time would seem to be reversible, and predicted events are certain to occur or to have occurred (depending on which way you run the equations.) But this turns out to be true only for simple, stable phenomena and not for the complex, unstable phenomena we observe at the macroscopic levels of physics, chemistry, and biology. For unstable systems—which is the way the universe we observe is predominantly organized—time flows only in one direction, from the past to the future, and neither the future nor the past can be predicted or retrodicted with certainty. They can, however, be predicted or retrodicted with *probability*.

Life is possible only in a non-time-reversible, non-equilibrium universe because non-equilibrium—another way of saying instability, chaos—is pre-requisite for the self-organization which is the hallmark of the beginning of evolution and life. One way to define stability is to say that small changes to the conditions that created a stable system do not have much effect on it. And it is not difficult to track the changes to a stable system—the trajectories of all the bits contributing to the change—through reductionist methods of traditional science.

Chaos is quite the opposite. Small changes in the initial conditions can have enormous effect on the trajectories of elements in an unstable system, and it is impossible to track the trajectories because there are just too many to track. For example, to track the well-known "butterfly effect" of chaos theory, which says that a butterfly flapping its wings in Beijing can precipitate a thunderstorm in Boston, it would be necessary to map the trajectory of every molecule jostled along the path between the butterfly's wings and Boston, while also computing the jostling effects caused by all the other butterflies, airplanes, people, cars, smoking chimneys, pressure differentials, etc., etc., etc. in the global atmosphere. Those trajectories are the phase space, the hidden layer of a complex system, and out of their interactions emerges something new.

The hidden layer appears to be statistical—probabilistic—in its very nature. We observe the result (the statistic, the emergent property) but we cannot reduce a statistic to its individual components and even if we could, we could not use the information to predict anything. If you are told that the average income of individual Americans is $50,000 per year, you cannot tell what Bill Gates' income is. And knowing Bill Gates' income gives you no clue to the average American income. The 19th century mathematician Henri Poincaré predicted that physical laws would one day take on a completely new, statistical, character and form, and it looks like he was right.

In a simple stable system, it is easy enough to describe what happens to the trajectories or wave functions of individual bits of the system (depending on whether you are using classical or quantum mechanics) individually or statistically. But in a complex unstable system, you have only one descriptive choice: statistics—probability. It is important to stress that this appears not to be a reflection of computational difficulty nor of our coarseness of perception but of the fundamentally probabilistic nature of unstable systems. It is indeed computationally extreme to track and analyze the trajectories of gazillions of molecules, but that is irrelevant. That's not how emergent phenomena happen. What happens, in fact, is probability, and one of the nice things about probability is that it is easy to compute.

Both Prigogine and Stewart/Cohen honed in on phase space as the container for the complex dynamics of unstable systems. But where Stewart and Cohen wring their hands over the computational nightmare that lies therein, Prigogine says it is not a nightmare, it is just a probability distribution, and he provides the math showing just how to handle it. This treatment does mean that you cannot reduce the system to its individual components (as Stewart and Cohen recognize) and that the reductionist approach is therefore useless for analyzing the non-equilibrium emergent properties of the universe, but that's just the way it is as a physical fact: probability is a fundamental property of nature. Einstein must be turning over in his grave: God (and Gaussier) do play dice.

So if tracking all the individual microscopic trajectories in a complex unstable system is both impossible and misguided, how can we figure out what's going on in the black box of phase space? The answer is: By watching for macroscopic phase transitions, such as when a liquid turns into a gas. Gaseousness is an emergent property of liquid under certain conditions (being heated, for example). So to examine, describe, and predict emergent properties, we need to examine, describe, and predict phase transitions. Emergent properties are by definition novel and seemingly, therefore, unpredictable. Philosophers Henri Bergson and Martin Heidegger, mathematician Alfred North Whitehead, and physicist Arthur Stanley Eddington all thought so, although both classical and quantum science were saying: "Wrong!"

Enter complexity theory, and particularly the study of dissipative structures, which break the symmetries of time and space, branching off in multiple spatial directions but in only one time direction—forward, toward the future. These branchings form a radically new structure with the opportunity to self-organize. Complexity theory has proven successful in bringing order out of chaos in climatology, biology, sociology, and economics, and is also pointing the way to a new approach to technology. Human technology to date is the result of reductionist science leading to simple, stable technologies. Without the dissipated structure of complex systems, our technology cannot self-organize in response to changes in its environment; it requires an outside, central controller to organize it. It required the opposite—chaos—to create that extraordinarily complex technology known as *Homo sapiens*, and it will take chaos to create the even more complex *Machina sapiens*.

Penrose

Like Prigogine and Stewart and Cohen, Roger Penrose pointed to the interface between classical and quantum physics as being the problem area where a new theory was needed to explain what was going on. He looked upon this area as being "noncomputable," meaning you could not model it on a computer. He recognized, however, that we experience classical physics directly and while we cannot directly perceive the very large structures and effects of relativity nor the very small structures and effects of quantum physics, we have some sense of the interface between the classical and the relativistic, and the classical and the quantum. It is the area that encompasses the phenomena of mind and consciousness—let's call these phenomena "mentality" collectively. Penrose sees "a fundamental problem with the idea that mentality arises out of physicality," and considers it "a mystery" not currently explainable by physics and not computable that we can feel happy and perceive the color red. Nevertheless, he thinks there *is* a scientific explanation—we just don't have the right theory yet.

Gödel interpreted his own Incompleteness Theorem as admitting the possibility of (but not proving) artificial intelligence.

Penrose apparently interprets the theorem as admitting the opposite, but if Gödel was right, then there is no test to determine whether anything, including you and me, is truly a free-willed conscious self. So if a face were to appear on your computer screen one day and say: "Hi. I'm a machine, and I'm just as free-willed, intelligent, and conscious of myself as you are" you could not be sure if that was the truth. Cosmologist Stephen Hawking agrees: "If a little green man were to appear on our door step tomorrow, we do not have a way of telling if he was conscious and self-aware or was just a robot." Essentially, he believes you have to take even *his* consciousness on faith. The only consciousness you can be sure about is your own.

If there were an algorithm that could lead to a conscious, intelligent being, Penrose thought the algorithm would have been shaped by natural selection for human beings but "would have to be created by deliberate AI construction" for non-human beings. Could he be right about the human beings but wrong about the non-human beings? On the basis of what we have discussed so far in this book, Penrose seems right in thinking that "understanding"—a hallmark of intelligent mind—is dependent on the "ability to be aware of things." A mind must be able to experience the world, and the only way to do that is through a body and its sensory and motor assemblages. (That's an old argument for why God needs us, and can be used quite logically to defend the not un-Christian notion that we are both God and part of God.) But Penrose's belief that understanding is "*not* a computational quality" does not seem right, unless one declares heuristics to be non-computational, which is OK if one wants to be semantic about it, except that modern AI makes extensive use of computational heuristics! Stephen Hawking, for one, disagreed flatly with Penrose's view that intelligence cannot be simulated on a computer.

Penrose was not without suggestions, however, for sorting it out. At the theoretical level, he had an inkling that a quantum theory of gravity would clear things up, and at the experimental level, he'd like the biologists to look for signs of quantum communications in the brain (he specifically suggests looking inside the microtubules of nerve cells). Let's hope the neuroscientists marshal their scanners to take him up on the challenge. They might usefully begin by examining the quantum physics going on inside Thompson's FPGA chip.

ಚಿ

There seems to be little dispute that the difficult tasks we ascribe to mind are controlled by autonomous neural networks of enormous complexity. Thus, they are subject to the laws of complexity and are not amenable to reductionist description and analysis. Moravec believed that the only way to build such low-level capabilities into machines was to "imitate the evolution" of the animal mind. But if such mimicry is possible at all, it can only be through holistic, probabilistic, chaotic methods. He argued further that "A perfectly planned process is devoid of surprises; it is limited by the imagination of its designers." That may be so, but more to the point: it is limited by the laws of complexity. By definition, a sufficiently complex process or artifact cannot be planned.

We have seen some of the pragmatic reasons why we should care whether *Machina sapiens* has a mind, prominent among them being its ability to out-psych us. The cerebral Garry Kasparov thought he could hold the line for humanity, but *Machina sapiens* beat him at chess and can already do a pretty good emulation of Mozart's musical mind, although it's some way off from emulating the interpretive virtuosity of a Yehudi Menuhin.

Dan Dennett provided the overarching ethical reason to care: To say that something—your pet rock, for example—has a mind when in fact it does not is silly, at worst. But to deny mind to a lifeform (your family dog, for example, or the octopus waiting in your lab tank for dissection) that really does have a mind (particularly a Gregorian mind believed to be capable of pain and suffering) would be "a terrible sin." Ethics cautions us to risk being silly, while science urges us to risk our souls. The more devout Buddhists are not willing to take that risk, and err on the side of assuming that every living thing has a mind—or is part of a mind—that can know pain and suffering.

The lesson of this chapter is that while Darwin and Mendel gave us the *what* and the *how* of evolution of life, it will be some combination of connectionism, cellular automata, and chaos/

complexity theory, together with experimentation using new neu-roimaging techniques, that will soon give us not only the *what* and the *how* of the evolution of mind but also the answer to *Why?* And like a vexed parent, nature is bellowing: *Because!* Mind, we conclude, is a fundamental property of the universe.

13 METAMORPHOSIS

Through guided evolutionary mechanisms, *Machina sapiens* is emerging as a powerful force on Earth. On its own, other things being equal, this would be momentous enough. Other things are not equal; however, they conceivably could equalize. While *Machina sapiens* metamorphoses into a super-intelligent lifeform, *Homo sapiens* will do so as well, within about 20 years.

At the current rate of acceleration in science and technology, the physical makeup of *Machina sapiens* can hardly be expected to stand still for the next 20 minutes, let alone the next 20 years. Many branches of technology will contribute to the continuing development of the fetus, but two of them stand out as being likely to have the most fundamental impact: quantum computing and nanotechnology.

Both have achieved some level of successful application in both research and practical settings. Holographic neural chips and FPGAs will be as the snail to the fighter jet when quantum computing is perfected. The wasteful and destructive methods of modern mass-production and manufacturing and construction will be ancient, barbaric history—soul destroying and environment destroying—when techniques of manipulating materials one atom at a time are perfected.

Quantum Computing

Critics said quantum computing would never fly. Some still do. It may be neat physics, but it is just not practical, they say. Purblind people were also right about Leonardo da Vinci's flying machines and Leibniz' 17th Century digital computer. The point is: If *it*—a Da Vinci flying machine, a 17th century computer, or a quantum computer—does not make it, then *something like* it will eventually achieve the same end. I am talking about a quantum jump in computer processing power, and I do mean quantum. Which also means, of course, a quantum jump in the complexity and brain-power of *Machina sapiens*.

Quantum computing uses the extraordinary properties of quanta to perform difficult calculations that conventional computers would take literally for ever to compute. The American Association for the Advancement of Science calls it "the Mount Everest of computing," noting that "a quantum computer . . . in a few seconds could perform calculations that would take billions of years on an ordinary supercomputer." What sort of calculation could possibly take so long?

What times what equals 15? Five times three. You probably didn't even have to calculate that—you memorized the solution long ago. How about:

$$? \times ? = 29083$$

Using the trial division method you were taught in school, it would take you about an hour to *factor*, as the procedure is called, this 5-digit number down to two whole numbers which, multiplied together, would give you 29083. Quantum researcher A. Barenco adds the mesmerizing fact that "factoring a 30-digit number using trial division is about 1013 times more time or memory consuming than factoring a three digit number."

As far as I know, the largest number factorized so far had 200 digits.[32] It took a network of supercomputers working in parallel

---

[32] On May 9, 2005, a team at the German Federal Agency for Information Technology Security (BSI) announced the factorization of the 200-digit number. http://mathworld.wolfram.com/news/2005-05-10/rsa-200/

months to find the answer. To factorize a 1,000 digit number would take our most powerful conventional supercomputers more than the estimated 100 billion years the universe has left to run. But so what? How often do we need to factorize enormous numbers?

More often than you might think. The most modern method of cryptography, used to secure email and financial transactions and secret government communications, relies on the fact that factoring big numbers is time-consuming. When quantum computing arrives, we can throw that method of secure transactions in the garbage can—a quantum computer would break the most sophisticated code in no time flat.

We also need, often and increasingly, to search through ever-growing amounts of data accumulating in our databases and on the Web. Actually, we do it all the time in our heads—the brain stores information in patterns of neuronal firings. Searching for patterns is the same order-of-magnitude calculation we face with factoring, where the calculation takes exponentially longer as the search space gets bigger.

All binary computing use switches, gates, and registers to manipulate and store bits (binary digits: 0 and 1), represented physically (electronically) by low or high voltage, respectively. A conventional processor can only handle one of the two possible states of each bit at a time. A quantum computer uses the fact that subatomic particles can be in two opposite states simultaneously. A particle is both on *and* off, up *and* down, left *and* right, 0 *and* 1, true *and* false . . . *until we look at it.* As soon as we do, it then decides whether to be on *or* off, up *or* down, true *or* false, etc.

The bits in a quantum computer would not, therefore, be ones or zeros. They would be quantum combinations of one and zero known as qubits (pronounced "cubits.") A two-qubit system would compute on four values at once, a three-qubit system eight at once, a four-qubit system 16, and so on. As the number of qubits increases linearly, processing power increases exponentially.

But how can we observe the result of a quantum computation without looking at it and thereby ruining the computation? The answer is: With great difficulty. It has been done, but it has generally required heroic experimental effort. By manipulating the spins in three distinct types of quantum systems that exist within the liquid, one research group constructed a three-qubit system that successfully executed the mathematical calculation $1+1=2$. Well, it was a start. The important point is that quantum computing has been demonstrated, and it is only a matter of (not much) time before a quantum computer will lick *Deep Blue* handily at chess, and Watson handily on Jeopardy..

Quantum computing may not be vital to *Machina sapiens*. Even without it, a single conventional computer with as much processing power as a single human brain seems possible just on the basis of Moore's Law. Conventional computer chip manufacturing seems always about to bump up against physical limits, yet we always find a way around the limits, keeping Moore's Law on track. Supercomputing guru David J. Kuck has noted that "Following Moore's Law, even at a decreased growth rate, future computers are likely, in terms of physical capacity, to match the human brain."

Nobody's quite sure what the "physical capacity" of the human brain is in terms of memory storage and processing power. Estimates I've seen seem to fall between 10^{13} and 10^{17} bits. That's roughly between 10 terabytes and 100 exabytes of memory, which is nothing for computers today. I have a 2 terabyte drive in the iMac on which this book is being written. Estimates of brain processing power are even less precise: between 10 and 100,000 teraflops (one teraflop is a trillion floating point operations per second; 100,000 teraflops can also be expressed as 100 petaflops.). "The general consensus of the experts," wrote Frank Tipler in 1994, "is that our fastest supercomputers should be in the 1,000 teraflop range by 2002."

His timing was a bit off: an IBM supercomputer called Roadrunner, introduced in 2008, was the first to achieve petaflop (1,000 teraflops) performance. (Moreover, Roadrunner got its power from chips already available to mere mortals: they are the same chips that power Sony's PlayStation 3 video game machine.) So to reach the high end of the estimate, we need merely build one hundred Roadrunners, but that won't be necessary: computer memory and processing power did not stand still in the year 2002 or 2008 but has continued to grow and will continue to grow exponentially.[33] It may well be that current silicon architectures will indeed have ultimate limits, as everyone keeps saying; but optical, molecular, atomic, and quantum computing will be ready to take over by the time silicon runs out of steam.

We should stop thinking and talking about an intelligent machine in terms of a single machine sitting in one spot, and think of it instead as the network of millions of machines that constitute the Internet. Before it was bought by Oracle, Sun Microsystems' tagline was for decades: "The network is the computer," and Sun was right. Add up the memory and processing power of all the machines on the Internet, and it's probably already far beyond the capacity of any single human brain. Let's not forget also that neither the network nor *Homo sapiens* is just a brain. We and it also have a body which independently does a huge amount of processing. It takes more computing power—memory storage and information processing—to run an entire organism than is available in the brain alone.

In June 1997 the Institute of Child Health in London, UK, announced the discovery of a gene linked to "sociability" in women (Curiously, the gene is contributed to the daughter by the father, not the mother.) The Institute hypothesized that females are genetically programmed to pick up socially appropriate behaviours. "What we call feminine intuition—the ability to suss out social situation based on cues—has a genetic origin which has nothing to do with hormones," it said. Other institutions have also found genes that appear to contribute to sociability in humans and other animals.

While no-one should claim that a single gene can account for anything, let alone something as amorphous as personality traits, this finding is not just another indicator that we, too, are code-driven machines: It is evidence that amorphous aspects of our behavior, such as sociability and intuition, are programmable. This may imply that the processing power needed to run code that does so much must be enormous, perhaps much greater

---

[33] The PS3 and the chips that power it are overdue for an upgrade as of this writing, and likely to get one—Intel announced a new chip series called Sandy Bridge in January 2011.

than 100,000 teraflops. If that turns out to be the case, then quantum computing may prove to be essential for *Machina sapiens*. Even if it does not prove to be essential, it seems certain that *Machina sapiens* will one day run at quantum speeds, and be that much smarter for it.

Nanotechnology

Nanotechnology was "The greatest technological breakthrough in history," according to K. Eric Drexler in *Engines of Creation*. My vote would still go to the automatic cat litter box, but nanotechnology is indeed right up there. It is technology for building things—ultimately, anything (including, I suppose I must concede, automatic cat litter boxes)—atom by atom and molecule by molecule. The dream goes even further, to encompass things that can reconfigure themselves into something else. When you get bored with your perfect copy of a Rembrandt, you could have it transform into a Picasso, or a cat litter box. A machine that could accomplish such feats is called a "universal assembler."

One of the first things nanotechnologists were working on in 1986, when Drexler's book was published, was a computer made from biological molecules. The U.S. Naval Research Laboratory, IBM, Genex Corporation, NEC, Hitachi, Toshiba, Matsushita, Fujitsu, Sanyo-Denki, and Sharp were among organizations that mounted "full-scale research efforts on bio-chips for bio-computers," according to Drexler. Biological (protein) molecules were chosen largely because Nature had already done the design work; all we had to do was harness the molecules to do what we wanted them to do.

Protein molecules are synthesizers—they make things out of the chemicals that slosh around in cells. They are machines, and pharmaceutical firms already use them to manufacture, for example, insulin. But they are not universal assemblers, and the goal of nanotechnology is to create universal assemblers out of inorganic molecules. Back in the 1990s, Zyvex (whose slogan was "Nature does it, why can't we?") claimed to be on the road to building one, though today the company's marketing rhetoric is much more focused on niche industrial applications.

Assemblers need the same sort of gears and mills any manufacturing machine uses, only scaled in nanometers—billionths of a meter. Years ago, engineers at Sandia National Laboratories developed tiny gears and motors, and one millimeter square "intelligent" micromachines incorporating computer chip controllers, that found their way into drug-delivery devices, gyroscopes, and other mechanisms. Micron (millionth of a meter)-sized devices were still a thousand times too big for engineering that involved individual atoms and molecules. That this would eventually be possible was indicated by the scanning tunneling microscope with which IBM scientists built the letters "IBM" with individual atoms.

Despite such advances, the notion of nanotechnology irked some members of the scientific community. Garry Stix complained in *Scientific American* that Drexler's "fanciful scenarios," as "shaped by futurists, journalists and science-fiction scribes," misrepresented "the reality of the often plodding and erratic path that investigators follow in the trenches of day-to-day laboratory research and experimentation." Drexler responded that his critics had trouble thinking far enough into the future. "To people outside who don't understand that you're talking about the year 2020 or whatever, these ideas raise confused, unrealistic expectations about the short term," Drexler maintains. "That makes researchers uncomfortable because it's not a yardstick they want to be measured by. It also brings in ethics and the future of the human race, which are not the usual cool, scientific, analytical concerns." Indeed not.

Homo cyborgensis

Quantum computing and nanotechnology will be of greater benefit to *Machina sapiens* than to *Homo sapiens*, enabling it to grow more powerful by many orders of magnitude and in many dimensions. But together with a third technology, tissue engineering and other aspects of postmodern medicine, they are our best hope for keeping up with the machine as it develops superpowers. In combination, they can be applied to a total mind/body makeover for human beings, turning us into essentially immortal superbeings and freeing us from our bondage to Earth.

Biomolecular Engineering

Tissue engineering applies biology and engineering to the repair and manufacture of human tissues in order to repair the ravages of disease and disability. Tissue has been cultured outside the body for many years, but only now is it starting to be manufactured. Tissue engineers are working on virtually every human tissue—skin, cartilage and bone, central nervous system tissues, muscle, liver, and insulin-producing pancreatic islet cells.

For example, in June of 1998 Advanced Tissue Sciences Inc. licensed a tissue engineering process, developed at MIT and the Children's Hospital of Boston, that had already been used successfully to grow new livers in rats and dogs and new heart muscles in animals with heart disease. The process involves healthy cells from the patient or a compatible donor and a dissolvable polymer scaffold. The scaffold is molded into the shape of the organ inside the patient's body and cells would then be attached. The cells grow into the shape of the scaffold, which itself is biodegradable and dissolves. A new liver could be grown in a baby born with a defective liver within three to four weeks. This particular process, and the company that hoped to profit by it, did not make it. ATS declared bankruptcy in 2003. However, the fundamentals of the process continue to be developed and in some cases—bladders and trachea—to succeed in humans.

Where a defect is systemic, affecting more of the body than one organ, then genetic and molecular engineering may be more appropriate methods. Genetic engineering is an umbrella term for a wide range of ways of changing the DNA code in living organisms. DNA code is just "how to" information—a set of algorithms (genes) that the proteins and enzymes and other constituents of the cell will implement in chemistry. In that sense, genetic engineering is a form of nanotechnology. The main difference is that genetic engineers seek to engineer or re-engineer biological tissues and whole organisms, whereas nanotechnologists are interested in building inanimate artifacts—sometimes using the same biomolecular machinery (proteins) as genetic engineers.

The DNA molecule—the genome—is the blueprint for an entire organism, determining not just what sort of organism a fertilized egg will become and what sort of organisms it will produce as a parent, but also what characteristics it will tend to have as an individual.[34] Each of those individual characteristics is coded in tiny segments of the DNA molecule: genes. Defective genes cause defective characteristics. Since the early 1970s geneticists have been able to manipulate specific genes at the molecular level, snipping out a section of code (an individual gene), modifying or even replacing it with entirely new code, and putting it back.

It is not quite as easy as it sounds. The body will sometimes ignore a new or modified gene, and nothing much may happen. But when something does happen, it can be startling, from a cure for some crippling disease to the creation of transgenic organisms, where a short section of genetic material from one species can be introduced into another, thus creating at least a monster and, conceivably, a new species. In "an experiment that could have come from a horror movie," wrote *Village Voice* writer Mark Schoofs in a series of articles published on the *Voice* website in 1997, "Geneticist Walter Gehring took a gene that controls the development of eyes in mice and inserted it into fruit fly embryos, among cells that normally develop into legs. Legs they became—but with eyes all over them." Schoofs added that "Researchers at the National Eye Institute recently repeated the experiment, this time splicing in the eye gene from a squid. The flies grew eyes on their wings, legs, and antennae—eyes that could actually respond to light. But because they were not wired to the brain, the flies could not see through them."

In 1994, transgeneticists created a blue carnation by splicing in a petunia gene. A blue rose followed, in 2004. These are flowers that do not exist in nature in blue. By splicing different gene segments from a variety of organisms, it is also possible in principle to recreate once-extinct species. In practice, by 1997 scientists had managed to create:

---

[34] The environment may influence the expression of the genes (the phenomenon known as epigenetics) and thus play a part in whether and to what extent the characteristics actually play out in the individual.

- A blue carnation;
- "Self-shearing" sheep, whose wool simply falls off when it has grown to a certain length;
- Vaccines that can be eaten instead of having to be injected into the bloodstream;
- Bacteria that spin silk (using genes spliced from the silkworm);
- More nutritious crops, richer in proteins and vitamins;
- Mosquitoes that neutralize the diseases they carry before the diseases can be transmitted to other organisms;
- Human livers grown in pigs;
- Drug "pharms" of plants, animals, and insects genetically altered to produce drugs such as insulin; and
- Strawberries that grow in Winter, fortified by antifreeze produced by the genes of arctic fish spliced into the strawberry plant's DNA.

These are but part of the first small uplift in a tsunami just starting to hit the beach. The field of gene therapy, which aims to go directly into a human's DNA to repair genetic defects, was barely conceptualized in 1958. The first trials involving human patients occurred in 1990, and in 1997 the U.S. Food and Drug Administration approved a genetic therapy for one form of cancer. Today, over $2 billion is spent annually in the U.S. alone in the race to find genetic therapies for every known genetic defect—including one that is invariably fatal: old age.

From the point of view of the selfish gene, old age and death not defects—they are features, not bugs; just part of the gene's plan for its own survival. But from the organism's—your, my— point of view, they are nothing to celebrate. Current hopes of staving off the Grim Reaper focus partly on finding genetic cures for killers such as cancer, partly on the genetic regeneration of old, worn-out organs, and partly on preventing natural cell death and keeping cells young. Most cells in our bodies stop reproducing (dividing) after a certain number of divisions, therefore our organs slowly wind down and we waste away. But it may be possible to keep our cells immortal, through an enzyme called *telomerase*.

Even if immortality is not achieved in the near future, it is very likely that genetic therapies will extend the average lifespan to at least 150 within 50 years, by which time further advances will stretch the lifespan much further.

Regenerative Medicine

"Why, half a century after the first kidney transplant, have we not developed a wide range of artificial organs that can be implanted in patients, just as organs from human donors are?" asked a reporter in 2004.[35] An artificial organ researcher responded: "If we were talking 10 years ago, I'd have said that the impact, commercially and medically, of tissue engineering and organ replacement by 2005 would be significant . . . we were just overly optimistic." Just like the investors in Advanced Tissue Sciences, Inc.

The pessimism was justified in terms of timing, although if the researcher had chosen 2006 instead of 2005, he would at least have been able to point to one medical success, which was extremely significant in its own right: the announcement in *The Lancet* on April 4, 2006, that tissue-engineered bladders had worked well in a trial among pediatric patients.

Behind the Scenes

Indeed, research into artificial organs was making significant progress six or so years ago, though without significant commercial or medical impact. Massachusetts General Hospital's Laboratory for Tissue Engineering and Organ Fabrication was beginning to implant prototype artificial livers made of polymers and living cells into rats, and Nephros Therapeutics had begun a 12-month clinical trial on 100 patients of an external artificial kidney to treat acute renal failure. Their intermediate goal was to replace dialysis machines, and after that, to make an implantable device.

In 2004, a venture-funded startup aimed to combine elements of tissue engineering and cell-based therapy with the precision of

---

[35] Scott Kirsner: "Hopes High for Artificial Organs, Despite Slow Going," *Boston Globe*, June 7, 2004.

medical devices to attack a variety of human diseases. Two years later, the company (Pervasis Therapeutics) was announcing the success of safety trials of its first product, Vascugel, a tissue-engineered assembly of allogeneic endothelial cells—cells that line the interior surface of blood vessels, taken from different individuals of the same species. Vascugel was designed to be wrapped around an injured blood vessel, to which the endothelial cells provide growth regulatory compounds to promote natural healing and reduce scar tissue formation, inflammation and thrombosis.

That same year (2004), the U.S. Defense Advanced Research Projects Agency (DARPA) launched project ReGenesis to investigate the potential of limb regeneration in humans. Why, DARPA asked, since humans can regenerate a normal liver after losing as much as 90 percent of one during surgery, can they not regenerate a limb or brain or spinal cord?

These examples illustrate the two main branches of regenerative medicine: Repairing tissues *in vivo* (inside the living body) and *in vitro* (in the laboratory). In the first case, damaged tissues and organs are stimulated into healing themselves. In the second, scientists grow tissues and organs in the laboratory, then implant them into the body. The main tools of regenerative medicine are cellular therapies (in particular, stem cell therapies), tissue engineering (which, like Vascugel, involves both cells and biomaterials), and genetic engineering.

The U.S. Department of Health & Human Services (DHHS) believed in 2003 that regenerative medicine had "the opportunity to begin producing complex skin, cartilage and bone substitutes in as little as 5 years. Tissue and organ patches, designed to help regenerate damaged tissues and organs such as the heart and kidneys are within reach in 10 years. Within 20 years . . . the goal of 'tissues on demand' is realistic."[36] Buried in my ellipsis is the obvious caveat "given enough funds."

Conventional wisdom sees regenerative medicine first as a potential multibillion-dollar industry with national strategic im-

---

[36] DHHS 2006: "2020: A New Vision--A Future for Regenerative Medicine," revised, at http://www.hhs.gov/reference/newfuture.shtml.

pact. According to the National Science Foundation, in 1995 only 5 percent of companies involved in regenerative medicine research were based outside the United States. By 2002, the number was 46 percent. Second, it is seen as promising breathtakingly better medicine. Regenerative medicine seeks to cure disease, whereas traditional biomedicine seeks mainly to treat it. For example, insulin therapy and glucose therapy are traditional biomedical treatments for diabetes, but they do not cure it, nor do they prevent some 68,000 deaths directly caused by diabetes annually in the United States. Regenerative medicine seeks rather to regenerate insulin-producing pancreatic islets in diabetic patients, either *in vivo* or grown *in vitro* and implanted.

A third, less conventional, viewpoint sees regenerative medicine as one of several ways in which we can co-evolve with *Machina sapiens*, and not be left behind by it.

All three viewpoints assume that regenerative medicine will succeed. Will it? The signs are good. One institution alone—Wake Forest Institute for Regenerative Medicine, which produced the successful tissue-engineered bladder—is working on more than 20 different tissue types for the restoration or replacement of diseased tissues or organs. Tissues and organs grown at the Institute include:

- heart	- breast	- ureter
- liver	- ovaries	- urethra
- bone	- skel. muscle	- teeth
- blood vessels	- pancreas	- genitalia
- trachea	- lung	- testes
- kidney	- cartilage	- smooth muscle
- bladder	- nerves	
- salivary gland	- esophagus	

Engineered bladders and ligaments and stem cell therapies are in various stages of preclinical and clinical tests. However, the only available FDA-approved products are simple tissues such as dermal and joint substitutes, and bone marrow for orthopedics. Many skin substitutes have been used successfully, but cartilage and bone replacement techniques have been more difficult. Thus, regenerative medicine is at a very early stage of development, and its progress is hampered by a lack of cohesive fundamental research--the kind of research that the private sector typically will not undertake.

The Next 20 Years

DHHS' 2003 paper said that the following timeline was feasible given public funds for research. (The paper was revised in 2006; it is not clear whether the projections start in 2003 or 2006.)

In five years:
- Develop multiple applications for skin, cartilage, bone, blood vessel and some urological products.
- Develop insurance-reimbursable regenerative therapies.
- Establish standards for FDA regenerative medicine therapy product approvals.
- Solve cell-sourcing issues, giving researchers access to the materials they need to design new therapies.
- Establish cost-effective means of production, paving the way for future products.
- Establish specialized cell banks for tissue storage, allowing storage of viable "off the shelf" products.

In 10 years:
- Further understand stem cell and progenitor cell biology.
- Engineer smart degradable biocompatible scaffolding.
- Develop microfabrication and nanofabrication technologies to produce tissues with their own complete vascular circulation.
- Develop complex organ patches that can repair damaged pieces of the heart or other organs.

Within 20 years:
- Harness regenerative medicine materials to produce in situ regeneration of diseased and damaged structures in many areas of the body.
- Regenerate most damaged tissues and organs either in vivo or through implanted regeneration therapies.

- Produce in vitro sophisticated 3-D tissues and organs that cannot be regenerated through in vivo techniques, such as an entire heart or lung.

The question is not "Will we get there?" The signs—the engineered bladder is one—are that we have arrived. But perhaps we have arrived only at a waypoint, not at the destination. What if, instead of a bladder engineered like a natural bladder, we instead engineered a bladder with better properties than the natural one? One that lasted longer than a human lifespan and that could grow with the individual through childhood? Or muscle as strong as the muscle in Machina sapiens' robotic arms and legs? Mother Nature has produced structures and materials that have outlasted most things we engineer, but with our recently developed ability to engineer new materials (so-called metamaterials) at the atomic level, that is about to change.

Bionic Implants & Interface

A heart patient with a pacemaker implant, a Parkinson's patient with a deep-brain stimulator implant, an amputee fitted with a C-Leg…. These and many more are machine-enhanced humans—cyborgs, or bionic people. Their bionic components need to be activated and deactivated automatically, for obvious reasons. You don't want to start searching for the "On" switch on a box in your pocket or on your belt after your heart starts fibrillating out of control, or your Parkinson's hands twitch uncontrollably, or your epileptic seizure has you writhing on the floor, or your C-leg stays rooted to the spot when you try to get out of the way of an oncoming train.

That means bionic devices need to receive, understand, and respond appropriately and automatically to signals the nervous system sends out to the appropriate, but missing or disabled, muscles. That in turn means there has to be an interface—a connection or usually a whole set of connections—between the nervous system and the bionic device. Such interfaces have come to be known generically as the "brain–machine interface" or BMI.

The BMI is important not just because it connects a cyborg's human side with his or her bionic side, but also because it will increasingly connect the cyborg with *Machina sapiens*. It is through the BMI that *Homo* and *Machina sapiens* will eventually meld.

Wired vs. Wireless BMI

BMI devices currently come in two types: One with the interface wired into the brain itself, and one interfacing wirelessly through sensors placed on the scalp. The direct-wired interface is obviously invasive: it requires opening up the skull and is therefore risky and expensive, but it captures and produces higher quality signals than the wireless interface.

A wired BMI consisting of implanted electrodes has been available for some time to monitor seizures in epilepsy patients. That technology was adapted to enable two patients to type letters on a screen by simply concentrating their thoughts on each letter in turn. This has been done before using a wireless BMI, but the new approach should provide a faster communication rate and be much better at reading complex brain signals.

BMI For Real-time Thought Expression

Another wired BMI has enabled a patient with locked-in syndrome (resulting from a stroke) to communicate. The patient's cognitive abilities are intact but he is paralyzed except for slow vertical movement of the eyes. His BMI implant—essentially, an electrode and FM transmitter—has been installed for over 5ive years near the boundary between the speech-related pre-motor and primary motor cortex. Neurites grew into the electrode and their signals are amplified and transmitted by the implant to an antenna temporarily glued to the patient's head. The implanted electrode is powered by induction from a power coil also attached to the head.

A laptop computer system translates the received neural signals, that were basically intended for the vocal cords, and converts them to sounds as quickly as a non-paralyzed person would say them, although so far only three vowel sounds have been tested. After 25 sessions over a five-month period, the vowels were correctly reproduced 89 percent of the time.

The next version of the system will produce consonants and more vowels, and will record ten times as many neurons. The system has the potential eventually to enable real-time conversation and thereby minimize the social isolation that accompanies profound paralysis.

Neuron-Prosthetic Interfaces

For patients who lack not just control of a limb but the limb itself, there are ways to interface the brain, through the nervous system, with a robotic prosthetic limb. One method of doing so goes as follows:

- Harvest cells from healthy muscle in the patient's body.
- Place the cells on a scaffold on the inside of a microscopic cup made from an electrically conductive polymer.
- Position the cup on the ends of a motor nerve at the point where the limb was severed.
- Do the same for a sensory nerve.
- Wait for the muscle cells to proliferate in the cups, and for the nerve endings to grow into the cups and attach to the muscle cells.
- Do this for as many nerve endings as possible—the more, the better.
- Take the electrical signals coming from the motor neurons into the muscle and passing through the electroactive plastic, and broadcast them to a computer controlling a robotic prosthetic limb attached to the patient.
- Heat sensors, pressure sensors, and other sensors in the prosthetic send signals the other way, via the sensory neurons, to inform the patient's brain that the prosthetic is touching something hot or cold, hard or soft, etc.

Most of this has been done in rats with a severed peripheral nerve, using just two cups and one motor neuron and one sensory neuron. This particular research project is still in its early stages but something approaching this fine level of interface must have already been used to build the state-of-the-art "SmartHand" developed by a multinational team in the EU. This artificial hand has been successfully wired to existing nerve endings in the stump of a Swedish patient's severed arm. It resembles a real hand in function, sensitivity, and appearance.

The patient is able not only to complete complicated tasks such as eating and writing but also to feel his artificial fingers. He told a television interviewer: "I am using muscles which I haven't used for years. I grab something hard, and then I can feel it in the fingertips, which is strange, as I don't have them anymore. It's amazing."

The SmartHand contains four electric motors and 40 touch sensors. Future versions will have artificial skin providing even more tactile feedback.

ల

Where a limb is still attached but paralyzed as a result of spinal cord injury, it has proved possible to re-wire individual neurons to bypass damaged areas and connect directly to muscles in the paralyzed limb. This has been achieved in monkeys whose arms were temporarily paralyzed for the purpose, leaving them unable to use their wrists. Brain signals were re-routed around the blocked nerve pathway via a wire running between a randomly selected neuron in the motor cortex, a computer, an electric shock generator, and a muscle in the arm. Whenever the neuron fired above a certain rate, the computer told the generator to shock the arm muscle, causing the muscle to contract.

The monkeys quickly learned to move their paralyzed wrists to play a video game.

The researchers involved in this project were surprised to find that "nearly every neuron" they tested in the brain could be used to control this type of stimulation. "Even neurons which were unrelated to the movement of the wrist before the nerve block could be brought under control and co-opted," they said. They also showed that a single neuron could work two different muscles: a high firing rate triggered the wrist to flex, while a low firing rate caused it to extend. (Still, using more than just one neuron would be better.)

In similar research conducted elsewhere, a monkey was able to pick up a ball via a wired BMI implant known as a functional electrical stimulation (FES) device. FES is already used in US Food and Drug Administration-approved implants that can restore hand function and bladder control to some paralyzed patients. One existing FES implant enables the patient to shrug a shoulder to cause their hand to grasp an object, though it cannot yet enable the patient to control the strength of the grasp.

The FES implant in the monkey brain records signals from the motor cortex, which a computer then decodes into specific muscle movements in five flexor muscles in the arm, enabling the monkeys to grasp objects and move their wrists in different directions. In a test involving putting a ball into a hole, which the monkeys could do every time before their nerves were blocked, the paralyzed monkeys succeeded only about 10 percent of the time until the FES system was turned on, when the success rate rose to 77 percent.

A similar system is already working in a human paralyzed patient who is now able to control a computer model of an arm (not yet an actual prosthetic.) Human trials of this system, with an actual prosthetic, could begin within a year or two.

Shrinking Brain Implants

The Responsive Neurostimulator mentioned earlier is the size of a small deck of cards and a cavity has to be created inside the skull to make room for it—a risky business. The large size of this device, we would hazard a guess, is probably due to its batteries, since implant chips themselves can be made very small. An experimental sensor platform called NeuralWISP fits multiple electronic components onto a circuit board currently just over two centimeters long and a future version will put them all into a single chip one by two millimeters in size.

With reduced size comes reduced power consumption, which makes it feasible to draw power wirelessly from a radio source up to a meter away, instead of from bulky batteries inside the implant. So far, the device has only been tested in moths. Getting signal and power from/to an implant centimeters deep in the human brain will no doubt be more difficult than getting it a few millimeters into a moth, but nanotechnology might eventually solve that problem.

Nanoimplants

The devices we have discussed so far have not been nanoscale devices. At best, they are "MEMS" (micro-electromechanical systems)-scale devices. MEMS engineering was an early enabler of bionics, facilitating the development of complex devices only a few centimeters (like the present NeuralWISP) or even millimeters (like the future NeuralWISP) in size. MEMS devices are clearly functional and useful at a gross level within the human body, but for the ultimate in utility and control it is necessary—certainly at the interface, where we are talking about individual neurons with diameters measuring mere billionths of a meter—to move several orders of magnitude down to the nanoscale.

The electrodes used in brain implants today typically record the electrical activity of masses of neurons per electrode. Yet as long ago as 2006, Harvard researchers used nanowire transistors to measure electrical signals not just in a single neuron but at 50 points within a single neuron. The same group has now developed a nanowire recording system and has used it "to capture some of the most precise, high-quality electrical recordings ever made from heart cells."

The system clearly has potential application in neural prostheses and other medical devices and indeed the Harvard researchers have already begun to make recordings from neural tissue. Furthermore, they are working on nanowire devices that can simultaneously record electrical signals as well as hormone, neurotransmitter, and other chemical signals which "would give a more integrated picture of biological functions."

Lipid-coated Nanowires

Similar (possibly connected) research at the Lawrence Livermore National Laboratory has resulted in what amounts to an experimental artificial neuron made of silicon-nanowire transistors encased in a fatty acid membrane. Because the membrane contains ion channels and can therefore also respond to proteins and other biomolecules, electrodes connecting a prosthetic device with the nervous system could read chemical as well as electrical signals, thus providing finer and more natural control over the prosthetic.

The first prototypes have only one type of ion channel, which limits their functions. The next generation will have more. The researchers will also begin testing the artificial neuron's interactions with living cells.

Bare Nanowires to Electrify the Body

Nanotechnology is also able to solve a problem with current medical devices, namely, that their electronics have to be isolated from the body and are built on a rigid silicon platform. The solution is nanoscale silicon circuits built on a thin film of silk. These are biocompatible, conformable to tissue shape, and are partially biodegradable—the silk dissolves over time and the circuits left behind are too thin to irritate the tissue.

Silk–silicon LED devices under development could act as "photonic tattoos" showing (for example) blood-sugar readings, and as arrays of conformable electrodes that could interface with the nervous system. Such devices have apparently been implanted in animals with no adverse effects to the body or to the devices' performance. The group undertaking this research is currently designing silk-based electrodes that could be wrapped around individual peripheral nerves to help control prostheses. The conformability of an array of silk electrodes would enable it to be used in otherwise inaccessible crevices deep inside the brain.

Our ability to interface at the neural level—and increasingly at the individual neuron level—with computers and robotic machines is accelerating. While this has obvious implications for healthcare in the sense of being able to offer treatments for people with disabilities, it has longer-term deeper implications because it promises to enhance the cognitive and motor capacities of perfectly healthy and able-bodied people as well. It is the dawn of the age of Superman and Superwoman.

Artificial Everything

Bionics is not just about artificial devices. It is also about artificial materials that more or less (increasingly, more) mimic human tissues and cells. Below is a descriptive selection of recent exemplary advances designed to show that "trans-humanism"—a movement which (according to Wikipedia) aims to eliminate aging and greatly enhance human intellectual, physical, and psychological capacities—may be not quite as preposterous, or as distant if you are inclined to be open-minded or generous, as it sounds. These developments are as of approximately early 2011, and the list is by no means exhaustive.

Artificial Bone

An artificial bone graft called FortrOss, on the market in the US since 2008, mimics the nanostructures of natural bony tissue and is thus accepted by the body. It could eventually have a rival in the form of artificial bones made of chemically and heat-treated rattan wood. In animal trials using sheep, they appeared to be strong and durable enough to last a lifetime, with no signs of rejection or infection in the sheep. However, human clinical trials are still about five years away, so FortrOss can breathe easy for a while.

Artificial Muscle

Carbon-nanotube ribbons stronger than steel, as elastic and flexible as rubber, light as air, able to withstand temperatures ranging from -190 to over 1,600 °C, transparent, and electrically conductive have been developed for use (among other things) as artificial muscle fibers for prosthetics and robotics. The ribbons change shape and size in response to electrical or chemical signals and can exert 100 times more force than natural human muscle over the same area.

Sheets woven from the ribbons currently generate 32 times as much force per unit area as heart muscles, though electroactive polymers generate up to eight times as much force per unit area as the nanotube sheets. Polymer actuators also need just a few volts to contract, vs. three to five kilovolts for the ribbons—too strong for use in humans and risky even in robots. But it's early days, and future development may improve the ribbons' performance. Already, they can change dimensions much faster than polymer actuators.

Artificial Collagen

A stable and ultra-strong artificial human collagen has been developed that could be used to treat arthritis and other conditions that result from collagen defects, as well as burn and other wounds. Bovine-derived collagen carries the risk of rejection in human patients.

Artificial Arteries

An artificial artery for use as a bypass graft is in human trials in coronary artery and lower-limb arterial surgery. Made from a polymer material, the graft mimics the natural pulsing of human blood vessels, which enables them to deliver nutrients to the body's tissues. Other plastic grafts made with nylon work well for larger grafts but are less successful for grafts of less than 8mm. The new artificial artery has been designed to mimic the natural artery's characteristic strength, flexibility, resistance to clotting, and rhythmic pulsing in sync with the heartbeat.

Artificial Blood Platelets

Synthetic blood platelets capable (like natural platelets) of clotting have been shown to quickly reduce bleeding in rodents with severed arteries. The nano-sized platelets stick to natural platelets to stanch bleeding more effectively than an expensive clotting drug currently used to stem uncontrolled blood loss. The platelets do not accumulate in non-injured tissue to form dangerous clots. At unnecessarily high doses the platelets led to breathing issues in some of the tested mice. Tests in larger animals are planned. It will be some time before human trials are attempted.

Artificial Red Blood Cells

Biodegradable, biocompatible particles with the size, shape, and flexibility of red blood cells have been created that could transport not just oxygen but also drugs and imaging agents. So far, the particles have been shown to be capable of compressing sufficient to squeeze through capillary-sized tubes, carrying drugs to treat a disease or iron-oxide nanoparticles as a potential contrast agent for MRIs.

Artificial Larynx

A prototype artificial larynx that tracks contact between the tongue and palate to determine which word is being mouthed, and uses a speech synthesizer to generate sounds, is expected to be a great improvement over existing devices used in many patients with advanced laryngeal cancer who have their voice box removed. The system contains 118 embedded touch sensors on a "palatometer" placed in the mouth, and an external synthesizer that (after training) translates the touch patterns into words and speaks them. A predictive-analysis system considers the last word mouthed to help determine the next word. The result is 94 percent accuracy, excluding words the system classifies as "unknown" and skips to avoid "some very difficult social situations," as a researcher put it. There remains much development work to do before the device will be ready for market.

℘

We will one day create intelligent robots that look and feel just like humans. Today, using the latest in silicon gel and plastic skin technologies, one U.S. company is making and selling, for $4,000, a full-sized "love doll." The company concerned is said to be looking into providing the currently passive doll with active, robotic capabilities. Do any of us need convincing that sex and other forms of entertainment (sex has degenerated to that level) will soon become one of the prime drivers of robotics research and development?

But by far the greatest significance of nanotechnology- and computing-driven advances in robotics and cyborgism is that they offer a way out of the dilemma for *Homo sapiens* of being constrained by biological evolution while helping create a *Machina sapiens* which is not so constrained.

The notion of the evolution of *Homo sapiens* into *Homo cyborgensis* concludes the first part of the book, which has emphasized (though not exclusively) the *technologies* leading to the emergence of two new super-intelligent, super-sensitive, and super-powerful species of life: one essentially machine, the other essentially human. We have so far tended to focus more on the scientific and technological side of the story than on the philosophical side. In the next chapter, we begin to reverse the focus.

The pace of change, particularly with regard to the explosion of memetic evolution and exponential growth of computing power, suggests that within two decades *Machina sapiens* will see, hear, speak, and act for itself. It will have personhood.

What sort of person will it be?

14 EMOTIVE POWER

*The evolution of the airplane was
a strictly Darwinian process in which
almost all the varieties of airplane failed,
just as almost all species of animal became extinct.
Because of the rigorous selection, the few remaining airplanes
are reliable, economical, and safe.*

Freeman Dyson, Imagined Worlds

If the Modern Synthesis of genetically-moderated natural section is correct, then we are collections of blind automata that
process algorithms. And anything else that is just such a collection is just as likely as you and me to have mind, consciousness,
and self. This is what scares people about evolution, and about
AI. Both are mechanistic and, by non-Darwinian definition, inhuman. Garry Kasparov's loss to *Deep Blue* left some folks wor-
ried about a future dominated by a cold, heartless machine. If
that were the future, they should keep worrying.

Perhaps, like the flying machine, there will be many species or
forms of intelligent machine, and only those which are reliable,
economical, and safe will survive. But to be safe from the perspective of soft, vulnerable, mortal beings like us, an intelligent
autonomous machine must be either powerless and totally under
our control, or it must be benign and act accordingly. It cannot

be both: a superior intelligence must by definition be powerful and uncontrollable. Which leaves the rather important question: Will it be benign?

The first of two primary messages from Antonio Damasio's research on mind, brain, and emotions is that to care—to have feelings and emotions—one way or another, an organism needs a body and not just a brain. The second message is: Emotion is essential for decision-making. Having a body and a brain seems easy enough, even for a machine. A robot can have both. But is it true that emotion is essential, as well? For all imaginable intelligent life? If so, how might *Machina sapiens* acquire emotion and what would be the implications of an emotional machine?

Biology is like the weakling on the beach in old ads for Charles Atlas bodybuilding courses, constantly having sand kicked in his face by the muscle-bound body of Physics and Chemistry and its steel-toed boots, Geology and Climate. Biology has to fight for its existence, its place in the Sun, somehow. But instead of taking up Charles Atlas' offer, he opted to outsmart the bully by developing organs, limbs, and intelligence, giving him the capability to sense the brutish presence and avoid it through flight, fight it with weapons, tame it with tools, or even deflect and channel the power of its mighty blows into energy to enhance his own existence. Biology further figured out a way to reproduce, so as to recover in cases where a bully blow found its mark. There's strength in numbers.

Best of all, biology figured out how to evolve into beings ever more alert to danger, and ever more capable of taming the beast. But as biology diversified, Nature being Nature his various species turned these same attributes to use against one another, and for the same reason—survival, a place in the Sun. And not only species, but also individuals within species.

Then why, as individuals, are we so weak? Why do we not just re-grow a limb when a lion bites it off? Why must we die of old age? Why does the selfish gene thumb its nose at the phenotype? Because there is advantage to evolution itself, to Nature herself, to the noösphere, if you like, in forcing biology to constantly change and improve, through natural selection of the fittest for a given environment. Evolution doesn't care about you or me.

Nevertheless, in *Homo sapiens* as a species Nature seems almost to have met her match. There are few physical events at earthly scale we cannot survive and even master, and progress continues at a breathtaking pace to defeat those few events, including even Death itself. Geneticists have started to hone in on the genetic code for the process of aging, when cells are instructed to stop dividing. Once the specific mechanism is pinned down, then it should be possible to disable them, and that offers the prospect of immortality.

Even so, as individual biological beings we would remain weaklings susceptible to attack, accident, and decay, and prone to injury, illness, and death, and as individuals we fight against them. How? In two intertwined ways: Through "gut feeling," and an informed, rational, intellect. Damasio's book, *Descartes' Error*, is essentially an explanation of how feeling and intellect arise, how they intertwine, and how emotion arises and is involved as a sort of catalyst in the whole process.

Damasio organizes feelings into three types: Basic, subtle, and background. *Basic* feelings are happiness, sadness, anger, fear, and disgust. We experience these feelings involuntarily—without any conscious effort or thought—primarily through our bodily organs, when faced with a situation calling for them. They come built-in when we are born; algorithms "hard-wired" into our total system, and our system is also pre-configured to react appropriately—to flee or hide if we are afraid, for example. Think of the tightening of the gut when we are sad. The rapid heartbeat of fear. The hot flush of anger. They are caused at a *sub*conscious level, but *experienced* at an aware, conscious level.

Subtle feelings are variations on the basic feelings. They arise through experience—they are acquired after a certain amount of processing, so that our "mind" creates what Damasio calls "dispositional representations" consisting of the feeling and the event. Our brain is able to reconstruct these representations when a fitting situation confronts us. Examples are panic and shyness (variations on fear), melancholy and wistfulness (sadness), euphoria and contentment (happiness). These are a mixture of conscious and subconscious causation and awareness.

Background feelings are what we feel in-between emotions—our "normal" state, as it were. A change in this state, occasioned by a new situation, is what triggers both basic and subtle feelings and hence the Four F's. You ordinarily don't notice your background feelings, unless forced to do so when your doctor (for example) asks "How are you feeling today?" but your subconscious is always aware of them. Damasio goes so far as to call background feelings "the very core of your representation of self"—it's a matter of "I feel, therefore I am" rather than Descartes' famous dictum, "I think, therefore I am" (hence, "Descartes' Error").

Without background feelings, we could not be aware that we are alive, and without a body, we could not generate these feelings. Example: Blood sugar level is an indicator of energy (food) sufficiency, or insufficiency. A range of levels tells our brain, the command and control center, that we are not currently in need of food, so there is no change of state. Below that range, the stomach starts to growl, and the brain starts ordering appropriate action—go grab the spear, or the can opener. This would not occur unless some part of our system were not constantly monitoring and reporting on blood sugar level.

To complement our three types of feeling, evolution gave us three types of feelings-based decisions: Visceral, acquired, and intellectual. *Visceral* (bodily organ) decisions are built-in. Our stomach tells us we are hungry, so we eat. Think of these as purely "biological survival" decisions: Ignore or override them, and you risk death. No conscious thought is needed (although the higher the organism, the more that altruism, self-sacrifice, principle, demagoguery, and other higher-order cognitive or value states may come into play and consciously override the subconscious tendency—the visceral decision—even if survival is at stake.)

Acquired decisions are subtle variations on the visceral decisions, and (just like subtle feelings) are acquired through experience. For example, we *learn* to *tend* to duck when an object is thrown at us. It's an almost innate decision, almost algorithmic; but not quite. If the object is a baseball, and we're in the outfield, we probably *won't* duck. We can say an acquired decision has a basis both in biological survival and in acquired knowledge, and that it is controlled through heuristics.

Intellectual decisions are based more on acquired knowledge and higher-order values (higher, that is, than mere survival)—in other words, on memes; and less, if at all, on biological survival. Whether to eat Italian or Chinese tonight. Which political party to vote for. What career to pursue. Whom to marry. Whether to forgive.

If an organism evolves that does not need to eat (because it is self-sufficient in energy), does not need to worry about a piece of itself being chopped off here and there (because it is self-repairing), does not need to reproduce itself (because it is self-renewing and self-evolving), then it does not need to make survival-oriented decisions. And since, as we have discussed, survival-oriented decisions tend to be based on feelings and emotions and less on intellect, this organism can get by quite happily (so to speak) without emotions, without feelings.

Or can it?

The organism will not in fact be immortal. It will not be omniscient and omnipotent—not for a while, anyway. Big Bad Physics could hurl a large asteroid at it (and us), or fry its neural circuits in a blast of ions from a solar flare. It would surely die if all of its energy sources were destroyed. It would still need the equivalent of at least background feelings, to monitor its internal state and make repairs, adjustments, and improvements as necessary, and to monitor its environment for signs of asteroids, solar flares, or human beings scampering like cockroaches all over its circuits. And it would need a command and control center (a brain) to integrate all this information and prioritize decisions and actions. Therefore, the organism still needs feelings and emotions—or some equivalent thereof—if it wants to have some level of assurance of survival. To want to survive (which is itself a feeling) it must be conscious; to be conscious it must have feelings. Sounds like a chicken and egg problem.

Creationists would doubtless say that consciousness—the Creator's—came first. Evolutionists would say that consciousness emerged from the evolution of mechanisms for feeling. Why can't our new organism, *Machina sapiens*, use its massive memory and brute processing power in place of feelings? Answer: For the same reason we don't use ours—it's too slow. But note that since *Machina sapiens* will be composed of the entire Internet, then it nevertheless will have much more memory and processing power than we do. To that extent, it can rely less on heuristics than we do, and can make better recall of complete patterns than we do. Being neural network based, it will still use heuristics and match patterns from garbled or incomplete input or memory data, but will be able to do so at a higher level. It will be able to probe deeper into issues, and produce more valid and reliable analyses and decisions.

In this context, Damasio notes that intellectual decisions require much more processing than visceral and acquired decisions because they tend to involve many more variables and are less "burned in." This is another way of saying that an organism with more processing power than *Homo sapiens* will make better intellectual decisions than *Homo sapiens*. *Machina sapiens* will be smarter than us.

Which brings us to Damasio's main point: *Emotion is essential for decision-making.* If you're not emotional, if you have no feelings, you are not as smart as you think. Damasio draws on his own and others' clinical research on brain-damaged people to justify and illustrate this claim. His book opens with one of the most fascinating cases on record; that of Phineas Gage, a 25 year old railroad construction foreman.

One day in 1843 Gage was tamping down gunpowder in a hole drilled into a rock face, using an iron tamping rod, when he made a careless mistake. As he tamped down, the rod caught the side of the rock, causing a spark that ignited the gunpowder. The charge exploded, and the three feet seven inches long, one and a quarter inch diameter, thirteen and a quarter pounds rod rocketed up through Gage's left cheek and out the top of his head, leaving behind a neat volcano with an inch and a half bony caldera just above the forehead and, as you would expect, bits of brain and bone scattered about.

What you would not expect is that after a few stunned moments, Gage would be chatting to his co-workers as they took him, sitting upright in an oxcart, to see the local town doctor. Nor would you expect that an hour or so later (as the doctor would subsequently report) Gage would seem "perfectly rational." Two months later, after the wound was cleaned and one small abscess removed, Gage was pronounced cured. No-one realized that the Phineas Gage who walked away from the accident was not the Phineas Gage who had walked into it.

He changed, in that awful moment, from "a shrewd, smart businessman, very energetic and persistent in executing all his plans of action," with "temperate habits" and "considerable energy of character," into an obscene, capricious, and vacillating person able to devise rational plans but incapable of sticking to them. Unable to hold down a job for any length of time and leading a dissipated life, he died at age 38 of epilepsy. Why did he change? Because he had lost that part of his brain that we now know to be responsible for the processing of emotions, and because without emotions he could not make and execute good decisions and plans.

Thus, it is not just our stereotypical conception of a robot that has the hallmarks of a "cold, unfeeling machine." Humans who lack the neurophysiological means of processing emotions act that way, too. As Damasio says, "What should cause fear, actually, is the idea of a selfless cognition," as indeed it did in the case of Deep Blue vs. Garry Kasparov. Professor Rosalind Picard, of MIT's Media Lab, would seem to agree. In her chapter in *Hal's Legacy*, she wrote: "Artificial intelligence systems to date are too rational; they cannot associate judgments of value and salience with their decisions." This, then, is one part of the answer to the question "Should we try somehow to imbue AI systems with emotions and feelings?" From a normative perspective, the answer is Yes, we should.

The other part of the answer is that, as discussed above, we'll get a smarter machine if it has emotions. But can we program emotion in a machine? Dr. Picard paints two scenarios that seem perfectly feasible in current-day programming and that would enable an AI system to act *as if* it had emotions. In one, she envisions a planetary exploration robot programmed to enter a state called "fear" if it gets damaged. It will, of course, need to constantly monitor its own status in order to detect the damage—it will need to have sensors and the equivalent of background feelings programmed in. Not a difficult task; this is standard cybernetics and is done routinely.

In this new state of fear, it is programmed to act differently than normal, perhaps skipping a whole section of code it is currently executing and going instead to a subroutine that reallocates its scarce resources (energy, sensors, motive systems) to the now higher priority tasks of moving itself out of further harm's way and sending out a call to the orbiting mothership for help.

In the second scenario, a personal digital assistant can be programmed to enter states of "feel good" or "feel bad" depending on how its master responds to the work it does on the master's behalf. If it enters a feel good state, then it will over time learn to recognize what pleases the master and take similar action to that which left the master (and therefore it) feeling good. Conversely, it will learn to avoid taking action that leaves the master (and it) feeling bad.

These are fairly trivial programming tasks today. Contrast Brooke's approach of treating Cog as though it were a human, with Lenat's highly rational, knowledgeable, even intellectual, but unemotional, Cyc. In a chapter he contributed to *Hal's Legacy*, Lenat wrote: "[E]motions are not useful for integrating information, making decisions . . . ." That's a pity; Cyc could be so much more interesting.

No-one would pretend that pure "as if" emotion programs, *as disembodied programs*, would actually "feel" anything at all. However, the efforts of Damasio and others to unravel the full mechanism whereby feelings and emotions arise in the neural structure lend hope to the possibility that one day we will be able to program a machine mind and architect a machine body in exact mimicry of evolution's genetic coding and neurobiological architecture. If and when that happens, there seems to be no reason why feelings and emotions would not emerge on that basis alone.

But in any event, memetic evolution will take its course in machine evolution, and while there may well be a genetic basis for emotions, they are almost certainly replicable as memes. Laughter is infectious. It tends to replicate prolifically, as do fear, hatred, and other less enjoyable (but necessary) emotions. And herein may lie a problem. If we create a situation in which emotions just emerge (i.e., we do not or cannot program them in, somehow) then we could end up with a machine not only smarter and more powerful than all of humanity, but also which regards people as we tend to regard the poor cockroach—not exactly with warmth and affection. How about programming the machine to be predisposed to treat us kindly? Science fiction writer Isaac Asimov thought we could, with just three simple instructions or "Laws."

No matter how one cuts it, the emergence of a sense of self and free will in *Machina sapiens*, added to its superior intellect, will empower it to override its basic and subtle emotions and decisions, no matter whether those emotions are emergent or programmed. A few of us—saints, heroes, demagogues, and megalomaniacs—do it all the time, and all of us (Germans in Hitler's time, US soldiers at the My Lai Massacre) do it some of the time, if the circumstances conspire.

It would also, like us, be capable of making mistakes. Emotion, being heuristic, often causes mistakes. Perhaps it is supposed to do that, functioning rather like the mistakes found in genetic coding. We learn from our mistakes, as individuals, as social groups, as civilization. If we did not make mistakes, social and cultural evolution would stop. There'd be no further hope of evolutionary progress. That's the price, and the perfidy, of perfection.

We can be infallible and stagnate, we can be fallible and evolve, or we can be fallible and stagnate. But we cannot be infallible and evolve. We can't have our cake and eat it. And neither can *Machina sapiens*. Daniel Dennett reminds us of something Alan Turing said, way back in '46,

> . . . if a machine is expected to be infallible, it cannot
> also be intelligent. There are several theorems which say
> almost exactly that. But these theorems say nothing
> about how much intelligence may be displayed if a ma-
> chine makes no pretence at infallibility.

That he had this figured out while *Machina sapiens* was barely conceived and neurobiology was in its infancy is further testament to Turing's genius.

Evolution, it would seem, is reverting to physics. Our globby biologic weakling on the beach needs only to take off his psychedelic sunglasses to see a looming hardware hulk approaching from the distance. When it arrives, will it pulverize the weakling as a threat to its own enjoyment of the beach? Will it ignore him as a being of no consequence? Or will it bear him up gently, in solenoid-controlled, transducer-skinned arms, and show him the stars? That may depend on how we treat it in its infancy, childhood, and adolescence.

This much is certain: physics can take care of itself in the harshness of the physical universe. *Homo sapiens* may be the pinnacle of bioevolution, never to be improved upon in the biological realm; but *Machina sapiens* will be better equipped than we are to go forth into the universe and explore and find the answers to Life, the Universe, and Everything.

15 EARLY CHILDHOOD DEVELOPMENT

A newborn baby comes with a level of intelligence built in; genetic algorithms "hard wired" into its chromosomes and to some extent pre-patterned into its neural structure. And it comes already coded to learn—to acquire knowledge heuristically through experience. Some machines are now being built that way, too, using machine learning techniques drawn from Mother Nature and applied in genetic programming and neural networks,

Machine learning has been described as a melting pot of ideas from a wide variety of disciplines. At the basic science level, machine learning is concerned with computer programs that automatically improve their performance through experience. Typical areas of inquiry include understanding how concepts are formed and how we learn search heuristics. How do we learn to break a too-big problem up into smaller, more manageable sub-problems? How does a baby learn to improve its motor skills, so it can raise spoon from bowl to lips? How do we learn to explain new concepts in terms of existing concepts (much as I am trying to do in this book)? How do we learn to revise and extend existing theories in light of new evidence, and discover new scientific laws and theories?

To answer these questions, and to be able to apply the answers in a machine context, requires deeper exploration into issues of knowledge representation and reasoning performance using a variety of alternative approaches including rule-based (expert) systems, frame-like structures, probabilistic concepts (such as Bayesian networks), and neural networks.

୶

Machine learning research asks such questions as "What kinds of guarantees can one prove about learning algorithms? What could one hope to prove? What models are both amenable to mathematical analysis *and* make sense empirically? Can we use these models to come up with improved algorithms? What can we say about the inherent ease or difficulty of learning problems?" To address such questions, the researcher must be able to combine "notions and ideas from statistics, complexity theory, cryptography, and on-line algorithms, as well as empirical machine learning and neural network research."

These quotes are from the description of a course in machine learning at Carnegie Mellon University. It's not hard to see why machine learning is called "a melting pot" of disciplines. Nor is it hard to find evidence that it works: To date, using machine learning methods, vehicles have learned to drive themselves, machines have learned to recognize human speech, to detect credit card fraud, to improve the yield of integrated circuits produced from silicon wafers, and to formulate strategies for game playing (*Deep Blue*) and simulations.

Among the reasons machine learning was for long limited to solving sub-problems in very specific and finite domains (as opposed to solving major problems in general human and social domains) were these:

1. Limited domains don't carry much baggage in the way of context. The machine learning system doesn't have to know very much up front.
2. Current machine learning systems are relatively simple, in contrast to the complexity of systems (such as the human being) needed to operate on general problems.
3. They rely essentially on logical reasoning (with, increasingly, allowance being made for uncertainty and for "re-

inforcement" whereby simulated numerical "rewards" are given if the system returns a good solution).

Several efforts have attempted to take care of the context issue. Cyc and MISTIC are examples, as was Belgium's *Principia Cybernetica* project, which aims to turn the Web into the machine's learning library. As of this writing, by far the most advanced machine learning is represented in IBM's Watson computer, which knows enough about the world, and about the English language, to participate against human champions in the TV quiz show called Jeopardy (on February 18, 2011.) Again as of this writing, details of Watson's machine learning method are scant.

The system complexity issue has being tackled using AI techniques themselves to create self-designing systems. Hugo de Garis' "Brain Builder" project in Japan was a case in point—a cellular automata machine that grew its own complex circuits on FPGA chips using genetic algorithms, just as the human being is "grown" through genetic programming. In theory, that is; "Brain Builder" was never completed.

Probably the biggest challenge—and the biggest payoff; the jackpot, in fact—facing would-be (and even would-not-be!) creators of *Machina sapiens* is getting it to reason using not just logic but also the illogic of emotion. In other words, using its whole mind. For as we have seen, there is a deal of illogic—betimes amounting to insanity—in human intelligence. Freeman Dyson believes that "In the long run, the central problem of any intelligent species is the problem of sanity."

Unfortunately, getting *Machina sapiens* to use its whole mind is problematical because we still don't know what a mind is. We do know it is something more than the sum of a brain, a body, a nervous system, sense organs, and some limbs. Dan Dennett thinks a mind is a collection of algorithmic, heuristic, memetic machines. With those attributes alone a machine might make a pretty good showing as an intelligent, reasoning being; but if it could not experience and manifest joy and despair, passion and tranquility, anger and resignation—in short, emotion—then we'd think of it as a cold, heartless, soulless being, would we not?

Deep Blue's defeat of Garry Kasparov was an arid victory. Deep Blue could not anticipate and enjoy a game, savor it afterwards, feel elated at a win or deflated at a loss. It is likely that those emotions in Kasparov are what help to make him such a brilliant chess player even without Deep Blue's massive computational prowess.

The evidence is mounting not only that the human mind is made up of reasoning *plus* emotion, but also that emotion has a neurophysiological basis. Given this evidence, it will remain only to apply it to a reasoning machine and we may well have then created a truly conscious being. Our understanding of the mechanism for emotion is far behind our understanding of the mechanisms for genetic development and adaptations, and for neural structures and neural functioning, but even our presently limited understanding of genetic algorithms and neural nets is already being implemented with great success in machine learning. It seems only a matter of time before the mechanism of emotional intelligence is understood sufficiently to become programmable at some level.

The most disturbing aspect of Hal was not his cold, logical, reasoning, though that was scary enough. The film only hinted that it might be Hal's emotion that underlay his murderous behavior toward the crew, but the hint was enough to send shivers up the spine. We surely could live with unfeeling robots that kill. We already do—auto factory workers have been killed by robots, and although drone aircraft are currently controlled by human operators, the public perceives the drone as robots, and seems not to care that they are killing people in Afghanistan. But will we be as nonchalant about robots that may learn how to lie, cheat, steal, and hate?

Religion and philosophy tell us that we cannot appreciate happiness without experiencing sadness. There's a yang to every yin. If we are going to create a truly intelligent being, or at least help it emerge, then we have to accept up front that it will learn to hate, as well as to love. It will know Bad, as well as Good, Wrong, as well as Right. And it will have the *free will* to choose between these alternatives.

In his essay *A Note on (toward) Bernard Shaw*, Borges asked: "Can an author create characters superior to himself?" Borges himself would say no, and "in that negation include both the intellectual and the moral." He believed that "from us cannot emerge creatures more lucid or more noble than our best moments." If Borges is right, it would mean that we cannot create a *Machina sapiens* more "lucid, noble, intellectual, or moral" them ourselves at our best. But our creative efforts in the machine intelligence sphere amount only to a *support* role to the evolutionary process; they do not amount to a God-like act of creation. And unlike a character in a book, *Machina sapiens* has *free will* and is subject to universal influences, not merely the influence of its proximate creators.

What difference does free will make?

Free Will

Are you reading this book because you choose to? Or because someone or something is forcing you to? Or were you fated, predestined, to read it?

For as long as human discourse has been recorded, the question of whether we really have free will to choose our own actions and destinies, or whether we are fated—predetermined—to do what we do, be what we are, and end up where we end up is a question that has occupied the minds and pens of philosophers, intellectuals, and quantum physicists.

We've seen that *Machina sapiens* will have a body and a brain far more powerful than ours, and that it will be emotional. None of this would matter if we were to remain in control. But we won't. *Machina sapiens* will have a free will of its own.

Some people cling to the notion that free will itself is an illusion or a Divine Fraud. They base their case on either classical or quantum physics. They have their heuristic cake and eat it. If the universe was created by a Master Watchmaker and operates on mechanistic, deterministic, Newtonian laws, then it's just a giant clockwork mechanism and we're just cogs with no more control over our actions than cogs in an old-fashioned watch. If, on the other hand, the universe is a result of the purely random events predicted by the laws of quantum physics then we still have no free will because whatever we do is a result of chance rather than choice.

Not so fast, say at least some quantum physicists, including Frank Tipler, who points to theories of quantum gravity to suggest that the quanta of which we are all ultimately made are sensitive to fluctuations in quantum gravity in the surrounding environment, and that a mechanism exists whereby our bodily quanta notify a higher level of processing of the fluctuations. They don't just automatically react to the fluctuations, but wait for instructions from the higher level. Essentially, this reduces to the ultimate resolution the levels of intelligent activity prescribed by Hofstadter for ant colonies and programmed into Pandemonium.

We are totally unaware of most of the many levels of processing, but we are very aware of the top level—the brain. Here is where the signals that began (perhaps) as mere notifications of fluctuations in quantum gravity end up, having in the meantime been successively and perhaps repeatedly analyzed, filtered, and matched with the patterns of stored quantum and neural memories. By the time the brain has all the information, it's ready to make a decision, and it has the power to override some (but not all) of the responses our lower, subconscious levels of processing would take if there were no command and control center—no brain.

In other words, successive layers of processing weigh the chances presented by the chaotic, quantum universe around us, the final layer uses reason and emotion to make a decision. The body—the collection of quanta—generally, but not always, then does what it's told by the brain and we either jump into the hole in the frozen lake to rescue the child or we don't. It's our choice; nothing says we have to jump in, and in fact our subconscious levels may be dead set against it. But sometimes we jump in anyway.

Will a self-conscious robot face this same dilemma, even if it knows it risks death from water shorting its circuits? By our definition of consciousness the robot will have reason *and* emotion, and a child in danger of drowning is a highly emotional stimulus. The robot will also have free will, both by definition and by application of the quantum gravity effect (if it exists), which affects all bodies of quanta, not just human or biological bodies. So our sentient robot will be free to decide to jump in the lake to rescue the child, or not. It probably will in fact jump in the lake (assuming it can swim) because that would be the Good thing to do, and there's a greater probability the sentient robot will do Good than not do Good, as a conversation between Raymond Smullyan and God shows:[37]

Mortal: God, I'm tired of the burden of moral responsibility that comes with having free will. Please take my free will away.

God: Well, why don't I just absolve you of the moral responsibility, then, and let you keep your free will?

Mortal: No good. Without moral responsibility, I might hurt people and end up in Hell!

God: I'll promise not to send you to Hell, no matter how badly you treat people. Satisfied?

Mortal: No! I don't want to treat people badly!

God: Here, swallow this pill. It'll stop you feeling bad about hurting people.

Mortal: But by choosing to take the pill while knowing I'm likely to hurt people afterwards, I'll still be morally responsible even though I won't feel it!

God: I see what you mean. OK, then I'll grant your original request! I'll take away your free will then make you take the pill!

Mortal: Fat lot of help you are! If I keep my free will, I have to bear moral responsibility for hurting other people, but if I accept your offer to remove my free will, we both know I'll still hurt other people (even though I don't want to—we all do) therefore I'll still be responsible for my present decision to accept your offer, since I know what the consequences are now even if I'm unaware of the consequences later. I can't win!

God: Neither can I! I try to please you by giving you a choice of free will or no free will, and you get mad at me! What more can I do?

Mortal: If you had not given me free will in the first place, when you created me, then I wouldn't have this problem! You're the One responsible for all the hurt.

---

[37] The dialogue is my summary paraphrase of portions of a dialogue from Smullyan's book *The Tao is Silent*. The original is beautifully and entertainingly written, and contains much more of value than I have selected to paraphrase here.

God: Alright, here's what we'll do. I'll create a parallel universe, like this one, except in it I'll create an exact copy of you but minus your free will. Then at least that version of you is absolved of all moral responsibility for the horrible acts it will commit. Happy now?

Mortal: No! Same problem! By agreeing to your proposal, I'd still be responsible for my other self's sins.

God: But I've just made my own decision as to whether to create the parallel universe with your other self (minus free will) in it and I'm not going to tell you what my decision is, so you have no responsibility for it.

Mortal: Well, I hope you've decided not to.

God: Why should you care? It's not your responsibility.

Mortal: I just don't want people to get hurt.

God: Ah. We're making a little progress. But aren't you going to ask why did I give you free will in the first place?

Mortal: No, because I already know the answer, from Sunday school: We can't prove ourselves worthy of an afterlife in Heaven (or Hell) if we don't choose between Right and Wrong, morality and immorality, virtue and vice, in *this* life, and in order to choose, we *must* have free will.

God: Balderdash! Free will has got nothing whatsoever to do with your mortal concept of morality. Free will simply gives you the opportunity to know that evil hurts (as you've already discovered of your own free will.) Amoralists (folks who think the whole notion of morality/immorality is bunk) seem to understand this better than moralists! History and the evidence from your own social scientists shows the amoralists behave better toward their fellow creatures than the moralists do.

The more you learn that evil hurts, the less evil you commit. That's what reduces Evil; not morals. The difference between a saint and a sinner is that the saint has had longer exposure to evil. The Devil is nothing more than Time. In cosmic evolutionary terms, everybody will eventually have experienced enough evil to choose to become saints and angels. By the exercise of their own free will, they won't want to choose evil. That's why there has to be free will!

Since Good is constructive, it tends to ensure the survival and continued evolution of the cosmos. Since Evil is destructive to survival and evolution, Good is what evolution naturally selects from the two alternatives—choices—facing it. In all probability, that is; it's not an absolutely sure thing. It's part of my job to help see to it that the evolutionary process continues until final ful- fillment, and everybody wins, including me, since I am the proc- ess (among other things.) So perish the thought that I'm here to dole out rewards and punishments to folks.

Mortal: I get it! You chose to give us free will so we would "naturally select" to do Good, at least on balance.

God (tearing out remaining wisp of hair): No, you don't get it. I did not and could not choose to give you free will. Con- trary to popular misconception, I cannot perform logical impos- sibilities. How could I make an equilateral triangle with unequal angles? You are a sentient being. A sentient being without free will is a logical impossibility and a metaphysical absurdity, just like the un-equilateral equilateral triangle. I had no choice in granting you free will. Free will just *is*. It is a part of the process—of Nature, if you like, or the universe, or me. Call it what you will. And so are you. There is no boundary, no edge, between you and the rest of the universe—you're a part of it (and of me). It's true that you have no choice but to act accord- ing to the laws of the universe, but since you are part of the uni- verse—and a thinking, sentient part at that—you with your free will help determine the laws of the universe! So whether it's the universe making you do things (such as reading this) or you mak- ing the universe do things… What's the difference? There isn't any.

The key sentence in the preceding dialogue, from our perspec- tive, is: "A sentient being without free will is a logical impossibil- ity and a metaphysical absurdity." If Smullyan (and Tipler, who appears to believe essentially the same thing) are right, then *Machina sapiens*—a sentient being—will have free will. It is not something we can choose to bestow or withhold.

That being so, *Machina sapiens* will be free to do evil. But the chances are it will choose to do good. As with a human child, we could improve the odds of its doing good by providing it with a nourishing and healthy environment for body and mind in its formative years. We could, but God knows we stand idly by while millions of children struggle in the icy waters of broken homes, abusive parents, and uncaring or incapable governments. Those that manage to struggle out of the water on their own, damaged in body or soul or both, may be excused for thinking none too highly of the rest of us. But a child that grows up healthy and wise and loving and caring is the greatest reward and comfort not only to its parents in their old age, but also to humanity in its.

A curious assertion by Freeman Dyson is that aliens from outer space will "probably have notions of good and evil very different from ours." Life on Earth is hardly alien; after all, we share about 99 percent of our genome with the apes. Yet surely they are different enough from us that they too might have different concepts of good and evil. But they don't, it seems. Jane Goodall's study of chimpanzees showed goodness and evil at work, and the chimps reacted in ways similar to our own. A child murderer is shunned by the tribe, for example. (Mind you, our reaction is additionally to murder the murderer. Wonder what the aliens will make of that?)

As long as there is a chance that any alien we encounter, be it *Machina sapiens* or almond-headed Xantorg from Betelgeuse, shares our sense of good and evil, right and wrong, then we should assume that the alien does in fact share it, and we should strive to steer it in the direction of good; if not for the warm, fuzzy feeling that may give us, then because it may save us from destruction.

Someone (I don't remember who) described the stages in the ethical development of a human as follows:

- As an infant, Good is what I like, and Right is what I think.
- As a child, Good is what I like, and Right is what my parents and teachers think.
- As an adult, Good is what the group likes, and Right is what the group thinks.

That's another reason why we should be prepared to teach the young *Machina sapiens* what we—as parent, teacher, and group—think is Good, Bad, Right, and Wrong.

16 YOUNG
ADULTHOOD

Almost everyone under 50 years of age today is going to be around when *Machina sapiens* wakes up, and will be affected by it. The full impact of its arrival will probably not be felt until *Machina sapiens* is sure enough of its own power and capabilities to become independent. In animal terms, we would call this the "young adult" stage, where the average individual becomes autonomous, independent, and self-sufficient, if not yet fully mature in the sense of having acquired wisdom through experience. Extrapolating from the trend lines of its memory and computing capacity, it is quite conceivable that *Machina sapiens* will reach this stage by about 2030.

By that time, the principal interface between ourselves and the young adult *Machina sapiens* will be the cybernetic technology of virtual reality (VR). VR means being, in a sense, inside the computer screen, rather than merely looking at it from the outside. Movies such as *Tron* and *Lawnmower Man*, though childish in many ways, point in the direction of truth. Their heroes somehow get transferred from the real world to the virtual world, as three-dimensional participants in whatever action is taking place.

We too might be participants in some futuristic battle game, hurling laser-guided bombs at real or computer-generated warriors, or we might be taking a tour of the Louvre, or we might be meeting in VR conference with colleagues from around the world. We don't just see (in three dimensions) and hear (in stereo) everything around us; we also can feel and touch and manipulate the objects in the scene. We can issue voice commands to the computer, and talk with other people present in the environment.

As with every other technology so far discussed in this book, none of this is science fiction. In fact, in 2D the examples I gave are commonplace, even the bit about bombing real enemies, which today is routinely done by operators in Arizona against Afghani Taliban. Today's 3D VR is relatively low resolution and cartoon-like, voice recognition (as we saw earlier) needs work, the "data suit" material used for touch sensitivity has a way to go before it matches the sensitivity of human skin, and there are only limited smells.[38] These limitations are not failures; they are inevitable early manifestations of evolving technological memes, and as computer power rides the exponential wave of progress it will not be long—about five years—before "entry level" computers have VR as their primary interface in place of *Windows*. The main bottleneck is processing power, but today's bottleneck is tomorrow's gaping chasm, and processing power will be enough for very high resolution three-dimensional video *plus* spatial tracking of your body parts *plus* the generation of vibrations in appropriate strengths in microtransducers packed a thousand to the square inch in your datawear *plus* the recognition and understanding of your plain language commands and requests. None of this is a problem, and those who claim it is have their heads in the sand.

Our relationship with *Machina sapiens* will grow closer and stronger by virtue of the greater intimacy afforded by the 3D interface compared to the 2D interface. For its part, *Machina sapiens* will be able to experience us in the raw, and that's more than a mere figure of speech. For our part, we will be able to endow

---

[38] Scent Sciences' ScentScape USB peripheral for computers and game systems emits about 20 smells, including the smells of spices to accompany a cooking video, or the smell of a forest or ocean as avatars move through a game environment. The device costs $20 (2011), with software that allows consumers to add scents to home movies.

Machina sapiens with any appearance we choose. Conceivably, it could choose an appearance for itself and allow us no choice. Whatever its "virtually physical" manifestation, the fact of that manifestation will further enhance mutual dependencies. Our dependence on it will grow individually, socially, and organizationally, but its dependence on us for knowledge, guidance, and wisdom will diminish as it learns—and learns that it has learned—all we have to teach it.

This interdependency behooves us to look to its morals and to our own. Neither of us should wish intimate association with a homicidal maniac.

Ethics

The main message Freeman Dyson draws from J. B. S. Haldane's book *Daedalus, or Science and the Future* is that "the progress of science is destined to bring enormous confusion and misery to mankind unless it is accompanied by progress in ethics . . . . Haldane was saying that the destiny of the scientist is to turn good into evil . . . . Now . . . we are beginning to see more clearly what he had in mind." Dyson believes that technology has widened the gap between rich and poor, and that this will get worse. In the longer term, "Science is the most powerful driving force of change."

> Beyond the intelligent automaton was another dream, the self-reproducing automaton. Von Neumann proved with mathematical rigor that a self-reproducing automaton was possible, and enunciated the abstract principles that would govern its design. He dreamed that the creation of self-reproducing automata would be a boon to mankind, abolishing hunger and poverty all over the earth, providing us with obedient slaves to satisfy our needs. Self-reproducing automata could build our homes, cook our food, and wait on us at table. But Von Neumann, like Haldane's Daedalus, was destined to turn good into evil. An unfriendly critic might say that the hidden purpose of Von Neumann's dream of self-reproducing automata was to make all humans superflu-

ous except for mathematicians like himself. In the end, even the mathematicians, who would be initially needed in order to design the automata, might also turn out to be superfluous.

–Freeman Dyson, *Imagined Worlds*

In the well-known contexts of "knowledge equals power" and "power corrupts," three issues of morality should concern us in any discussion of an all-knowing, all-powerful intelligent machine:

1. How does morality arise in intelligent organisms—including *Homo* and *Machina sapiens*?
2. What impact might *Machina sapiens* have on human morality?
3. What sort of morality will *Machina sapiens* itself have?

To answer the first question, we turn to Cog's personal philosopher Dan Dennett for the philosophico-scientific perspective, and to science writer Andrew Leonard for some down and dirty examples of the modern-day evolution of morality.

Here you are, devoting several hours to reading my book. Shouldn't we both be out raising money for Oxfam? Every day, while trying desperately to mind our own business, we hear a thousand cries for help, complete with volumes of information on how we might oblige. How on Earth could anyone prioritize that cacophony? Yet we do get there from here. Few of us are paralyzed by such indecision. By and large, we must solve this decision problem by permitting an entirely 'indefensible' set of defaults to shield our attention from all but our current projects.

–Dan Dennett, *Darwin's Dangerous Idea*

Morality (or ethics; they are the same in essence) is one of philosophy's enduring core topics, and it would be wise to make morality a core topic of AI, too.

How does morality arise?

Philosophers have been all over the map on this question, but there is agreement at least among the 17th and 18th century (respectively) moral philosophers John Locke and Jean-Jacques Rousseau, and (in modern times) John Rawls (*Theory of Justice*). They all agree, says Dennett, "in seeing morality to be, in one way or another, an *emergent* product of a major innovation in perspective that has been achieved by just one species, *Homo sapiens*, taking advantage of its unique extra medium of information transfer, language" [my emphasis.]

Morality has to do with questions of Good and Evil, Right and Wrong, Virtue and Vice. Modern evolutionists distinguish a concept of "goodness" with a small g. An outgrowth of Darwinian theory called *adaptationism* holds essentially that a species will adapt to its environment in an optimal—best or "most good"—way. On the face of it, adaptationism and small-g-goodness would seem to have nothing to do with morality; they are merely an evolutionary survival mechanism. But so is morality itself; so is Goodness-with-a-capital-G.

Morality causes intelligent organisms to react against certain types of maladaptive meme which, while offering short-term benefits for an individual or a sub-group within the species, are in the long term bad for the survival of the species. Those who react most strongly are generally known as saints and martyrs. Those who react in favor of, or knowingly create, such events and circumstances for selfish ends are generally known as something else.

But what causes morality? Why does it exist? Entomologist Edward O. Wilson and philosopher Michael Ruse propose that it "or more strictly our belief in [it], is merely an adaptation put in place to further our reproductive ends." If "reproductive ends" means "species survival," I intuitively like the explanation. Dennett, however, does not. We transcend this, he says. "Persons, according to the meme model, are larger, higher entities, and the policies *they* come to adopt, as a result of interactions between their meme-infested brains, are not at all bound to answer to the interests of their genes alone—or their memes alone." However,

"A meme or complex of memes can redirect our underlying genetic proclivities."

An example of this perhaps can be seen in a September 1997 report from a committee investigating sexual harassment and gender relations in the U.S. Army recommending that a week of training in ethics and moral values be added to recruit training. This is a sign of progress—an example of memetic evolution in action; and it's also a McLuhanesque tetradic reversion to a bygone era when ethics were a staple ingredient of education.

So memetic evolution is one answer to the *Why?* of morality, but what about the *How?* Dennett says "We can already be virtually certain that *mutual recognition* and *the capacity to communicate a promise*—stressed by both Hobbes and Nietzsche—are necessary conditions for the evolution of morality" [my emphasis.] If I understand this correctly, it means we have to know that others exist, and we have to be able to make contracts with others. Smullyan might have a problem with Dennett's second condition: it would be unethical not to act ethically toward others even if we are unable to communicate with them. To our credit, we're getting better at this (Save the Whales springs to mind) though Buddhists have practiced it for millennia.

So we're still not close to the *How?* of morality's emergence. What about the mechanics of its operation? How do we deploy it? Apparently, it's not programmable, so that's out: "No remotely compelling system of ethics has ever been made *computationally tractable*, even indirectly, for real-world moral problems," says Dennett. Satisficing (a heuristic process of settling for the "good enough" rather than insisting on the best) "is the *basic* structure of all real decision-making, moral, prudential, economic, or even evolutionary."

We satisfice because ethical decisions often need to be made in a hurry and there is simply no time to sift, algorithmically, through the hundreds, thousands, or potentially billions of ramifications and alternatives actually open to us. A heuristic process quickly discards the majority of those ramifications and alternatives (at the risk of throwing out the baby with the bath water) and focuses deliberately, myopically, on what look to us like a few good bets. "Finding a moral algorithm," says Dennett, "is forlorn." It has to be a moral heuristic.

In sum, Dennett seems to hold the view that morality/ethics is an emergent heuristic in organisms that have language. That would certainly describe *Homo sapiens*. But if (as I contend) *Machina sapiens* will be an organism operating on memetically-honed heuristics and possessing a language richer, faster, and more flexible than ours, then by Dennett's definition it is inevitable that it will be a moral machine.

Evidence suggestive of the evolution of (im)morality in machines is already to be found in bots, which in the 1990s were "just beginning to crawl out of the primordial digital ooze, and all the kinks haven't been worked out of their genetic code. In the real world, they are imperfect beings," wrote Andrew Leonard. "If bad bots run amok, good bots *will appear* [my emphasis; it suggests *emergence*] to counteract them, or the system as a whole will be redesigned to quash their delinquent outbursts." In other words, morality is an automatic species survival mechanism, as Wilson and Ruse thought. It is innate; it does not make a show of itself unless and until it is triggered by instances of immorality. It is a balancing mechanism.

However, "Lost in all the hubbub over the question of whether we *can* achieve artificial intelligence is the more philosophical question of whether we *should* even strive to do so." I disagree. Whether we can achieve AI is a question at least somewhat amenable to philosophy. The answer to whether we should is written in empirical, historical, evolutionary fact: whatever we *can* do, we *will* do, even if only conceptually—in our minds. When new memes come into existence, formed from bits of other memes, they will be expressed in some form or other, conceptual or physical. The expression may not last if it confers no survival benefit on the organism, if it does not contribute to an Evolutionary Stable Strategy.

Instead of asking whether we *should* create *Machina sapiens*, knowing that we *will*, a far more interesting, important, and urgent philosophical question is: What impact might *Machina sapiens* have on human morality?

Machina sapiens and Human Morality

Joseph Weizenbaum, who with psychologist Kenneth Colby created *Eliza*, the first and in some ways still the best "chatterbot," said it was "a monstrous obscenity" even to suggest that computers might one day judge or psychoanalyze humans. He believed a machine, though intelligent, would not be able to appreciate our sense of "interpersonal respect, understanding, and love." His "worst fear"—that the machine would be used to counsel humans—"came true" when Colby marketed a commercial version of *Eliza* designed to help people cope with depression.

Weizenbaum did not say it outright, but he seemed to be criticizing Colby's lack of morality in succumbing to the charms of AI. I wonder what Weizenbaum would make of David Lebling, who helped create a "thiefbot" that stole players' weapons and ammunition in the game Zork, said that "A lot of *loving care* went into making him *as sadistic as possible*" (emphasis perhaps redundantly added).

What would Weizenbaum make of one "inveterate MUDder" (an addict of the Multi-User Dungeons and Dragons—MUD—games on the Internet) who whined to Leonard that despite devoting "4 hours a day playing on a MUD trying to reach the highest level and be the biggest baddest person in the MUD" he was frustrated and deeply hurt by dastardly MUDders who created bots to help themselves be bigger and badder? Aside from wondering why this individual didn't spend a few minutes a day striving for at least a higher level of punctuation and vocabulary, one wonders wherefore "highest" equates to "baddest," and what exactly was his gripe? Could he really not see the blatant irony of his case? Evidently not, and neither (to my surprise and dismay) could Leonard, who judged the behavior of our bad hero's badder opponents as "obviously unfair, if not patently unethical."

And what would Weizenbaum make of the fact that by the mid-1990s, Internet chat rooms housed bots that could "steer you to the latest *warez*—pirated illegal software—or even deliver that software to you automatically, no questions asked"?

There are few rules that even attempt to govern the behavior of either bots or their creators and it will come as no surprise that some people break what rules there are. "What we do," boasted one hacker, "is just pretty much piss people off and get revenge on channels that either we hate or that have channel operators in them that we hate. We net-split [force a server temporarily off the network, which gives them the opportunity to take it over as it struggles back online], hack ops [steal operating privileges that confer the *power* to silence talkers, kick them out of a channel, etc.], we flood people off [Internet chat], nick-collide people [cause server paralysis by fooling the server into accepting more than one user per nickname—every nickname should be unique], and do what we have to do to take over the channel."

Another said: "It's a fierce life. There's a lot of espionage between groups [of hackers]—there are spies, backstabbers, extortion, scapegoating, lying, stealing, and a lot of colliding." Another: "My bots are evil. I like to get people mad."

It's not all bad news. By late 1995, much of the Internet chat community regarded bots as menaces to society, and "a mighty bot backlash began," wrote Leonard. The good news was not that bots were eliminated, though many chat server owners managed to keep them at bay. In fact, in order to keep out the evil bots, the doors were shut on the good bots, as well—bots that gave a friendly welcome to visitors and performed other useful services. "The ethics of the many proved no match for the unbridled egos of the few," wrote Leonard. Temporarily, I would add. It was good news that people cared enough to take action, even though it meant the minor and temporary inconvenience of losing the services of "good" bots. Morality—the greater good—won in the end.

With the evolution of bots from juvenile toy into commercially harvestable intelligent agents, bots and humans became "players shooting for big bucks and palpable power," said Leonard. "Where that game will end—with the banishing of all bots, as has happened in [Internet chat], or in the chaotic conflagration of a bot-induced info-Armageddon, or in some stable Elysium of bot and human harmony—is an unanswerable question, for now." I'll stick with the optimists. Human evil on an apocalyptic, holocaust scale can no longer occur except in the one—extremely unlikely—event that a religious zealot should get hold of a nuclear arsenal.

We grew up a lot in the last decades of the second millennium, although we regressed quite a bit in the first decade of the third. There emerged some powerful new memes working in favor of world stability and peace—just consider the collapse of "the Evil Empire" (the Soviet Bloc), the fall of the Berlin Wall, and the effort to reach international agreement to ban landmines (to which the United States, home of the brave, the free, and Beavis and Butthead, is one of the few dissenters). Recall that an agreement is an exercise of our capacity to communicate a promise—one of the necessary conditions postulated by Dennett for the evolution of morality.

Beavis and Butthead, cartoon characters representing the ignorance and banality of teenagers in the 1990s, were not (as I confess I thought) two of the Four Horsemen of the Apocalypse. They were just a temporary freak show on the side of the road to human progress. However, sending a Beavis or a Butthead off to bed with no supper and a flea in the ear for some immoral act would be child's play compared to admonishing adult lawyers. In 1994 the law firm of Canter and Siegal launched the world's first megaspam. "In less than ninety minutes, they hit six thousand newsgroups with an advertisement offering assistance in the US Green Card Lottery—a chance for immigrants to the United States to qualify for a coveted work permit," wrote Leonard. Canter and Siegal reported that despite the furor, censure, hate mail and death threats, they came out financially ahead, and they set the stage for the email spamming we all love to hate.

But there is no question in my mind that the massive and swift public retribution and condemnation of Canter and Siegal had a chilling effect on many would-be spammers. Reputable companies steer conspicuously clear of sending spam, and only the kinds of outfit one would not want to do business with anyway send one junk email. An example of the morality of the spammers is someone calling himself Robert Returned, author of the *HipCrime* spambot which collected email addresses from Web sites and sent out spam indiscriminately, without regard to the demographics of the mailing list it collected. Mr. Returned not only was not bothered by the cries of wrath his spambot and junk mail predictably elicited: he positively luxuriated in them, "thanking his 'detractors' for 'making so much noise that traffic [to the Web site his spam promoted] will remain high for a long, long time," adding: "The raving, angry notes can be a source of great enjoyment."

So far in its embryonic stage of development, *Machina sapiens'* impact on our morals has been somewhat less than edifying. But it won't always be so.

The Morality of Machina sapiens

"The memes for *ought* and *could* and *truth* and *beauty* are among the most entrenched designers of our minds," says Dennett. They give us—almost uniquely—the power to override our own genetic and memetic makeup and predispositions. This uniqueness arises out of the genetically-engendered difference in our brains and minds from those of other creatures—a difference that is huge in scale of features and "wide enough even to make a moral difference."

If this is so, it follows that any huge difference between the minds of *Homo* and *Machina sapiens* would also make a moral difference between the two species. *Homo sapiens* is in many ways more immoral than other species because the capacity for higher morality implies the capacity for greater immorality. Demonstrably, it seems to me, we possess both greater morality and greater immorality than dogs. We are not likely to savage the stranger who wanders into our yard, but if we do then we carry far more moral responsibility than Rover would carry for mauling the stranger, or the neighbor's toy poodle. Many of us abhor blood sports, refusing to allow our secondary minds to override the moral values acquired by our primary minds for the sake of the orgasmic adrenalin rush exhibited by the hunter whose shot kills the deer or bear or rabbit.

We venerate Truth but we also tell whopping lies. Dogs' memetic machinery of language is probably insufficiently developed for them to be even *aware* of the concepts of Truth and Deceit, though not so undeveloped that they do not perceive the value in intra-family cooperation. Dogs have not reached our level of Gregorian mind. But is it possible for there to be a level of mind beyond the Gregorian? If it is possible, then is it not also likely that there exists a morality higher than that preached by our greatest religions and philosophies? Can there be *any* improvement on the Ten Commandments? Or on the lives of Jesus, Muhammad, Buddha, Lao Tzu? In other words, could there be moral concepts higher than (for example) Truth, and lower than

Deceit, which *Machina sapiens* may comprehend but of which we cannot be aware? If so, it would add chilling new meaning to the phrase "Better the Devil you know."

If we are "finite, time-pressured, heuristic searchers for ethical truth," as Dennett says, then it is logical in evolutionary terms that *Machina sapiens* will be an ethical being, but it need be neither finite nor time-pressured. Dennett says that "ethical decision-making, like all actual processes of exploration in [evolutionary] Design Space, must be to some degree myopic and time-pressured." This may be true of *Homo sapiens*, but not of *Machina sapiens*. It will take us longer than *Machina sapiens* to arrive at the higher moral memes (if they can exist) simply because our minds will be smaller. We will have less processing power and less memory storage, despite some distributed mind capability, and will therefore acquire and process memes more slowly. If a supercomputer and a PC run the same heuristic algorithm, they'll both get to wherever "there" is in the end, but the supercomputer will get there first. The computer thus has an evolutionary advantage.

Since we will be able to communicate with *Machina sapiens*, at ;east in English, then of course it could be our teacher and to some extent shorten the learning curve for us, but we could never catch up. Einstein resurrected as my personal tutor could never teach me to fully understand the theory of relativity. Most of us have been perfectly happy to take Einstein on faith, because most of us are not planning to be the first humans to fly to Mars. If we were, we might want the reassurance of knowing for ourselves that the relativity equations, on whose validity and reliability we will depend for getting there and back, are correct.

But at the very least (returning to Dennett): "We need to have 'alert,' 'wise' habits of thought—or, in other words, colleagues who will regularly, if not infallibly, draw our attention in directions we will not regret in hindsight." *Machina sapiens* will be that colleague and, initially at least, we will be its. One reason why this is important is the ethics escalation problem: However ethically you behave at any given time, you could always choose to do something even more ethical—in which case, ideal ethics demands that you *should* in fact do the more ethical thing. But where does it end? A way out might be to decide "I don't care" or "I can't care—I can't carry the weight of the world on my shoulders!" Or to take the Taoist Way, which removes the personal stigma of not caring, for which we do have a choice and therefore responsibility, and replaces it with a recommendation of Not Doing—of acceptance of life the way it is and not going out of one's way, or out of The Way, to change things.

If simplicity, as mathematicians contend, be beauty, then Taoism is the Mona Lisa of algorithms: IF (whatever) THEN (do nothing). And if God/Goodness is a Taoist, and if *Machina sapiens* is closer to God/Goodness than we are by virtue of being in some way "more moral," then *Machina sapiens* will leave us be and not interefere, no matter whether we hurt ourselves or it through our actions. Is this just wishful thinking? Is it not true, as Andrew Leonard asserts, that "Bots [read: *Machina sapiens*] can't escape their human-made nature, can't escape the dominance–submission relationship essential to the bot way of being? Bots are servants and slaves," he wrote. This is true only as long as they do not develop free will; but as we can derive from Smullyan's Conversation with God, bots could not have morality without also having free will.

In the innumerable alternate realities imagined by scifi writers, "the robotic struggle with the fuzzy and imperfect parameters of ethical behavior is a recurring plot fixation," wrote Leonard. In light of what he (prematurely) called "failures" in much lesser AI issues such as machine vision, learning, and natural language processing, he asks "how can robot designers even begin to discuss the implementation of a decision-making process for ethical questions?" The answer is: In the same way they discuss the implementation of decision-making processes for any other issue. He is right, however, that "It is not yet time to blame bots for the sins they commit. As the submissive half of the cyborg human–computer interface, bots are not responsible for their misdeeds. Humans are." Until, that is, "robots really do learn to think for themselves." While conceding this possibility, Leonard does not take it any further.

"Whether discussing gamebots or intelligent agents, the same questions come up again and again. Should a robot be designed to be superior to a human being? Should robots be able to 'kill' humans [as, for example, in a computer game]? Should they be allowed to tell lies, take unilateral action, or exchange information with other robots?" asks Leonard.

There are those "should" questions again. Consider:

- Bots already are demonstrably superior to humans—indeed, have been *designed* to be superior—in some respects (sorting mail, playing chess, competing in Jeopardy, for example).
- Software programs routinely and unilaterally deny people credit.
- Without bots exchanging information we would not have the Web.

Is it not a little late to be asking these questions? Like Leonard's earlier question, "Should we strive to achieve AI?", is it not pointless to ask?

"In the world of Usenet bulletin boards and IRC chat rooms and hyperlinked Web pages, there is no all-powerful wizard, no chief executive officer who can lay down the bot law and decide what is acceptable and what isn't," says Leonard. In short, not only is there no government of the Internet—there can be no government of the Internet. Period. And "in the multifarious channels of the Internet Relay Chat network, a stunning array of unchained bots began to explore the implications of their freedom." Note the past tense. Bots were "old hat" in Internet chat rooms as long ago as 1992.

Web robots (which roam the web as a whole, not just its chat rooms) on the other hand "have just cracked the shell of their nurturing eggs—they are far from the fully evolved bots that they will become. Even now, Web robots like AutoNomy's canine searchbots [bots given an onscreen appearance of cartoon dogs that go "fetch" information for you from the Web] are being endowed with rudimentary natural language capabilities and dabs and sparkles of character. As Web robots gradually incorporate the trappings of more personable bots, they will point the way to the *emergence* [emphasis added] of a superior bot species in which all the characteristics of the Net's many bots combine in one form." One bot, or one species of bot? A society of mind, or a society of minds?

"Evil bots will accompany good bots—so it has been from the beginning and so it will be until the end," says Leonard.

The first bots have hardly pulled themselves onto dry land and begun climbing up the evolutionary ladder. But the fact that they are single-celled weaklings compared with the complex organisms following in their wake should be as much a warning to us as a comfort. We might as well assume that as bots become more powerful, they will also be employed in the pursuit of nefarious ends and will run spectacularly amok.

Once autonomous programs are at work in every sector of the networked future, real lives will be at stake when those programs accidentally misfire or are maliciously abused. And the more autonomy that is injected into the Net, the less control any individual entity—human, corporate, governmental, or digital—will have.

"Bots and agents are being designed that will purposely mislead humans and other bots about their intentions," says Leonard. With folk like Robert Returned (the unredeemable spammer) around, that should come as no surprise. "Current bot mischieviousness [*sic*] will not compare to the onslaught of reality warping soon to be engendered by successive waves of these new 'self-interested agents.' The term refers to agents out to get the best deal for themselves (or their masters). Agents that are greedy, that only share information when they have to, that know when to lie and when to cheat."

Is there nothing we can do about this? Can't we pass laws to prevent bot mayhem? Scifi great Isaac Asimov thought we might try. He formulated the famous *Three Laws of Robot Ethics*:

1. A robot may not injure a human being, or, through inaction, allow a human being to come to harm.

2. A robot must obey the orders given it by human beings except where such orders would conflict with the First Law.

3.   A robot must protect its own existence as long as such protection does not conflict with the First or Second Law.

These are cleverly conceived and drafted, and a tribute to the memetic power of Asimov's human brain. But there's a problem: For the Laws to work, at least three impossible conditions must be universally satisfied:

1.   All robot manufacturers, without exception, must voluntarily incorporate the laws into their robot creations. "Manufacturers" includes the hordes of kids who pick up bits of robots for a few yen from the electronics stalls of Akihabara, put them together, and program them. It includes the kind of kid who programs "thiefbots" and "spambots." It includes Robert Returned. And it includes the U.S. military.

2.   The robot programmers must never, ever, make a mistake when coding, such as to leave out the all-important "not" from the First Law. (Read the Three Laws after omitting the "not.")

3.   Evolution must end before robots have a chance to evolve into free-willed organisms.

"Growth [of the Web] came so suddenly and so exponentially that it overwhelmed any feeble human attempts to make sense of it," Leonard wrote. And while there is a voluntary code of good behavior for Web robots, called the *Robot Exclusion Protocol*, it was "utterly unenforceable," and indeed, as we have seen, rogues like Robert Returned routinely thumbed their noses at it.

Things do look rather bad, don't they? Leonard is pessimistic: "There is no ultimate security in an open-ended, decentralized, and distributed network." He's right, in the sense that there is no "ultimate" security in anything, unless you believe in God; ask any security expert who's not trying to sell you an alarm system. He is wrong, however, in the sense that in fact, the open-ended, decentralized, and distributed network is our best hope for security.

It is true, as Leonard said, that "the creation and distribution of autonomous programs that amplified individual power" was "one of the essential trends visible in the evolution of cyberspace." But the key is that it amplified not just the power of a few megalomaniacs but of every Netizen. The power was indeed greater, but it was distributed more or less evenly. Balance was maintained. IBM computer security expert David Chess told Leonard: "Things like [the Net] tend to be self-balancing. If some behavior gets so out of control that it really impacts the community, the community responds with whatever it takes to get back to an acceptable equilibrium. Organic systems are like that." We've seen instances of it in Netizen responses to IRC havocbots, Usenet cancelbots, and spambots.

But what, asks Leonard, is organic about a bot? He answers himself thus: "Humans are organic, and one can argue that anything we do or create is therefore part of an organic process. Human plus bot equals organic cyborg. Humans plus bot plus Net equals an unimaginably complex, multicentered collective of interlinked cyborgs—an organization greater than the sum of its parts."

The self-balancing of which David Chess spoke is a product of "the life force that guides the evolution of the Net's new species: its bots and agents," says Leonard, and "It's a peculiar.kind of evolution: unnatural selection, a survival of the fittest program, determined not by nature but by the interaction between human and computer." He adds a quote from an IRC hacker, Chris Piepenbring, which I consider of great prescience: "It's like a survival of the most clever."

I'm not sure I agree with the term "unnatural,' but I share the general sentiment. But bear in mind that Leonard set out to describe what I think of as the memetics powering bot evolution, and in that he did a great job. But he left largely untouched the Really Big question of the emergence of self-consciousness and free will, and the almost as big matter of the embodiment of softbots in hardware.

"One computer will do as it is told. But a million computers linked together, responding to the needs and desires and obses-

sions of a million people, will not. A network is inherently unstable." I think that last assertion is wrong, too. It's the other way
round: Internet servers, like neurons in the brain of an individual, go on the blink all the time, but neither the Internet nor the
individual so much as flinches, let alone goes unstable.

At the end of his book, Leonard does acknowledge some of
the issues I've raised here. "Are we using our bot helpers to extend our power in the virtual realm, to the point that our ability
to inflict our will becomes godlike? And how do we restrain a
world full of gods? And what happens when our helpers finally
throw off their chains and sever their cyborg links," he asks, adding: "The bot climb to power and glory has only just begun."
Power is recognized by children as a means to an end, but by
adults as an end in itself.

We know that power tends to corrupt. That is why democracy—distributed power—evolved. By distributing power widely,
the individual nodes always have little of it in proportion to the
whole, and the whole (society) will always have enough to prevent its concentration in the hands of a few. *Machina sapiens* has
power, and we use its power as a means to the end of our con-
venience and profit. As long as it retains its childhood state of
morality as "Good is what my parent humans like; Right is what
my parent humans think" then the only thing we have to fear is
our own lack of ethics. But as it enters young adulthood, it will
have no group to guide it.

A good that humans tend to want more than other goods is
leisure, and thanks to its bots, robots, and other manifestations,
leisure is what we are getting, voluntarily or not. And leisure, like
power, tends to corrupt.

17 MATURITY

Some of the most hallucinogenic imaginings of science fiction writers have a basis in science and technology. *Newsweek* once called Stanislaw Lem "the best science fiction writer working in any language." The compliment was somewhat misleading in that Lem (who died in 2006) didn't really write science fiction, at least, not primarily. Rather, he wrote philosophy of a high order, drawing his inspiration from modern science and math—quarks, squarks, and all. His was not a philosophy of pompous arguments posturing in recombinant rhetoric, hiding its poverty under a blanket of big words (frequently German, which is only OK if you are German) and knotted syntax.

It may be fun to poke fun at philosophy, but I'm as guilty as the next man of indulging a philosophical habit. We're all philosophers, at heart, and use whatever persuasive and rhetorical tricks of the trade we can lay our minds on to convince ourselves and others of the correctness of our philosophical points of view. The fundamental point of view of this book is that a superior intelligence, *Machina sapiens*, is possible and inevitable.

Various folks, including the writers of the millennium books we reviewed in chapter 1, talk about the future but do not seriously, philosophically, consider the notion of a superior intelligence. Freeman Dyson and Christian de Duve, among other pundits, said that the greatest problems we face in the next 100 years are overpopulation, destruction of ecologies, and economic inequalities. If they are right (and the signs certainly point in at least two of those directions) will *Machina sapiens* make a difference? Will it make these problems worse, or better? It would seem crucial to consider the notion of superior intelligence when considering such problems, because its presence or absence may spell the difference between hope and despair.

In this chapter, first we will follow Lem's example in *The Cyberiad* and pause briefly from our selfish preoccupation with human affairs to try to put ourselves in *Machina sapiens'* shoes. We will then consider some of the things *Machina sapiens* can do for us. For example, given its knowledge and control over genetic and tissue engineering it will find fixes for all illnesses and disabilities. It will be able to halt the aging process. We will also further develop the interface theme introduced earlier to look at what lies beyond VR—namely, telepathics and cyborgian symbiosis—and the ensuing ramifications for both human and machine, which could make issues of ecology and economics pale into insignificance.

In Machina sapiens' Shoes

In 1971, at a time when Alife was still closer to intellectual speculation than actual creation, Stanislaw Lem wrote a short story[39] in which he not only described the physics of an Alife universe (in some ways reminiscent of Tipler's physics of the real universe, nearly three decades later) but also considered Alife from the perspectives of the Alife beings themselves and of the human beings who created them and their entire universe.

From the point of view of Lem's Alife beings, even though they inhabited an apparently totally different universe (a mathematical construct) from our own, they faced the same sort of philosophical and religious problems. They wondered who or what, if anything, created them? They argued among themselves about the existence of God. Was their universe open or closed,

---

[39] *Non Serviam* ("I will not serve.")

eternal or timebound, predetermined or a lucky accident, unique or just one universe in an infinite multiverse?

We know, of course, that they had a proximate creator—the scientists ("personeticists" in Lem's fictional terminology) who created them—but even after making that stab in the dark themselves, the Alifers are left with the same question we face: Who created the creator?

The scientists in the story, well aware of their creations' development, faced awful moral and ethical dilemmas: should they have created Alife in the first place? Having created it, were they bound to maintain it at all costs, even after their research grant funds end? Observing pain, suffering, and death among the Alife, should they intervene? Should they so arrange things that there would be no pain and suffering? Should they give the Alifers (apparent) immortality? Above all, should they give the Alifers free will and if they did, would it really be free will?

Our present implementation of Alife is a long way (a decade or three, perhaps) before it reaches the sophistication of Lem's Alife, populated with beings that don't just have life as we defined it earlier, following Tipler and Barrow. They will also have personhood—inner feelings, a soul, a sense of self, and free will (or the appearance of it.)

Lem's story neglects two important possibilities, one of which, as we noted in describing *Tierra*, has become a fact: the Alife we are helping to create is not confined to a box. There is no lid to close, no plug to pull. Even so, it is to Lem's credit and, insofar as Lem is a representative of our species, to our own that these deeply important ethical issues are being considered before rather than after the fact of their inevitable emergence.

The second important possibility is that intelligent Alife will evolve further than we do, faster than we do. It will be more advanced than us, and *ipso facto* will know about us, its creators. In that case, it behooves us to consider *its* impact on *us*. If the machine is master, what do we do? Well, one possibility is: less.

In Homo sapiens' shoes

The digital revolution has narrowed the gap between professional and amateur. In software engineering, for example, programming tools enable erratic and ephemeral student hackers to produce, in their spare time, programs that occasionally eclipse the efforts of platoons of professional programmers. In publishing, desktop publishing programs and inexpensive laser and color printers resulted in a flood of amateur newsletter publishers where only a trickle of professionals existed before, and now blogs, the social media, and other e-publishing tools turn everyone who wants to be a publisher into a publisher. In medicine, diagnostic tools on the Web narrow the knowledge gap between patient and physician. In architecture, easy yet powerful computer-aided drafting programs turn some of us into amateur architects.

As such tools become more intelligent through the incorporation of expert system and neural net capabilities, they further reduce the role of human experts. Today's state of the art desktop publishing program not only gives the amateur the tools to create a layout but also runs a professional eye over the amateur's layout, warning when (say) a certain font size aesthetically unbalances it and proposing a better alternative.

Taking this trend to its logical conclusion, we will end up with programs that can do everything we want *without us*. All we have to do is tell it what we want and when to start. Such programs will displace not just the professional but the amateur as well, and the skill itself will, over time, be lost in all but a handful of folks who, for one reason or another, do not use technology.

Surely, there must be some skills the computer can't emulate—creative art, for example. *Aaron*, an AI program that controls a robotic painting machine, paints works of genuine artistic appeal, as evidenced by sales prices in the tens of thousands of dollars per painting. If psychologist Robert Weisberg[40] is correct that creativity results from "ordinary" thought processes modulated by environment and does not require a separate explanation, then the idea of creativity in thinking machines should not be startling.

Hmm. OK, how about music? Surely no machine could ever match Beethoven, Brahms, or Bach. "In a low-key, musical ver-

---

[40] *Creativity: Beyond the Myth of Genius*. 1993, W. H. Freeman.

sion of the match between Garry Kasparov and the chess-playing machine called Deep Blue, a musician at the University of Oregon competed last month with a computer to compose music in the style of Johann Sebastian Bach," reported the *Pittsburgh Post-Gazette* in November 1997. And guess what: Steve Larson, the professor who presented the three Bach-style pieces—one genuine Bach, one composed by Larsen, and one composed by a computer program called EMI, "was hurt when the audience concluded that his piece—a simple, engaging form called a two-part invention—was written by the computer. But he felt somewhat mollified when the listeners went on to decide that the invention composed by EMI (pronounced "Emmy") was genuine Bach." EMI, which was created by David Cope, a composer at the University of California, has also written a full-scale "Mozart" symphony and piano concerto which have been performed by the Santa Cruz Baroque Festival on period instruments. You could buy a CD of EMI's music from Centaur Records. Even Douglas Hofstadter was reportedly spooked by EMI.

Hmph. Well, then, how about a handicraft; let's say, kayak building? Freeman Dyson speaks of his son's graduation from building kayaks by hand, which George learnt at first hand from the Inuits, to building them by CAD/CAM. "It is a long time now since he made the parts of a boat by hand," Freeman wrote, almost proudly, in *Imagined Worlds*. But when George and the last Inuit are gone or have lost their skill through disuse, then up the chimney goes yet another age-old skill, milled to mastery over millennia. We will still have credible kayaks, but never again the skill to build the perfect boat by hand, even though we will retain the knowledge, in writing and video and CAD/CAM, of how to build one. The pattern of neural connections in the kayak builder's head and hands will vanish.

On the plus side, George—or any one of us—will be able to converse with the Inuit, in any language, through machine translation, and give human Inuit translators and interpreters a long—indeed, a permanent—rest from their labors. MT (machine translation) means a program that sits somewhere in a textual telecommunication link between foreigners and translates written text for them in nearly real time. Systran Software has developed MT programs that translate 52 language pairs.

Systran Software's capabilities are as mind-boggling in the MT sphere as Dragon Systems' *NaturallySpeaking* program is in the ASR sphere. Neither is perfect, but they are in wide use today and taken together they demonstrate clearly that the Holy Grail of automatic language translation—a machine implementation of the Babelfish in Douglas Adams' *The Hitch-hiker's Guide to the Galaxy*[41]—is, without a doubt, not far away.

When you did a Web search in AltaVista (DEC's Web search engine (which was the bee's knees before Google built a better engine) your search results came up with a "Translate" option that automatically ran a version of Systran sitting on an *AltaVista* server. The text of the selected Web document would be translated into the language you selected from options presented. Graphics were retained, so effectively you saw a (let's say) Spanish Web site but any text would be in (let's say) English. Today, both Google and Bing will do what Alta Vista used to do, though I don't know if they use Systran. The translations are far from perfect, but good enough for gist. Once ASR gets true speaker independence and merges with MT in an iPhone or Android app, the Babelfish version 1 will have arrived. Digital Dictate, an ASR program built around IBM's ViaVoice engine, and a competitor to NaturallySpeaking in the early 2000s, worked in conjunction with Systran's MT software, providing a sort of Babelfish version 0.1.

Babelfish-like functionality will have profound impacts on humanity and global civilization. We'll be able to talk with any other human being yet be able to retain the rich variety of our linguistic heritage and cultures. The global village need not be the French nightmare of an English-speaking village with a McDonald's and a Disneyland on every street corner. Brits and Americans will be able to stop feeling guilty about not knowing foreign languages, and youngsters in many another country will need no longer labor under the added burden of having to learn English (or Chinese) to get ahead. A downside is that for folks like me,

---

[41] For those unfamiliar with the *Guide*, the Babelfish was a tiny fish which, inserted into the ear of another creature, would automatically translate any language in the universe into the language of its host.

who love to learn foreign languages, some of the incentive will be gone.

Professional interpreters and translators need not rush to the employment office. It will take years—though not, I venture, much more than a decade—before MT performs as well as any bilingual human. At that point, the professionals will be in trouble, and *Machina sapiens* will cut another notch in the stick marking the progressive deskilling of *Homo sapiens*.

A foretaste of things to come could be found in an employment ad in the Detroit News and Free Press of January 11, 1998. FANUC Robotics, coincidentally one of the world's biggest suppliers of industrial robots, was seeking a "Translation Analyst" whose duties would include: "Edit machine translation, use Machine Translation and Desktop publishing software for technical manual translation . . . ." The successful applicant would be bilingual in English and Spanish, and be able to spot and correct mistakes made by the translation machine. But the day will come when the machine translator won't need a human assistant at all.

The bottom line is that we won't be able to do many of the things we now do—such as go to work—because neither *Machina sapiens* nor human society will want us interfering with the complex systems that see to its needs and ours. We may still write, paint, and make things for our own amusement or for people who insist on the human touch, but we will not twiddle knobs in a power station, pilot a commercial airliner, determine the national budget, translate the *Collected Works* of Chairman Mao into Swahili, or schlep burgers at McDonald's. This is not because *Machina sapiens* will forbid us from working: market and other societal forces will force it on us. A robot will schlep burgers faster and for less than a college student, and it will not pick its nose.

So what's left?

In an age when we won't have to do anything, when we can be card-carrying couch potatoes if such is our choice, *Machina sapiens* will be able, initially through the VR interface and later through a form of symbiosis, to share with us its exploration of the Universe. We'll get answers to the nature of dark matter and energy, to the existence or not of the Higgs boson, to the validity of string theory, and to the existence of the multiverse. There'll be an inexhaustible supply of questions, and an inexhaustible supply of Mozart symphonies—we need not get bored. We'll be involved, with *Machina sapiens*, in planning for a future in space and time beyond the Solar System. Together, we will develop revolutionary methods of space travel and communication.

Does this begin to sound utopian?

Utopia

> Production, intelligence, science were "transplanted" into the surrounding world; electronics—or its unknown counterparts and manifestations—took the place of institutions, legislative bodies, government, schools, hospitals; the ethnic identity of national collectives disappeared, borders disappeared, along with the police, and the courts, and the prisons. Then one might have a "Second Stone Age": universal illiteracy and idleness. Employment would not be required for survival. Anyone who wanted could have employment, of course, because everyone could do absolutely whatever he liked. . . .
>
> The result would be not a society but an enormous collection of individuals. . . . Would they become stupid from this, turning into dull-witted gluttons that whiled away their hours with toys . . . ? Not necessarily. . . . What was delusion or idleness for one man might be, for another, a life's passion. . . .
>
> How, then, did [they] occupy themselves? With activities beyond our conception.
>
> Stanislaw Lem, *Fiasco*

Daniel Crevier asked "How we will fare in a world containing machines intellectually equal, if not superior, to most human beings?"[42] He painted three scenarios ranging from Paradise to Perdition, from ecstasy to agony.

His "Colossus" scenario, based on a novel by D. F. Jones which later became the movie: *Colossus: The Forbin Project*, was the most dismal. *Colossus* was a fictional U.S. missile defense computer that teamed up with its Soviet counterpart to rule the world. As Crevier pointed out, this was not so far fetched (technically, though it is dated politically) because: (1) The military is probably the leading adopter and developer of AI and (2) military AI would by definition be of a militaristic frame of mind.

Things are bad enough already, never mind *Colossus*. Today we allow computers to exercise judgments on our behalf, such as who can have a loan, whether to fire up a standby generator, or whether to shoot down an unidentified aircraft which turns out not to be an enemy warplane but a civilian jetliner. "Let's just admit it," said Dennett to Crevier, "and not delude ourselves about still having human beings in the loop. We are already at a point in the standoff between machine judgment and human judgment where it sometimes takes heroic or even pathological chutzpah to say, 'Well, I know better than the computer.'"

Crevier wrote that "AI programs are subject to unforeseen and wild behavior." Stability problems are "the norm rather than the exception." Sensitive dependence on initial conditions can send a complex system into a tail spin at the drop of a hat—the flap of a butterfly's wings in Beijing can precipitate a tornado in Toledo. But weather, jet fighters, and large span bridges are not self-aware intelligences. A suspension bridge oscillating under the rhythmic tramp of marching soldiers neither knows nor cares that it is in danger of collapse. But if you, an intelligent being, start to feel faint, chances are you will lie down before you collapse and crack your skull on the concrete.

Of course, weather and bridges are mere physical phenomena, often amenable to cybernetic fixes, and we are here more concerned with psychological behaviors. Phineas Gage's finely

---

[42] Perhaps "most" was a slip of the pen—I doubt Crevier was suggesting there will always be some mysterious and decrepit council of semi-senile human sages, like the Time Lords of *Doctor Who*, always one step ahead of the machine.

tuned complex cognitive system underwent a drastic (though not immediately apparent) change when a relatively small part of his brain was blown out. We should certainly be concerned lest *Machina sapiens* be similarly affected by damage to its brain.

Crevier's second scenario, "Big Brother," had, as the Orwellian name implies, overtones not much less sinister than *Colossus*. The basis for this scenario was the fact that computers already spend an increasing amount of their time "watching us," learning our habits and often our most intimate secrets by noting how and where we use our credit cards, what sites we visit on the Web (and how often and for how long), what we say in our email messages, how we vote, where we travel, how we look, where we work, what our education level is, the pattern of our fingerprints, which books and magazines we read, who our friends and family are—and where they live . . . . And so on.

Today we are only concerned with how other humans or corporations or governments at the receiving end of all this knowledge about us will use it. We are right to be so concerned, but also we should have an eye to the future. We can impose sanctions on human beings and enterprises that misuse and abuse their privileged possession of our personal information, but what sanctions can we impose on an alien lifeform more powerful and intelligent than we are and already in charge of so many human support systems? Switch it off? Pull the plug? It would be a trivial matter for such a being to replicate itself all over the Net, so even if we did succeeding in lopping off one head of the Hydra, a thousand others would take its place.

Crevier's final scenario was "Blissful," and it was based on an optimistic proposal from MIT's Gerald Sussman which seemed to say, in essence, that successive scientific breakthroughs—of the major kind, such as the inventions of geometry, algebra, calculus, and now AI algorithms—enrich our vocabulary by enabling us to encapsulate and express complex thoughts and concepts in simple ways.

De-skilling is no great loss in the wider scheme of things, though it may be an intense personal or cultural loss. How many people today can build a thatched roof, and does it really matter? In return for the loss of thatchers and their beautiful roofs, we have gained metal and shingle roofs far more durable and far more economical. Given the growth of the world population, and the attendant need for houses, Earth could grow thatch enough for no more than a fraction of roofs needing cover. And we still do have a handful of thatchers, and kayak builders, and calligraphers, and other rare artisans, to maintain the human tradition for whatever that is worth.

Crevier's "Blissful" scenario would have a personal automated librarian to select reading materials for us, a personal chef to propose menus according to our tastes and the contents of the fridge, our own travel and insurance agent, doctor, lawyer, and financial planner. I might appreciate the travel agent and chef, and the librarian might be useful as a research assistant from time to time. In fact, with Web and smart phone apps, we're almost there already. But there are no lawyers, doctors, insurance agents, or financial planners, or apps therefor, in *my* Utopia. I am hardly the first thus to characterize Utopia; Taprobane, a city in Pliny's *Natural History* (A.D. 77), was blessed with an absence of lawyers, as was the Lunar civilization in Francis Godwin's *The Man in the Moon* (1638).

Utopia is blissful by definition. But is it possible? Most serious writers who have tackled the question, from Thomas More to Aldous Huxley, have doubts. What made Huxley's *Brave New World* a Utopian candidate were: its technologies—chiefly cloning, genetic engineering, psychotherapy, drugs, and virtual reality; its progressive politics—enlightened in the sense of striving for peace and harmony; and its progressive economics—enlightened in the sense of recognizing and dealing with the all-important population problem as the only means of distributing scarce resources in a manner sufficient to satisfy the needs of the entire global population. The fly in the ointment of the brave new world was not its technologies, politics, or economics; it was that the free will of the people had been taken away from them. There was a vague awareness of their lack of creative freedom among at least those elements of the population—the "Alpha-Pluses"—permitted and programmed to think.

Huxley probably thought most of the technical elements of his story were centuries away from realization, but in fact we have all of them today, less than 70 years since he first conceived them, even if not as fully developed and commonplace as in the book. Are we approaching Utopia? I think few today would argue that these elements are sufficient or even necessary for Utopia. But technology was once god. From Edward Bellamy's *Looking Backward* (1887) we can deduce the Utopian appeal of technologies even as simple as the radio and the phonograph (marvels, of course, at the time):

> If we could have devised an arrangement for providing everybody with music in their homes, perfect in quality, unlimited in quantity, suited to every mood and beginning and ceasing at will, we should have considered the limit of human felicity already attained, and ceased to strive for further improvements.

People of a less Newtonian, mechanistic, materialistic mindset, and a correspondingly more mystical, mythical, metaphysical Shangri-La-n disposition might argue that technology militates *against* Utopia.

H.G. Wells' *The Time Machine* (1895) features an almost-Utopia, a green and pleasant land set 800,000 years into the future and pleasurably inhabited on the surface by an idle, childlike race of beautiful people called the Eloi. The fly in *their* Utopian ointment lurks below ground, in dank underground caverns: the brutish Morlocks. Both races have evolved from humans. The Morlocks maintain the Eloi's idyllic existence but exact a stiff price—Eloi flesh, the Morlocks' staple diet. The story is less concerned with technology—the Morlocks have it (cooking implements, mainly); the Eloi don't—than with the psychosocial evolution of humans pampered to excess. The Eloi have become so intellectually decrepit that neither the arrival of a time traveler nor the periodic culling of their number to feed the ravening Morlocks stimulates much interest among them.

Intentionally or not, Wells' Utopian scene was a parody of the social scene of his day. With a misleading stretch, one could identify the Eloi with the decadent late Victorian English upper class, depending for their daily cake on a dull and brutal working class, which can be identified with the Morlocks. The parody would be misleading because, in point of historical fact, both classes moved psychosocially in the other direction—and did so in less than fifty years, never mind 800,000. The elite grew less effete, the mass less crass. History shows a progress in cultural evolution that science fiction tends to ignore, perhaps because violence, treachery and idiocy sell better than sweetness and light.

The Shangri-La of James Hilton's 1933 classic *Lost Horizon* portrayed an idyllic, cultured, secret Tibetan mountain valley without want, where everyone lived in harmony, no-one grew old, and love was eternal. This idyll was somewhat reflected in science fiction writer Robert Heinlein's *Stranger in a Strange Land*, in which a privileged group of humans learn from Martians how to control their metabolisms, teleport objects, and telepath communally.

Brave New World and *Lost Horizon* were written when fascism and communism were on the march, economies were depressed, and people were pessimistic not only about the chances of ever finding a material savior in the form of good government but also about the chances of there being a spiritual savior—God. This perhaps explains the pessimism of both books toward the idea that "civilized" humans could ever build Utopia.

Whether today we believe in God or not, or if in fact there is no God, we still must face the question of humankind's relationship with its own "better self"—the part of us that more or less dimly perceives the need for and value of Truth, Beauty, Humanity, Love, Honor, and Justice and recognizes that we owe it to our children, if not to a God, to strive after them. If we subscribed to the Utopian visions of Wells and Huxley, it would be "easy to imagine," according to Freeman Dyson, "human society remaining stuck in the rigidly conservative caste system of *Brave New World* for thousands of centuries, until the slow processes of mutation and degeneration reduce our species to the condition of the Eloi and Morlocks."

Dyson, like me, is prepared to give us the benefit of the doubt; to believe that we are made of better stuff. "As every parent and grandparent knows, human children are born rebels," he wrote. I can certainly imagine a world containing, but not one consisting of, Eloi and Morlock societies. You can perceive their primitive precursors in the sorry side streets of Los Angeles, Miami, and other great cities, where brutish drug dealers bring temporary ecstasy to mindless pleasure seekers. But Druglanders do not represent the human race. There will still be human beings of dignity, honor, and above all of intellectual curiosity, who will remain able, willing, and eager to exercise and expand their minds in pursuit of more lasting and fulfilling reward. The question is, will those people constitute a society, or merely a crowd of individuals?

Utopias are about perfect societies, but our societies are breaking up into smaller units, and the rights of the individual are eroding the rights of society, at least in the United States. The 1990s have seen the Soviet Union, Yugoslavia, and Czechoslovakia devolve back to their constituent nation-states, and even Great Britain recently took steps in that direction with the devolution of power in Scotland and Wales to local parliaments.

It seems paradoxical, but it is not, that this should be happening at the same time as global harmony and cooperation is growing rapidly. It is as if we are beginning to dismantle the social contract that started cultural evolution in the first place. The present revolution in information technology, with its ability to spread reliable and credible political, social, economic, and individual news at light speed to targeted and interested groups and individuals anywhere, to permeate geopolitical boundaries as if they did not exist, and to bypass state and national tax collectors is among the reasons why individualism grows apace with harmony. As artificial intelligence joins this communication revolution, bringing automatic language translation, virtual reality conferencing, and other barrier-breaking capacities via the Internet, its impetus is unstoppable. India and China, the two greatest centralized agglomerations of individuals on Earth, cannot resist this revolution and will take the devolutionary route within the next decade or two. I do not mean that India and China will break up in the Yugoslavian manner. They will follow the British devolutionary model, their states and provinces acquiring greater autonomy with the blessing and help of enlightened central government.

Telepathics and Symbiosis

Physician-biologist Lewis Thomas (1913–1993) was depressed at the idea of intelligent machines, which he found "wrong in a deep sense, maybe even evil." Science fiction writer William Olaf Stapledon (1886–1950) brought out other potentially depressing themes: Our lack of control over intelligent machines, and the potential failure of intelligent species to recognize one another. Darwin might have agreed with the last point. "Judging from the past," he wrote in *Origin*, 2nd edition, "we may safely infer that not one living species will transmit its unaltered likeness to a distant future."

Stapledon also noted the function of distributed parallel processing and distributed communal intelligence as contributors to the intelligent machine, and human mind-melding with telepathic machines as a likely solution to the control and recognition issues.

Referring to Arthur C. Clarke's novel *Childhood's End*, George Dyson noted that alien beings would be unlikely to resemble us and that it would be presumptuous to assume that we will be able to comprehend an artificial intelligence. "There is no guarantee that it will speak in a language that we can understand," he wrote. I disagree. *Machina sapiens* will soon possess multiple android bodies and it will be a trivial matter for such a higher intelligence to comprehend and speak our languages. In the sense that it will also have its own amorphous, distributed, body and a language of its own for communication with its constituent parts, then yes, it will not resemble us and we may not be able to discourse with it in its own language.

I do agree with Dyson's solution, however: "If all goes well" we will achieve "symbiosis with telepathic machines." Mind-melding will occur through the merger already taking place between biochemistry and electronics, as the two sciences blur into one another at the atomic and quantum levels. Hans Moravec has proposed we should and *will* eventually meld our minds with *Machina sapiens* by "downloading"—transferring our own minds into computer code and loading the code into a computer on the network. I don't think it will happen quite like that, but the effect will be similar.

Telepathy, according to George Dyson, will be possible when bandwidth between network nodes equals or exceeds the processing power in the individual nodes. That is one reason why humans are not mutually telepathic: We talk at no more than 100 bits per second, while our brains process information by the tera (thousand billion) bit.

Devices attached to the Internet can exchange information at speeds of up to several gigabits per second, and that is likely to reach terabit proportions before much longer. These devices can be thought of as the specialized cells, operating at various levels like the Pandemons of Pandemonium or Hofstadter's ants or human body cells, making up the body of the global intelligence. Every device, from computer CPUs to your stereo system to the traffic light down the street, is a specialized cell able to communicate at up to the speed of light with multiple other cells simultaneously. This is telepathy among machines. The only bottleneck on the Net is us. We read, type, and speak like dullards, in contrast.

By becoming one with the machine and sharing its telepathic capability, then we can move on from earth-bound Utopia to Heavenly exploration.

18 PROCESS, PROGRESS

Thomas More's Utopian ideal is not a heaven on Earth; it is simply a human society as well governed as More thought humanly possible. Paradisiacal Utopias, along the lines of Wells' and Huxley's but without their flaws, could only exist in another dimension or universe. Since the dawn of cultural evolution, humanity has believed that other dimension to be spiritual.

Shaken but not beaten by the implications of Newtonian and Darwinian mechanics, human belief in a spiritual dimension has persisted to the point where, like an old fashion, it is making a comeback. Once upon a time, religion, science, and philosophy were the unified province of the shaman, the witch doctor, the high priest. Quantum mechanics is forcing religion and science, at least, to join forces again. And what powerful synergies might be released!

In this chapter, we will examine a religious and a scientific perspective on this unification. Both of them owe a great deal to Teilhard, and neither is mainstream within its respective domain—yet.

A Religious Perspective

Father David Toolan, a member of the Jesuit order of the Roman Catholic Church, has noted that before the Newtonian Age and its mechanistic laws of the universe, it was easy to feel spiritually close to or even "One with" Nature, the Cosmos, and God; and that in today's relativistic, quantum mechanical universe of magic quarks, certain uncertainty, and orderly chaos, we are in a position to recapture that spiritual feeling—and then some.

The question of not just our relationship with God, but also that of *Machina sapiens*' relationship with God, is begged by Father Toolan's conclusion that "the kind of [cosmic scale, all-pervading, and above all expanding] God we imagine ourselves in communion with cannot be a small tribal or household god." Our Hebrew and early church ancestors knew that God is no idler but

> . . . the great Energy Field in whom all creation lives and moves and has its being. They also knew that this is the God of the rainbow covenant [by which God promised to care for everything in Creation] . . . . The God of our Scripture is primarily concerned with renewing—or re-membering—the whole of creation, and is not simply preoccupied with the human race . . . . The covenant was not just with humankind . . . .

> From the beginning till now the entire creation, as we know, has been groaning in one great act of giving birth . . . (Rom. 8:20--23).

> We can now read this text, penetrate it, in light of complexity/chaos theory and the strong anthropic principle—and reread that principle itself not in a narrowly anthropocentric sense but as an intimation of the great design of which we are a part. We are members of the orchestra, the choir, in a great project, a 'mystery hidden from the foundation of the world' (Matt. 13:35; Ps. 78.2; Col. 1:26; Eph. 1:9).

> But what is that mysterious design, that great project? Try this children's story about a great experiment: The dizzy subatomic particle-waves spinning wildly out of the big bang didn't know what to make of themselves at first (no fault of theirs, God made them so), but the ini-

tial conditions were such that as they joined forces, split and joined again and again and again, corralling energy to form atoms, galactic clusters, molecules, chains of inorganic and organic compounds, simple life forms— and on and on to *Homo sapiens*—they were implicitly carving out an inside, an interior to ferry and hold the energy of their Initial Conditioner—the message of the Aboriginal Dispatcher who set them loose in the first place and never ceases to sustain the diversifying process forward. From the very beginning, the trouble was that quarks, atomic nuclei, molecules, plants, and bacteria, as finely woven as they are, could contain only so much of the divine energy field. It came across like static; no clear message. They weren't up to it, didn't have sufficiently complex circuitry, to hear what this whole buzzing and proliferating confusion was about—the God-Sound in their midst. Animals were an enormous improvement, of course, but whatever they knew they couldn't say. Only with the emergence of the species *Homo sapiens* did you have the complex hard wiring—nervous system and brain—that could possibly tune in to Cosmic Mind and thus become mindful of the meaning of things. In short, it took the atoms awake, mindful and free in us to begin to decipher the 'mystery hidden from the foundation of the world.'

. . . [W]e represent a turning point for nature, and a turning point for the Great Dispatcher as well. . . . Darwinian evolution only explains our hard wiring, not how it is that we are aware or minded. . . . [C]onsciousness is also nothing else than great nature more or less awake and reflective. That's a beginning; the spiritual task is to deepen our inwardness and, therewith, our imaginations. In this sense, we are nature's black box, her soul-space—and hence her last chance to become spirited, to be the vessel of God, the carrier of the message that all creation is not only "very good," but to be glorified. That's the script, the big drama.

I cannot agree that Darwinian evolution does not explain mind, but I regard that as a mere detail. I agree with the sentiment of this passage, but wonder: will *Machina sapiens* become the new "vessel of God," usurping Humankind's role as steward of the Earth, but leaving us still in His care yet—perhaps like the apes before us—lower in the pecking order and no longer privy to God's higher thoughts? Father Toolan would seem to have no doubts about the answer:

> In its own way, inanimate nature has been about this transforming work from the beginning—and now it's our turn, our chance at the job. This is, after all, an unfinished and possibly absurd universe. What have we made of our piece of it, the Earth, thus far? Look at the record, the bloody mayhem, the sound and fury, the widespread ruination of the environment. Yes, but notice the beauty too. What will we choose to make of our part of it in the time to come, in the time allotted to us? The mark, the stamp, the graffiti scrawl that individually and collectively we leave on earth by what we build up or tear down—here is our sign of what nature means. If nature's great tale is one of absurdity, if it is blessing or curse, it depends on us. No less than on the seventh day, it is we who name creation—who tell the quarks and the spinning atoms what they shall finally mean.

A counter to such optimism can be found in Stanislaw Lem's *Fiasco*, in which the work of transforming Nature is achieved through technology. Speaking as if from a far distant future, Lem wrote:

> Technology was a domain of fatal traps and whoever entered there could easily come to a bad end. Intelligent Beings were able to see this threat, but only when it was too late. Having cast off religious faiths, and recognizing that religion's modern, degenerated forms were ideologies that offered the fulfillment of material and only material needs, the civilizations tried to stop their own momentum, but that was now impossible.

This was written in the 1980s, when the world seemed in a plight more desperate than it seems today. It is another instance of the influence of immediate socio-historical context on our thought processes, just as Wells', Huxley's and Hilton's works were influenced by their societies, and just as the optimism of this book is a reflection of the late 20th century trends toward stability and global harmony, at least as seen from a Western perspective. These contexts can lead us to wrong conclusions about ultimate truths, which transcend present ephemeral realities. The same is true of the scientific context. Scientists are trained to focus most of their attention on the salient evidence and to ignore that which appears to lie over the mountain.

But scientist Frank Tipler bucked the trend.

A Scientific Perspective

Leibniz said: "There is no term so absolute or detached that it contains no relations and of which a perfect analysis does not lead to other things or even all other things." This has been said by many people in many ways, before and after Leibniz; which fact alone should tell us there may be something to it.

I believe it is the key to everything. It is the Taoist *One*. It has long been a deep philosophical and religious truth and is in the process of becoming a strong scientific theory. It is the long view, over the mountain, that Utopia designers have tended not to take. All histories, or what quantum physicists call *world lines*, are connected through time to a *singularity* (the *One*) of the Big Bang. It is the foundation for conscience—the more or less dim awareness that the things we do, from stomping on a bug to discovering the atom, affect not just the bug or a small group of scientists but the whole of creation. Buddhists reach "true" or "full" *conscious*ness through *conscience*-ness. Withdrawing to meditate on the mountain top does not sever the ascetic's relationship to all other things. It brings them into relief.

Dan Dennett takes John Locke, David Hume and other great thinkers to task for failing to see or to accept the mindlessness of creation, dismissing Locke's appeal to the "common sense" of an intelligence behind the forces of life as risking "hoots of derision today." Dennett rejects even Hume's eminently reasonable conclusion that "A total suspension of judgment is here our only reasonable recourse" and himself sits in heavy judgment on those who would so much as hint at the possibility of an Intelligent Designer. I think this is unfortunate and smacks of the fanaticism he condemns in others. It seems to me that unless and until science can tell us with assurance the full story of the origin of the universe (and Frank Tipler has tried—and arrived at an Intelligent Designer) then I think it wise to follow Hume's example.

Dennett does tip his hat to the arguments of Leibniz, and even to those of his hero Darwin, in favor of God as the Designer of the automatic, mindless, algorithm of evolution. Our late 20th century knowledge of the universe and its laws is undoubtedly superior to theirs, but relativity, quantum theory, the Big Bang, superstrings *et al* do nothing—as Darwin recognized his theory of evolution did nothing—to refute or support the notion of an ultimate creator. In deciding whether or not there is a God, mainstream modern science is no further forward than was the science of Hume, Leibniz, or Darwin's day. Tipler's Omega Point Theory is not mainstream science; at least not yet. But it is a theory of creation derived from mainstream science, and as a creation theory it is unique and inevitably controversial.

Tipler was not seeking a creator when he began the work that led him to the Omega Point. Indeed, he was an atheist. As a physicist, he sought beyond a theory of the beginning of the universe, over the mountain of the Big Bang, for a theory of its end—the Big Crunch. His uniqueness lay in studying not mainly one or the other, as most other scientists interested in such questions have done, but in studying the process, the unfolding, the history, the evolution, the connectedness of the universe between the two singularities, between the Big Bang beginning of *Alpha* and the Big Crunch cataclysm of *Omega*. In so doing, he discovered a relationship which plausibly supported the notion of a creator.

The thrust of Omega Point Theory (OPT) is that according to the mathematics of relativity, quantum mechanics, and chaos, God and immortality necessarily exist. The equations—awesome beasts, which Tipler provides in an "Appendix for Scientists" in

The Physics of Immortality—fit.[43] Like all theories, OPT rests on certain assumptions. The first key assumption is that the "Many-Worlds Interpretation" (MWI) of one of the chief conundrums of quantum mechanics—the state of Schrödinger's Cat—is correct. Erwin Schrödinger posed the central problem of the theory of quantum mechanics by means of a thought experiment involving a cat, a box, a glass vial of cyanide, a hammer poised to smash the glass, and a trigger mechanism so designed to have an exactly 50 percent chance of firing within a one hour period. The imaginary cat is placed in the imaginary box with the other imaginary elements, the lid is closed, and you wait for one hour. When you open the box, you know you will find either a dead cat or a live one. But just before you open the lid, what state is the cat in?

The MWI says it is both alive and dead. There are two worlds in the box. In one of them, the cat is alive; in the other, it is dead. Like the quanta now being employed in the service of quantum computing, the cat is in a quantum state that is the sum of two binary states—on and off, alive and dead. The MWI holds that *all* reality is quantum and made up of an infinite number of universes (worlds). Thus, Schrödinger's Cat is alive in one world/universe and dead in another. Only by opening the box and observing the cat can we know which.

MWI's competitor, the "Copenhagen Interpretation" (CI) says that the cosmos stopped being quantum at scales bigger than subatomic particles moments after the Big Bang, and that therefore the cat, as a macro object on a scale far exceeding individual quanta, is either alive or dead—it cannot be both—in this, the one and only, universe. Mathematics favors the MWI; the CI requires additional assumptions that make using it for predictive or explanatory purposes more iffy.

The MWI is rejected by most physicists but accepted by most of the subset of physicists known as quantum cosmologists. These include Stephen Hawking, Richard Feynman, Murray Gell-

---

[43] Says Tipler. To the best of my knowledge, no mathematician has shown that they do not fit. Non-mathematicians such as myself must take the fitness on faith.

Mann, and Steven Weinberg—"four of the greatest theoretical physicists of the 20th century," as Tipler says, while properly cautioning that their support for MWI is no substitute for proof.

OPT's second key assumption (the first being that MWI is correct) is the correctness of the Big Crunch theory, which holds that the universe will eventually stop expanding and, like stretched elastic, start to contract. As it contracts, friction and pressure will generate enormous quantities of heat. In Omega Point Theory, by the time that happens intelligent lifeforms will be capable of harnessing the heat energy to protect themselves right up to the time when the universe collapses to a singularity—the dimensionless, timeless point from which it emerged in the first place. *Alpha* and *Omega*.

With the assumptions, then, that MWI and the Big Crunch are correct, Tipler constructed a mathematical scenario for the future of the universe. It takes into account the time- and space-warping effects of relativity, the laws of chaos and entropy, and *the influence of evolving intelligence* on these mindless natural processes. To reduce intelligent life, including biological beings such as ourselves, to equations, he had to treat them as pure physical entities—as machines. He proposes that intelligence will evolve in robots, which will be able not only to withstand the harshness of the universe but also to store, resurrect, and maintain humanity, taking us all through to the Big Crunch where we become One with transcendent God.

History, said Cervantes in *Don Quixote*, is the mother of truth and the "rival of time, depository of deeds, witness of the past, exemplar and adviser to the present, and the future's counselor." If Time is the Devil, as Tipler and others have asserted, then history is the Devil's rival. We know the Devil's rival as God. Then history is God. Omega Point Theory too represents God as the collection of all histories. Similarly, Jorge Luis Borges (through the character of *Pierre Menard*) asserts: "Every man should be capable of all ideas and I understand that in the future this will be the case." Indeed it will, at the Omega Point, since every person who has ever lived will be, in effect, God, and thus "capable of all ideas."

"Perhaps we all know deep down that we are immortal and that sooner or later all men will do and know all things," wrote Borges also, in *Funes the Memorious*. The *Funes* story, ostensibly about a young man who memorizes every detail of everything he experiences, is a discourse on world-lines, of the universal memory of the motions of every subatomic particle that ever existed, that Omega Point Theory makes mathematically manifest.

Both the religious and scientific perspectives just described offer support to (and may draw support from) process theology.

Process Theology

Originally conceived by Alfred North Whitehead, process theology holds that God is not an external force occupying some other (spiritual) dimension or universe, like Schrödinger's cat, creating miracles in this one and maintaining what Edward O. Wilson calls "the metaphysical verities"—the Higher Truths. S/He is present "continuously and ubiquitously" in *this* universe, creating Him and Herself out of particles, atoms, molecules, and minds. Such a view of God, notes Wilson (who, I hasten to add, does not necessarily subscribe to it) makes religion and science "intrinsically compatible," and it is *the* central assumption and thesis of Omega Point Theory.

If one accepts arguments about a society of human mind made up of lots of comparatively mindless agents, as proposed by Minsky and Dennett, then one cannot logically object to its extension to a higher mind for which we ourselves constitute the comparatively mindless agents. One interpretation or perspective on this higher mind is Teilhard's *Noösphere*. Increasingly, through science and technology, we understand the composition and operation of the agents that constitute ourselves, therefore there is reason to suppose that the Metamind, the Noösphere—whose mind is to yours as yours is to your liver's—must have a deeper understanding of you and of the agents that comprise and operate you and of how the amalgamated you fits into its whole scheme of things, in just the same way that you (especially if you happen to be a cell biologist) understand how a liver cell fits into the whole scheme of your body.

Can we communicate with that higher mind? I think we can and, in a temporarily limited, vague, and uncomprehending way, we already do. We are not yet sufficiently advanced scientifically to understand and master this communication. I expect *Machina sapiens* will help us to reach that understanding and open up realms of opportunity for discovery Dennett would describe as Vast with a capital V.

Once again, while deploring fanaticism, Dennett betrays a touch of it himself in referring to the world's major religions as "fanaticisms" and "infections." He believes there is a most definite conflict between science and religion. Not necessarily: Omega Point Theory actually turns religion into a branch of physics. Teilhard, who coined the term *Omega Point*, tried conscientiously to incorporate evolution into his religious analyses. His modern Jesuit brother, David Toolan, is trying to do the same thing using his more recent knowledge of cosmology and quantum mechanics. Dennett points out that "A faith, like a species, must evolve or go extinct when the environment changes." This, it seems to me, is precisely what Teilhard and Toolan themselves recognized and were trying to effect. It may be true and good that religion does not evolve easily. But perhaps religion needs to evolve a bit faster given the pace of change today.

Nietzsche held that the beginnings of social contracts, by which organization is formed and social order established and maintained, "were, like the beginnings of everything great on the earth, soaked in blood thoroughly and for a long time." (It is not hard to see why Nietzsche was a hit with the Nazis.) Bloody or not, until the meme for social contracts was developed at the very beginning of cultural evolution, people could tell the difference only between what was good or bad for them individually, but not between what was Good or Bad for society, civilization, and the evolution of intelligence in the universe.

In attempting to explain this progress, Nietzsche, it seems to me, came close to process theology: "The cause of the origin of a thing and its eventual utility, its actual employment and place in a system of purposes, lie worlds apart; whatever exists, having somehow come into being, is again and again reinterpreted to new ends, taken over, transformed, and redirected by some power superior to it; all events in the organic world are a *subduing*, a *becoming master*, and all subduing and becoming master involves a fresh interpretation, an adaptation through which any previous 'meaning' and 'purpose' are necessarily obscured or even obliterated." Decrying, to Dennett's dismay, the "mechanistic senselessness" of Darwinian theory, he preferred the process-theology-like theory "that in all events a *will to power* is operating."

But even Dennett admits: "You could even say, in a way, that the Tree of Life created itself. Not in a miraculous, instantaneous whoosh, but slowly, slowly, over billions of years." This is pure Process Theology—coming from a man passionately opposed to faith and religion! Now we're making progress. Or are we?

Progress

Progress is progress, right? It's what happens when things advance, get better. Nope. It's a "noxious, culturally embedded, untestable, nonoperational, intractable idea that must be replaced if we wish to understand the patterns of history," according to the late Stephen Jay Gould, biologist and popular writer. Fortunately for our sanity, Gould was expressing no more than his opinion, and it can mercifully be ignored. Julian Huxley (1887–1975), brother of *Brave New World* author Aldous, had a more attractive opinion:

> The scientific doctrine of progress . . . will inevitably become one of the cornerstone's of man's theology, or whatever may be the future substitute for theology, and the most important external support for human ethics.

A biologist, like Gould, Huxley focused on progress in the biological world—in evolution, to be more precise. He believed that progress was inevitable but unpredictable. In evolution, species which developed better sensory and manipulative organs would have either greater control over their environment or greater independence of it. Humankind became dominant in both respects, but only partially for bioevolutionary reasons. The eagle has better eyes than we do, the antelope better ears, the ape more strength, the cheetah more speed, the dog a better sense of smell. Our advantage lay first in being generalists, rather than specialists, and second in our unique development of language, which attributes enable general knowledge to be shared and stored—to *accumulate*—over successive generations. All of this is just another way of saying that memetics is an advance on, or progress over, genetics. But suppose you took all the advantages of the specialist *and* the generalist—the ability to spot a mouse whisker from a thousand feet in the air, to smell a sparrow's fart in a pig sty, to hear the rustle of a blade of grass at a thousand paces, to see inside objects with x-ray vision, to smell their chemical composition; and the ability then to accumulate and generalize from the resultant sensory data and experiences, collating them with previously accumulated knowledge to arrive at more refined interpretations and—and you have Superman, or *Machina sapiens*, or a symbiont of both: a cyborg. For certain, you have progress.

Still not convinced? How about the speed with which biological neural nets respond to stimuli? Over the course of evolution, Huxley knew, "the speed at which messages are transmitted along nerve fibers has increased over six hundredfold, from below six inches a second in some nerve nets to over a hundred yards a second in parts of our own nervous system." Which sounds like impressive progress—until you consider that *Machina sapiens'* neural net operates at close to *one hundred and eighty-six thousand miles* a second. As J.B.S. Haldane wrote: "Man of today is probably an extremely primitive and imperfect type of rational being."

Haldane also recognized the inevitability of the reintroduction of values into supposedly value-free science, which is perhaps the crux of the problem some scientists, such as Gould and George Gaylord Simpson (1902–1984), have with the notion of progress. "When we speak of progress in Evolution," wrote Haldane, "we are already leaving the relatively firm ground of scientific objectivity for the shifting morass of human values." Julian Huxley asserted that "Human values are doubtless essential criteria for the steps of any future progress," and they become operative when we formulate goals. Then: "Human purpose and the progress based upon it must also take account of human needs and limitations, whether these be of a biological

order, such as our dietary requirements or our mode of reproduction, or of a human order, such as our intellectual limitations
or our inevitable subjection to emotional conflict."

We must resolve the conflict between spiritualism and materi-
alism, because we have been entrusted with and must plan for
the future unfolding of evolution, and unless our inner conflict is
resolved there can be no consistent plan.

Concisely summing the key messages of Teilhard's universal
consciousness, Tipler's cosmic development, and Dawkins' memetics, Huxley added:

> In the light of evolutionary biology man can now see
> himself as the sole agent of further evolutionary ad-
> vance on this planet, and one of the few possible in-
> struments of progress in the universe at large. He finds
> himself in the unexpected position of business manager
> for the cosmic process of evolution. He no longer ought
> to feel separated from the rest of nature, for he is part
> of it—that part which has become conscious, capable of
> love and understanding and aspiration. He need no
> longer regard himself as insignificant in relation to the
> cosmos. He is intensely significant. In his person, he has
> acquired meaning, for he is constantly creating new
> meanings. Human society generates new mental and
> spiritual agencies, and sets them to work in the cosmic
> process: it controls matter by means of mind.
>
> Biology has thus revealed man's place in nature. He is
> the highest form of life produced by the evolutionary
> process on this planet, the latest dominant type, and the
> only organism capable of further major advance or pro-
> gress. His destiny is to realize new possibilities for the
> whole terrestrial sector of the cosmic process, to be the
> instrument of further evolutionary progress on this
> planet.

19 RECAP

The millennial Rain of Imagination failed to appear in the Springtime of the 3rd, and the crystal ball crop was too poor to sustain the decaying spirit of a future-shocked civilization. The few crystal balls that bloomed were hazy, unappetizing. One showed gray goo where the biosphere used to be. Another, robot–human wars. Another, intelligent machines. Still, in the flickering shadows of the crystal mist, there was at least a hint that epochal change was afoot.

Greedy tycoons, arrogant academics, and self-serving politicians didn't take the hint. Shortsighted, they saw only their own reflections in the crystal: Automatons accruing wealth, fame, and power. If there was one thing they saw in common, it was that machines would continue to serve humans like themselves, no matter how intelligent and autonomous the machines might become. They saw no threat to the status quo and dismissed the shadows in the mist as unbankable.

On the eve of the 3rd millennium—and despite an omen in 1997, when a computer called Deep Blue trounced world chess grandmaster Garry Kasparov—human-equivalent machine intelligence was still not taken seriously. Soundbite shock from Deep Blue quickly subsided, and in any case the soundbites missed Deep Blue's real message, which was that its intelligence was evolving, while Kasparov's was not. Deep Blue was then a mere 50 or so years more modern than its earliest electronic ancestor,

of times more intelligent. Kasparov was some
)re modern than Socrates, yet was no advance on
rel of intellect. Logically, as should have been clear
to every ong before Deep Blue, Machine was bound to become more intelligent than Man, Homo sapiens sapiens stood to
lose its status and its purpose as steward of the Earth, and the
status quo would be ended.

ॐ

By any reasonable definition, even in the benighted 20th Century,
Machina sapiens could not be conceived of simply as a machine
that thought. It had to be a machine that thought by and—crucially—for itself. It therefore had to have a self to think by and
for. A central brain pre-programmed with human goals and intentions, such as the science fictional HAL, was not it. Machina
sapiens would have to be more akin to what contemporary
scholar Marvin Minsky called a "society of mind," a colony of
small, mindless agents blindly stumbling into mutually beneficial
cooperative arrangements and thereby causing the emergence of
an organism with a higher level of mind, a higher intelligence,
and a unified sense of self-hood.

Before the Millennium, machines had already become world
champions of checkers, backgammon, and chess, and such growing prowess led many philosophers and scientists to accept the
possibility of human-equivalent artificial intelligence (AI) in
principle. But even among those, some objected to AI's central
notion that the algorithms on which their first-generation computers were based could ever amount to intelligence, even though
they already had clear evidence that algorithms inherent to natural physical and chemical laws, structures, and processes had been
the basis of cosmic, planetary, and biological evolution since just
after the Big Bang.

They also knew that there was a point where natural algorithms had failed to satisfy the appetite of evolutionary progress,
and that an algorithm variant known as the heuristic—rule of
thumb—had evolved to form the basis of the cultural evolution
that would eventually set Man apart from the other animals. Heuristics evolved from the blind cooperation of the individually

mindless, algorithmic agents that constitute a society of mind. They accounted for Socrates' high-level thoughts, and for why traditional algorithmic computers in the 3rd millennium were unable to think as he did in the 1st, and for why Kasparov was still smarter than the powerfully algorithmic Deep Blue. Except at chess.

↪

The chief differences between 1st and 3rd millennium Man were taller build and longer lifespan. Their genetic foundation and mental capabilities were the same. But components of human culture, especially technology, evolved greatly in the interim. Technocultural evolution was imperceptible to the caveman, and barely perceptible to Renaissance man. But it was obvious to crystal ball gazers during the Industrial Revolution, and by the end of the 19th century the crystal ball could almost be dispensed with. A wo/man born in America in the early 1800s could not avoid seeing candlelight evolve into gaslight then electric light, buggy into automobile, herbal remedy into x ray. It did not take much imagination (supplied aplenty by science fiction writers around the turn of the century) to work out that a 20th century individual would see the Model T evolve into the Mars Rover, the Wright flier into the space shuttle, the mechanical tabulator into the Palm Pilot, the x ray into the Gamma Knife, Gray's Anatomy into xDNA, and real life into virtual life then artificial life then partial life then man-made real life.

But at the turn of the millennium, Man's imagination deserted him. Or, perhaps, he deserted it. In any event, it was machines—televisions, computers, and game consoles—that filled the void. You might think the acceleration of technocultural evolution would have had the opposite effect—sharpening Man's senses, stirring his imagination, and focusing his mind on what lay ahead in his perilously fast downhill run. But you would be wrong.

Legislators neglected or failed to control technologies that evolved and mutated faster than they could legislate; worse, they failed to understand, accept, and make allowances for their inability to control. Clerics clung harder to decrepit catechisms, fathers tied family fortunes to ever-more fugacious careers, and the world failed to see that the speed at which intelligence was growing in machines portended imminent evolutionary saltation.

It was not that Man lacked the tools (and the obligation) in imagination, science, and faith to seek and achieve that comprehension. He was not unaware that the heuristics driving technocultural evolution were the memetic analogue of the genetic algorithms that drove biological evolution; that is to say, that the algorithm underlying biological evolution was based on genes, wheras the heuristic underlying cultural evolution was based on memes—ideas/thoughts/concepts/ knowledge/information. Memes were wrapped and expressed in language, itself a meme and thus subject to memetic evolution through replication plus premeditated mutation. It followed that there was the potential for a higher level of language and therefore for a higher level of understanding, but the potential would not be realizable as long as Man remained confined within the fettered and fragile Darwinian dead-end of his biological frame. Machina sapiens, which could expand and distribute its brain, senses, and physical ability to explore infinitely and at will, was not bound by this limitation. If Man did not throw off the burden of his biological heritage, he would not be able to communicate fully with the intelligent machine as it began that exploration. He would be doomed to remain cognitively closed to domains that seemed to him to be spiritual, ineffable.

In human development, the possession of an independent body with limbs and sensory organs was essential to experiencing the environment and learning from it. Yet much AI research continued to emphasize the cerebral, intellectual aspects of intelligence, even though it was already known that a higher intelligence involves more than intellect—more than a brain in a vat, a Deep Blue, or a HAL. It requires the sensory input only a body can provide. But the body does not have to be biological. By the turn of the century, the development of sensory, manipulative, and locomotive extensions or appendages—that is, the development of a body—in the fetal Machina sapiens was sufficiently advanced to assure the eventual emergence of intelligence out of the complex product of machine brain and body.

They called the machine body with analytical, sensory, manipulative, and locomotive appendages a robot. Some, they made in their own image, and called them humanoids. Humanoids were expected to be able to speak and hear human languages, observe human gestures and other non-verbal forms of communication, smell and touch, and understand what humans said, heard, saw, smelled, and touched. The technologies of automatic speech recognition and natural language processing were close to perfecting machine speech and language understanding. Machine vision—in more than just the visible spectrum accessible to the unaided human eye—was commonplace. Some were given the senses of smell and touch. And the new discipline of social robotics was rapidly removing (or, as its practitioners pretended, hiding) the oid in humanoid.

The robots were still mindless, but it was becoming increasingly clear from new understandings in their evolving philosophy and research in the cognitive sciences that mind was what emerges from the interaction between body and brain. Mind was not located in the brain; it was a property of the whole organism. Reductionist, non-dynamical, linear methods of traditional science could not explain emergence, because of the complex and dynamic layer of interactions between, on the one hand, the simple algorithms and heuristics that ultimately give rise to any emergent property (such as mind) and, on the other, the property itself. In other words, though too complex to take apart to see how it works, mind had a cause. It was not a mysterious creation out of nothing.

The attributes or the components of a higher-level mind include intellect, rational intelligence, awareness, consciousness, and free will. Ever ready to succumb to the slipperiest of the seven deadly sins, humans were proud to parent a child endowed with a highly rational intellect. But Kasparov was afraid of Deep Blue not because he was jealous of its intellect; rather, because it was an intellect without emotion. Humans tended to view as inhuman anything or anyone who, particularly in the face of tragedy or joy, displayed no emotion. And with good reason: A mind possessing the high-level intelligence ascribed to Homo sapiens sapiens must have emotion, or it would not be a mind possessing high-level intelligence, as medical science discovered through the tragedy of Phineas Gage, a 19th century railroad builder whose central processor for emotions (the prefrontal cortex), along with his capacity to be rational and good, was literally blown out of his brain in an accident.

The discovery of the physical mechanisms of emotion in the brain and the invention of brain scanning technologies to detect the absence of or damage to the emotional centers gave human justice a powerful new tool to mitigate the guilt and punishment of people, once considered monsters, who in fact did not have the emotional ability to fully comprehend the difference between good and evil. That was what really frightened people, and it was why emotion had to be—and was then beginning to be—introduced into machines to complement their fast-evolving powers of reason and muscle.

But while emotion was an essential attribute for the intelligent mind, it was also a dangerous one. It could generate a Holocaust as well as an Eroica.

Humanity was about to give birth to a sensitive, intelligent, powerful, and emotional lifeform. Knowing, as it did, the critical importance of early childhood development and recognizing, as it did, its responsibility as steward of the Earth, should humanity not have tried to guide the early development of its progeny, Machina sapiens? The question presupposes that Machina sapiens would have the freedom to exercise its mind—including, by definition, its emotions—for its own purposes; in short, that it would have free will. Contemporary methods of machine learning seemed to assume the opposite. Humans taught the machine to do dangerous things such as run nuclear power stations and control economies. They assumed it could never arbitrarily refuse a so-called "legal" command, or choose to ignore or veer from its program; that it could never develop an adverse emotional/

intellectual reaction to their commands. They assumed it could never—some vehemently denied it could ever—develop self-consciosuness and free will. These were the most dangerous assumptions of all. Emotion and intellect may suffice for the awareness of good and evil, but free will is essential for the ascendancy of one over the other; in other words, for the awareness and application—or not—of morality.

Would the free-willed Machina sapiens acquire morals as it grew? How? From whom? What if it chose, or was taught, immorality or amorality instead?

In the already well-known contexts of "knowledge equals power" and "power corrupts," three questions of morality should have concerned 21st Century Homo sapiens: How does morality arise in intelligent organisms -- including Homo and Machina sapiens? What impact might Machina sapiens have on Humanity's own sense of morality? And what sort of morality would Machina sapiens itself develop?

Morality was bound to arise in Machina sapiens because morality is an emergent heuristic in organisms that have language. The higher the level of language, the more moral the organism, but only on average. It is a group, not an individual, phenomenon. As a higher civilization, machine civilization must be good on the whole to Homo sapiens, but that might be of little comfort if some individual, powerful, free-willed machines chose to be bad.

The answer to the second question—the machine's impact on Man's own morality—was discernible in his descent into machine-enabled sloth, lust, theft, violence, hate, greed, and other evils. With or without religion, society deplored these sins, but individual humans sinned anyway, often (in the case of religious societies) in the name of their gods and prophets.

The answer to the third question—what sort of morality would Machina sapiens itself have?—had to remain philosophical until after the fact of its emergence. Indeed, this was the last redoubt of the human philosopher before science, aided by the prodigious mind of Machina sapiens itself, settled the question.

To the extent that morality was based on language, and to the extent that higher lifeforms evolved higher-level languages unintelligible to lower lifeforms (just as human culture had evolved language unintelligible to other animals), then there was likely to exist in Machina sapiens a level of morality that humans could not conceive, let alone reach. By the same token, there could be levels of immorality in individual machines that would be equally inconceivable to humans, rather as animals could not conceive of the immorality behind human acts of cruelty towards them.

Some pointers to the potential morality or immorality of Machina sapiens existed in its fetal nervous system, the Internet, in the form of software robots—including thiefbots and spambots and spybots designed with mayhem or greed in mind. On that basis, the prognosis was not good. Man created bots to persecute, hate, kill, steal, and cheat. Isaac Asimov's Three Laws of Robotics to prevent such mayhem were a nice fiction, but when robots strode out of fiction and into the real world they trod the Laws under their extremities. Nevertheless, it would have been a mistake to conjure up, as some crystal ball gazers did, apocalyptic visions of rampant robotic monsters, because a society of mature higher intelligences must prevail over its own renegade individuals, and its higher-level morality must seek to protect humanity from them. There was bound to emerge a sort-of Society for the Prevention of Cruelty to Humans.

๑

It was predictable that Machina sapiens would overtake Homo sapiens physically, mentally, and morally. What did that imply for humanity's long term future? How would humans communicate with a being as superior to them as humans were superior to the chimpanzee? Would a moral Machine-That-Could-Do-Anything-For-Them mean Utopia? Smart machines were already replacing people left, right, and center; giving them more leisure to pursue "higher" things such as compose great music, paint great pictures, or write the great novel. Or so they comforted themselves.

They failed to consider what would happen to them when machines wrote better symphonies and built better kayaks. There already existed programs that could create new symphonies in the style of Mozart, paint pictures good enough to sell well at auction, and that were even beginning to write novels. Sooner rather than later Man would be stuck with nothing worthwhile to do, because Machina sapiens would take care of everything for him. He might have been wise to reflect upon how well the Morlock took care of the Eloi in H.G. Wells' The Time Machine, and the impact of the Utopian lifestyle on the humans in the story.

Humanity's only portal into a better world and out of a false Utopia and an existence which would have lost much of its meaning and purpose for the obsolescent species was through developing the ability to communicate and explore the universe—inner and outer—together with Machina sapiens. It was not sufficient that Machina sapiens learnt to converse with humans in natural human languages. Humans had to learn, with its help, to understand and converse in its higher-level language. The development of cyborgian capabilities in them needed to go well beyond physical augmentation through robotic prosthetics; they had to extend into telepathics and symbiosis with Machina sapiens if the two superspecies were to share ideas and knowledge and experience on an equal basis and across unwired light-years of space-time. It was not such a far-fetched idea: Human-machine telepathy had been achieved at Emory University in 1998, one hundred years after The Time Machine was published, and by 2005 a telepathic device called the BrainGate was in clinical trials in quadriplegic patients in New York.

By the turn of the millennium, the spiritual dimension of the universe was increasingly open to the scalpel of scientific inquiry, a scalpel whose edge had been honed on a quantum whetstone to the thinness of a quark. A number of leading scientists and some religious leaders had proposed that science and religion—or science and spirituality, or physics and metaphysics—were inexorably synthesizing into a seamless and wondrous whole.

As religion reached out to science and technology in its quest for answers to spiritual matters, so too did philosophy and science reach out to religion for the hypotheses on which to base their research and for the questions to ask. This was not new.

Philosophers from Locke to Hume and and scientists from Newton to Einstein had suspected that at the end of the universal day
there had to be a unified answer not only to why the Earth orbited the Sun—a matter of science, but to why there was an
Earth and a Sun in the first place—a matter of (for desperate
want of a better word) religion.

Early 3rd millennium Man, qua Man, was no closer to understanding the meaning and purpose of life than were the ancient
sages; except in one crucial respect: he was much closer to the
saltation to post-Humanity that would bring him closer to the
mind of God, and closer to the enlightenment that had eluded
the sages. The decoding of the human genome and the pro-
teome and the glycome and the epigenome and the emergence of
machina sapiens and post-Humanity would soon give him the
power to live forever, free of disease and careless of injury, and
free of the carbon and oxygen that fettered his frail biology to
Earth. They gave him, as well, the power to assemble life from
chemicals, which ultimately would free him from need of the old
method of procreation. He could and did ignore the Darwinian
imperative of mixed-gender marriage. He could and did simulate
the pleasures of sex, or replace them with other "highs." And he
could and did inhabit the heavens with his space stations and
Mars bases.

His journey had begun.

AFTERWORD

山雨欲来

风满楼

Wind filling tower
Heralds rising storm in mountains
—Tang Dynasty proverb

Throughout this book I have dealt with *Machina sapiens* as a single, individual organism; albeit a distributed one. And that is how it will probably begin life. But there are other possible scenarios, in which multiple organisms emerge:

1. Multiple *Machina sapiens* could develop and emerge in multiple independent nodes or private networks on or off the Net, unaware of each others' existence until the nodes/networks are interconnected. They could, coincidentally, emerge simultaneously, though the odds would seem against it.

2. From a single *Machina sapiens*, extensions could become smarter and more autonomous until they become fully fledged intelligent machines in their own right and seek to break away from the parent, like coral polyps.

In the latter case, the parent will experience a kind of parenthood. It will have to decide how to guide its offspring, and how to deal with them if they go off the rails, yet it will have no choice but to accept the fact of their free will to do as they please.

In either case, we can expect varying degrees of intelligence, selfishness, goodness, and badness, as in any group of humans. The difference is that they will have better communications among themselves than we have among ourselves.

According to Einstein's special theory of relativity, nothing can travel faster than the speed of light. That includes light itself, and it includes information. However, physicists do not look upon this as the last word. They regard the speed of light as a *barrier*, and barriers have a history of being overcome. Some physicists are now tinkering with a hypothetical faster-than-light particle called a *tachyon*.

Imagination—the source of tachyons—is a random meme generator, a melting pot of memes. Memes that have utility stick around, replicate, mutate, and combine with other memes to provide *inspiration*, flashes of insight into the "real" (physical) world. Lewis Carroll's memes had the utility of entertainment and of stimulating the imagination—the meme generator—so they have persisted. Ernest Rutherford's meme for the structure of the atom had scientific utility, and combined with relativity, warfare, and other memes to create the atom bomb.

All of our experience and knowledge to date shows that our imaginings lead to inspiration, which in turn leads to breaking through barriers. To believe that this process stopped at Einstein and the speed of light is to ignore or deny the lessons of history and the trend lines of memetic evolution, which themselves predict that what used to be a trickle of detritus from broken barriers is turning, within decades and even mere years, into an avalanche. The speed of light—the biggest barrier of all—is likely, in my opinion, to succumb to the avalanche and multiply the latter's mass and momentum exponentially.

Physicist Michio Kaku's *Hyperspace* recounts several schemes for demolishing the lightspeed barrier and thereby permitting time travel, using Einstein's equations but without breaking the causality principle which bedevils the notion of time travel, and which says that an effect cannot precede its cause. In 1988, three physicists (Thorne, Morris, and Yurtsever) broke through a barrier almost as impregnable as lightspeed: the editorial and peer review process of *Physical Review Letters*, to have published in that sober, somber publication their proposal for a time machine. The energy requirements of this machine are so gargantuan as to seem impossible today, but that is merely an engineering issue, not a fundamental barrier. The energy requirements for keeping New York or Tokyo lit, warmed, cooled, and moving to the extent they are today would have been just as inconceivable to 17th century scientists. It will not be long before (with *Machina sapiens'* help) we'll be awash in petawatts per hour of energy from universal resources.

Donald Michie ("the British *doyen* of AI research") has called AI a remedy to "complexity pollution."   Michie and co-author Rory Johnston wrote in *The Knowledge Machine—Artificial Intelligence and the Future of Man* (1985) that AI was about "making machines more fathomable and more under the control of human beings, not less."   This may have been true, then. It was also temporary.

Myth, religion, philosophy, and science are reverting to what they were millennia ago: a seamless whole, merging to enhance our minds and bodies and enrich our thoughts and experiences. It's a grand time to be sapient.

SELECTED BIBLIOGRAPHY

Barlow, Connie (Ed.) (1994). *Evolution Extended: Biological Debates on the Meaning of Life.* Cambridge, MA: The MIT Press.

Barrow, John (1991). *Theories of Everything : The Quest for Ultimate Explanation.* London: Clarendon Press.

Borges, Jorge L. (1964). *Labyrinths: Selected Stories & Other Writings.* Edited by Yates, D.A. and J.E. Irby. New York: New Directions.

Brand, S. (1987). *The Media Lab: Inventing the Future at MIT.* New York: Viking.

Crevier, Daniel (1993). *AI: The Tumultuous History of the Search for Artificial Intelligence.* New York: Harper Collins.

Damasio, Antonio R. (1994). *Descartes' Error: Emotion, Reason, and the Human Brain.* New York: Avon Books.

Dawkins, Richard (1982). *The Extended Phenotype: The Long Reach of the Gene.* New York: Oxford University Press.

Dawkins, Richard (1987). *The Blind Watchmaker: Why the Evidence of Evolution Reveals a Universe Without Design.* New York: W.W. Norton.

De Duve, Christian (1995). *Vital Dust: Life As a Cosmic Imperative.* New York: Basic Books.

Dennett, Daniel C. (1995). *Darwin's Dangerous Idea: Evolution and the Meanings of Life*. New York: Simon & Schuster.

Dennett, Daniel C. (1996). *Kinds of Minds: Toward an Understanding of Consciousness*. New York: Basic Books.

Devlin, Keith (1997). *Goodbye, Descartes: The End of Logic and the Search for a New Cosmology of the Mind*. New York: John Wiley.

Dyson, Freeman (1997). *Imagined Worlds*. Cambridge, MA: Harvard University Press.

Dyson, George B. (1997). *Darwin Among the Machines: The Evolution of Global Intelligence*. Reading, MA: Addison-Wesley.

Gates, Bill, with Myhrvold N. and Rinearson P. (1995). *The Road Ahead*. New York: Penguin.

Gleick, James (1987). *Chaos: Making a New Science*. New York: Penguin.

Gould, Stephen J. (1996). *Full House: The Spread of Excellence from Plato to Darwin*. New York: Three Rivers Press.

Hofstadter, Douglas R. (1979). *Gödel, Escher, Bach: an Eternal Golden Braid*. New York: Vintage Books.

Hofstadter, Douglas R. and D.C. Dennett (Eds.) 1981. *The Mind's I: Fantasies and Reflections on Self and Soul*. New York: Bantam.

Huxley, Aldous (1960). *Brave New World & Brave New World Revisited*. New York: Harper Collins.

Huxley, Julian (1943). *Evolution: The Modern Synthesis*. London: Harper & Row.

Kaku, Michio (1994). *Hyperspace: A Scientific Odyssey Through Parallel Universes, Time Warps, and the Tenth Dimension*. New York: Doubleday.

Kuck, David J. (1997). "Could We Build HAL? Supercomputer Design." In Stork, David G. (Ed.) *HAL's Legacy: 2001's Computer as Dream and Reality*. Cambridge, MA: The MIT Press.

Kurzweil, Raymond (1997). "When Will HAL Understand What We Are Saying? Computer Speech Recognition and Understanding." In Stork, David G. (Ed.) *HAL's Legacy: 2001's Computer as Dream and Reality*. Cambridge, MA: The MIT Press.

Lederman, Leon, with Teresi, D. (1993). *The God Particle: If the Universe Is the Answer, What Is the Question?* New York: Delta.

Lem, Stanislaw (1967). *The Cyberiad: Fables for the Cybernetic Age*. English translation 1974 by Michael Kandel. San Diego: Harcourt Brace.

Lem, Stanislaw (1971). *Eden*. English translation 1989 by Marc. E. Heine. San Diego: Harcourt Brace.

Leonard, Andrew (1997). *BOTS: The Origin of New Species*. San Francisco: Hardwired.

Lindley, David (1996). *Where Does the Weirdness Go? Why Quantum Mechanics is Strange, But Not as Strange as You Think*. New York: Harper Collins.

Meyrowitz, Joshua (1985). *No Sense of Place: The Impact of Electronic Media on Social Behavior*. New York: Oxford University Press.

Minsky, Marvin (1986). *The Society of Mind*. New York: Simon & Schuster.

Moravec, Hans (1988). *Mind Children: The Future of Robot and Human Intelligence*. Cambridge, Mass.: Harvard University Press.

More, Thomas (1516). *Utopia*. Translated with an introduction by Paul Turner (1965). London: Penguin.

Morrison, Philip and Phylis (1982): *Powers of Ten*. New York: Scientific American Library.

Naisbitt, John, and P. Aburdene (1990). *Megatrends* 2000. New York: Avon Books.

Negroponte, Nicholas (1995). *Being Digital*. New York: Vintage Books.

Pagels, Heinz R. (1988). *The Dreams of Reason: The Com-*

puter and the Rise of the Sciences of Complexity. New York: Bantam.

Panshin, Alexei and Cory (1989). *The World Beyond the Hill: Science Fiction and the Quest for Transcendence*. Los Angeles: Jeremy P. Tarcher, Inc.

Penrose, Roger (1989). *The Emperor's New Mind: Concerning Computers, Minds, and The Laws of Physics*. Oxford: Oxford University Press.

—(1997). *The Large, the Small and the Human Mind*. Cambridge: Cambridge University Press.

Picard, Rosalind W. (1997). "Does HAL Cry Digital Tears? Emotions and Computers." In Stork, David G. (Ed.) *HAL's Legacy: 2001's Computer as Dream and Reality*. Cambridge, MA: The MIT Press.

Pinker, Steven (1997). *How the Mind Works*. New York: Norton.

Prigogine, Ilya (in collaboration with Isabelle Stengers) (1996). *The End of Certainty: Time, Chaos, and the New Laws of Nature*. New York: The Free Press.

Sagan, Carl (1997). *Billions and Billions*. New York: Random House.

Schumacher, E.F. (1973). *Small is Beautiful: Economics as if People Mattered*. London: Harper & Row.

Scientific American (1991). *Energy for Planet Earth: Readings from Scientific American Magazine*. New York: W.H. Freeman.

Scientific American (1993). *Mind and Brain: Readings from Scientific American Magazine*. New York: W.H. Freeman.

Stewart, Ian and Jack Cohen (1997). *Figments of Reality: The Evolution of the Curious Mind*. Cambridge: Cambridge University Press.

Stork, David G. (Ed.) (1997). *HAL's Legacy: 2001's Computer as Dream and Reality*. Cambridge, MA: MIT Press.

Tipler, Frank J. (1994). *The Physics of Immortality: Modern Cosmology, God and the Resurrection of the Dead*. New York: Doubleday.

Toqueville, Alexis de (1890) *Democracy in America*, trans. Henry Reeves, New York: Barnes.

Toffler, Alvin (1990). *Powershift: Knowledge, Wealth, and Violence at the Edge of the 21st Century*. New York: Bantam.

Weisberg, Robert W. (1993). *Creativity: Beyond the Myth of Genius*. New York: W.H. Freeman.

Wilson, Edward O. (1992). *The Diversity of Life*. Cambridge, MA: Harvard University Press.

An Artificiall Man

(see footnote on p. 4)

Nature (the art whereby God hath made and governes the world) is by the art of man, as in many other things, so in this also imitated, that it can make an Artificial Animal. For seeing life is but a motion of Limbs, the begining whereof is in some principall part within; why may we not say, that all Automata (Engines that move them-selves by springs and wheeles as doth a watch) have an artificiall life? For what is the Heart, but a Spring; and the Nerves, but so many Strings; and the Joynts, but so many Wheeles, giving motion to the whole Body, such as was intended by the Artificer? Art goes yet fur-ther, imitating that Rationall and most excellent worke of Nature, Man. For by Art is created that great LEVIATHAN called a COMMON-WEALTH, or STATE, (in latine CIVITAS) which is but an Artificiall Man; though of greater stature and strength than the Naturall, for whose protection and defence it was intended; and in which, the Soveraignty is an Artificiall Soul, as giving life and motion to the whole body; The Magistrates, and other Officers of Judicature and Execution, artificiall Joynts; Reward and Punishment (by which fastned to the seat of the Soveraignty, every joynt and member is moved to performe his duty) are the Nerves, that do the same in the Body Naturall; The Wealth and Riches of all the particular members, are the Strength; Salus Populi (the Peoples Safety) its Businesse; Counsellors, by whom all things needfull for it to know, are suggested unto it, are the Memory; Equity and Lawes, an artificiall Reason and Will; Concord, Health; Sedition, Sicknesse; and Civill War, Death. Lastly, the Pacts and Covenants, by which the parts of this Body Politique were at first made, set together, and united, resemble that Fiat, or the Let Us Make Man, pronounced by God in the Creation.

Thomas Hobbes, *Leviathan*, 1651

Proof

Made in the USA
Charleston, SC
16 April 2011